MPH

MARK MILLAR
Writer & Co-Creator

DUNCAN FEGREDO
Artist & Co-Creator

PETER DOHERTY
Letterer & Colorist

MIKE SPICER
Coloring Assistance,
ISSUE 2, pages 16-21
ISSUE 5, pages 24-32

Covers by
DUNCAN FEGREDO

NICOLE BOOSE & JENNIFER LEE - Editors
MELINA MIKULIĆ - Collection Designer
DREW GILL - Production

image

IMAGE COMICS, INC.
Robert Kirkman – Chief Operating Officer
Erik Larsen – Chief Financial Officer
Todd McFarlane – President
Marc Silvestri – Chief Executive Officer
Jim Valentino – Vice-President

Eric Stephenson – Publisher
Ron Richards – Director of Business Development
Jennifer de Guzman – Director of Trade Book Sales
Kat Salazar – Director of PR & Marketing
Corey Murphy – Director of Retail Sales
Jeremy Sullivan – Director of Digital Sales
Randy Okamura – Marketing Production Designer
Emilio Bautista – Sales Assistant
Branwyn Bigglestone – Senior Accounts Manager
Emily Miller – Accounts Manager
Jessica Ambriz – Administrative Assistant
David Brothers – Content Manager
Jonathan Chan – Production Manager
Drew Gill – Art Director
Meredith Wallace – Print Manager
Addison Duke – Production Artist
Vincent Kukua – Production Artist
Sasha Head – Production Artist
Tricia Ramos – Production Assistant
IMAGECOMICS.COM

CHAPTER ONE

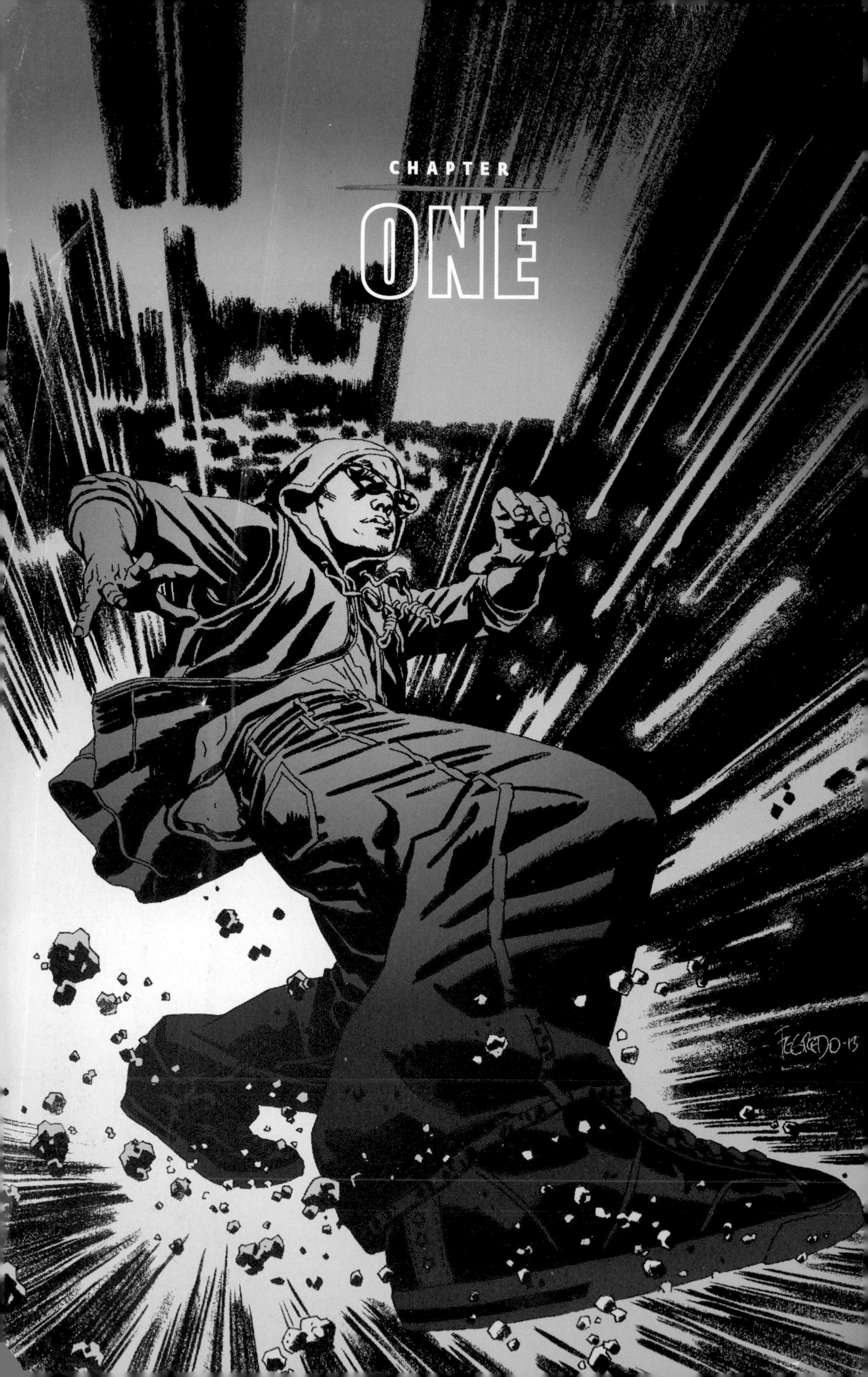

29 May

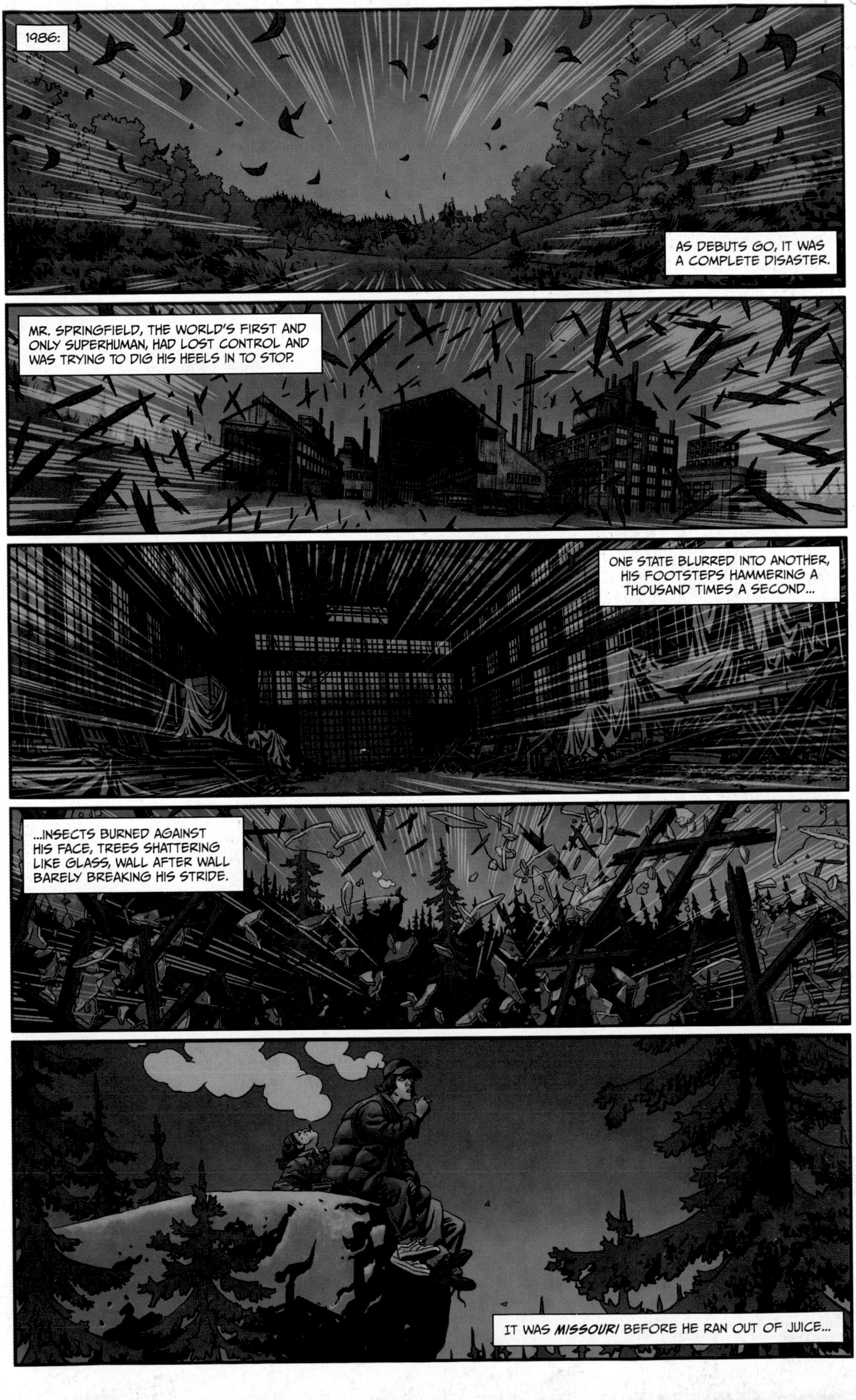
1986:
AS DEBUTS GO, IT WAS A COMPLETE DISASTER.
MR. SPRINGFIELD, THE WORLD'S FIRST AND ONLY SUPERHUMAN, HAD LOST CONTROL AND WAS TRYING TO DIG HIS HEELS IN TO STOP.
ONE STATE BLURRED INTO ANOTHER, HIS FOOTSTEPS HAMMERING A THOUSAND TIMES A SECOND...
...INSECTS BURNED AGAINST HIS FACE, TREES SHATTERING LIKE GLASS, WALL AFTER WALL BARELY BREAKING HIS STRIDE.
IT WAS *MISSOURI* BEFORE HE RAN OUT OF JUICE...

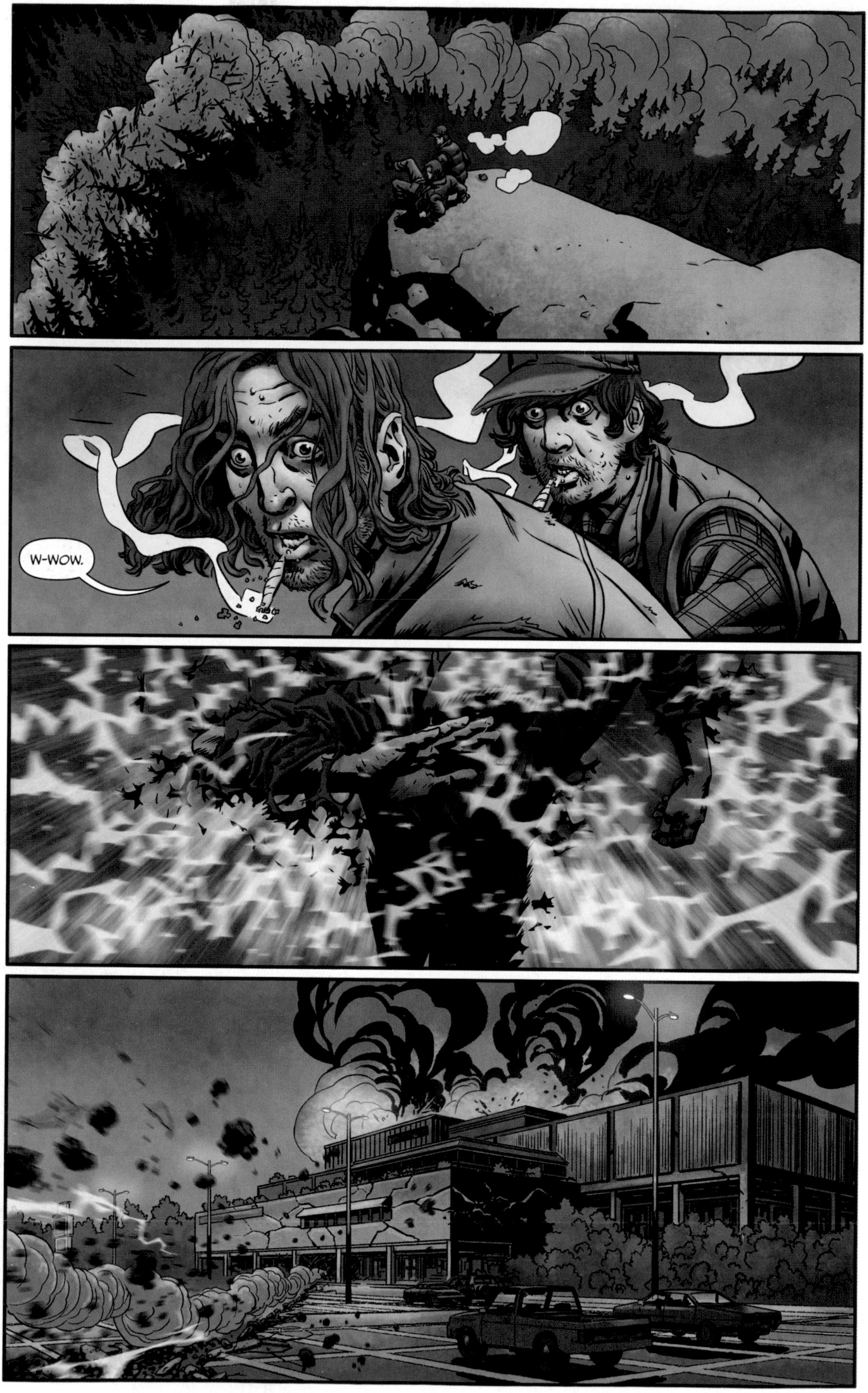
W-WOW.

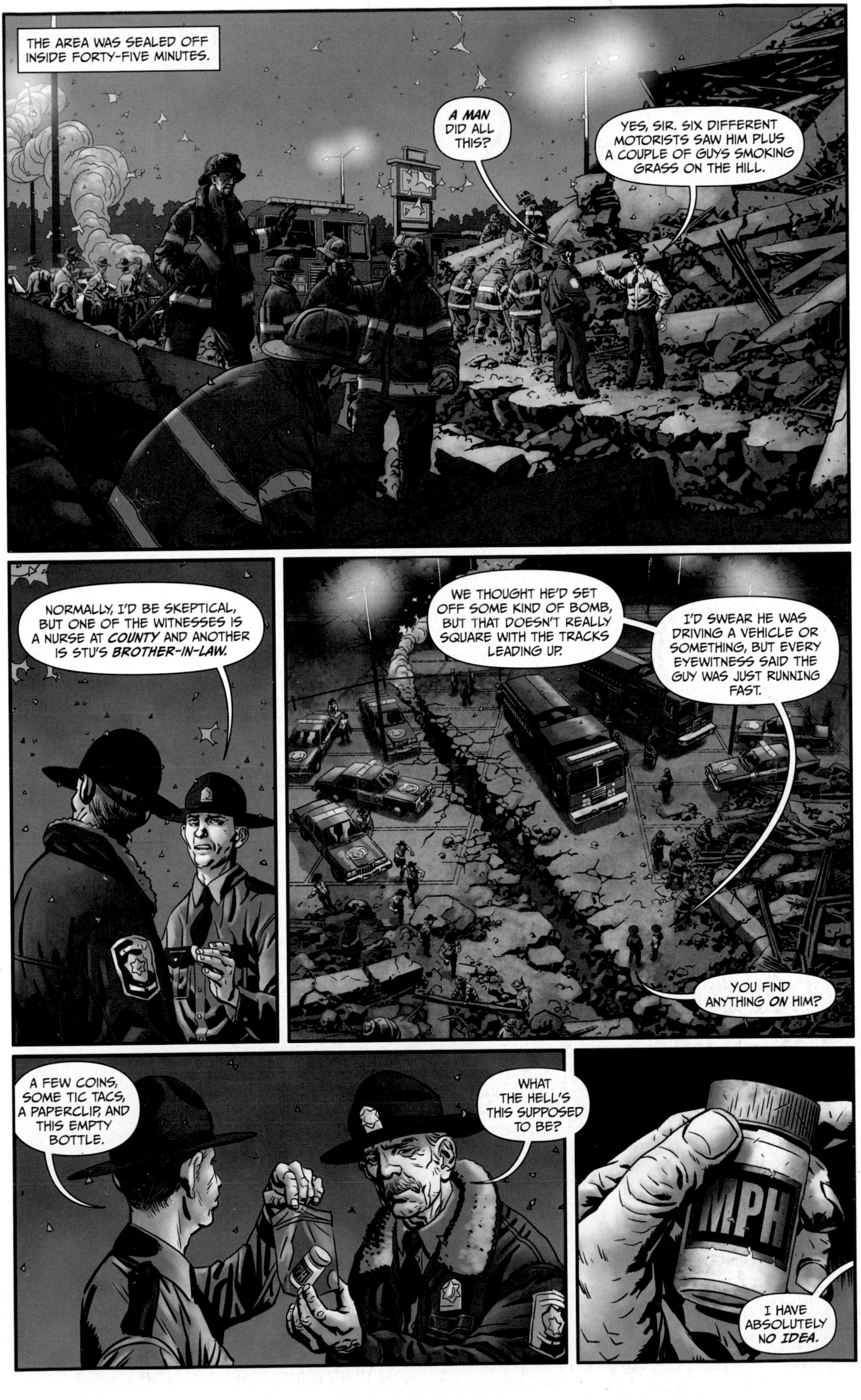
THE AREA WAS SEALED OFF INSIDE FORTY-FIVE MINUTES.
A MAN DID ALL THIS?
YES, SIR. SIX DIFFERENT MOTORISTS SAW HIM PLUS A COUPLE OF GUYS SMOKING GRASS ON THE HILL.
NORMALLY, I'D BE SKEPTICAL, BUT ONE OF THE WITNESSES IS A NURSE AT COUNTY AND ANOTHER IS STU'S BROTHER-IN-LAW.
WE THOUGHT HE'D SET OFF SOME KIND OF BOMB, BUT THAT DOESN'T REALLY SQUARE WITH THE TRACKS LEADING UP.
I'D SWEAR HE WAS DRIVING A VEHICLE OR SOMETHING, BUT EVERY EYEWITNESS SAID THE GUY WAS JUST RUNNING FAST.
YOU FIND ANYTHING ON HIM?
A FEW COINS, SOME TIC TACS, A PAPERCLIP, AND THIS EMPTY BOTTLE.
WHAT THE HELL'S THIS SUPPOSED TO BE?
MPH
I HAVE ABSOLUTELY NO IDEA.

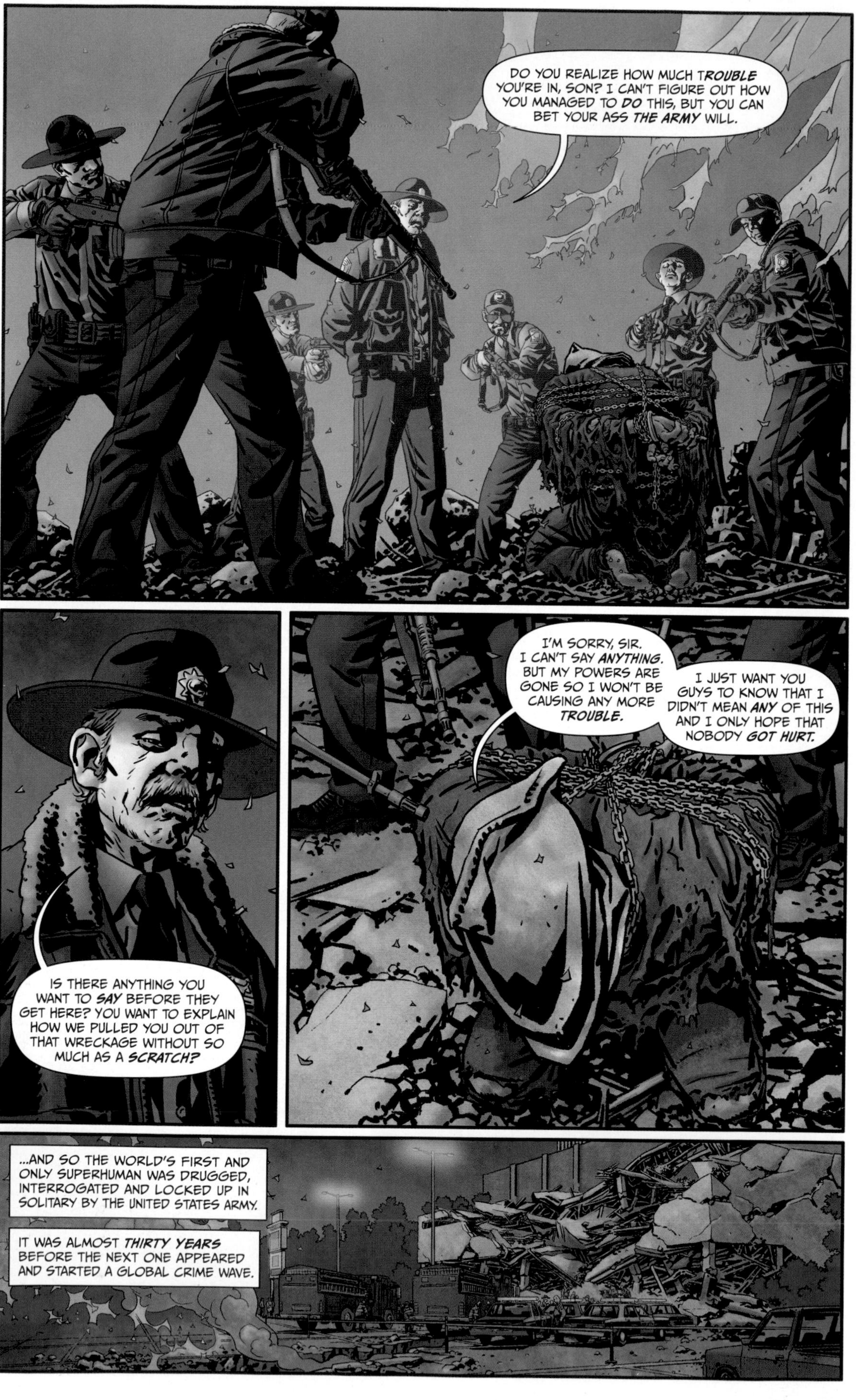
DO YOU REALIZE HOW MUCH TROUBLE YOU'RE IN, SON? I CAN'T FIGURE OUT HOW YOU MANAGED TO DO THIS, BUT YOU CAN BET YOUR ASS THE ARMY WILL.
IS THERE ANYTHING YOU WANT TO SAY BEFORE THEY GET HERE? YOU WANT TO EXPLAIN HOW WE PULLED YOU OUT OF THAT WRECKAGE WITHOUT SO MUCH AS A SCRATCH?
I'M SORRY, SIR. I CAN'T SAY ANYTHING. BUT MY POWERS ARE GONE SO I WON'T BE CAUSING ANY MORE TROUBLE.
I JUST WANT YOU GUYS TO KNOW THAT I DIDN'T MEAN ANY OF THIS AND I ONLY HOPE THAT NOBODY GOT HURT.
...AND SO THE WORLD'S FIRST AND ONLY SUPERHUMAN WAS DRUGGED, INTERROGATED AND LOCKED UP IN SOLITARY BY THE UNITED STATES ARMY.
IT WAS ALMOST THIRTY YEARS BEFORE THE NEXT ONE APPEARED AND STARTED A GLOBAL CRIME WAVE.

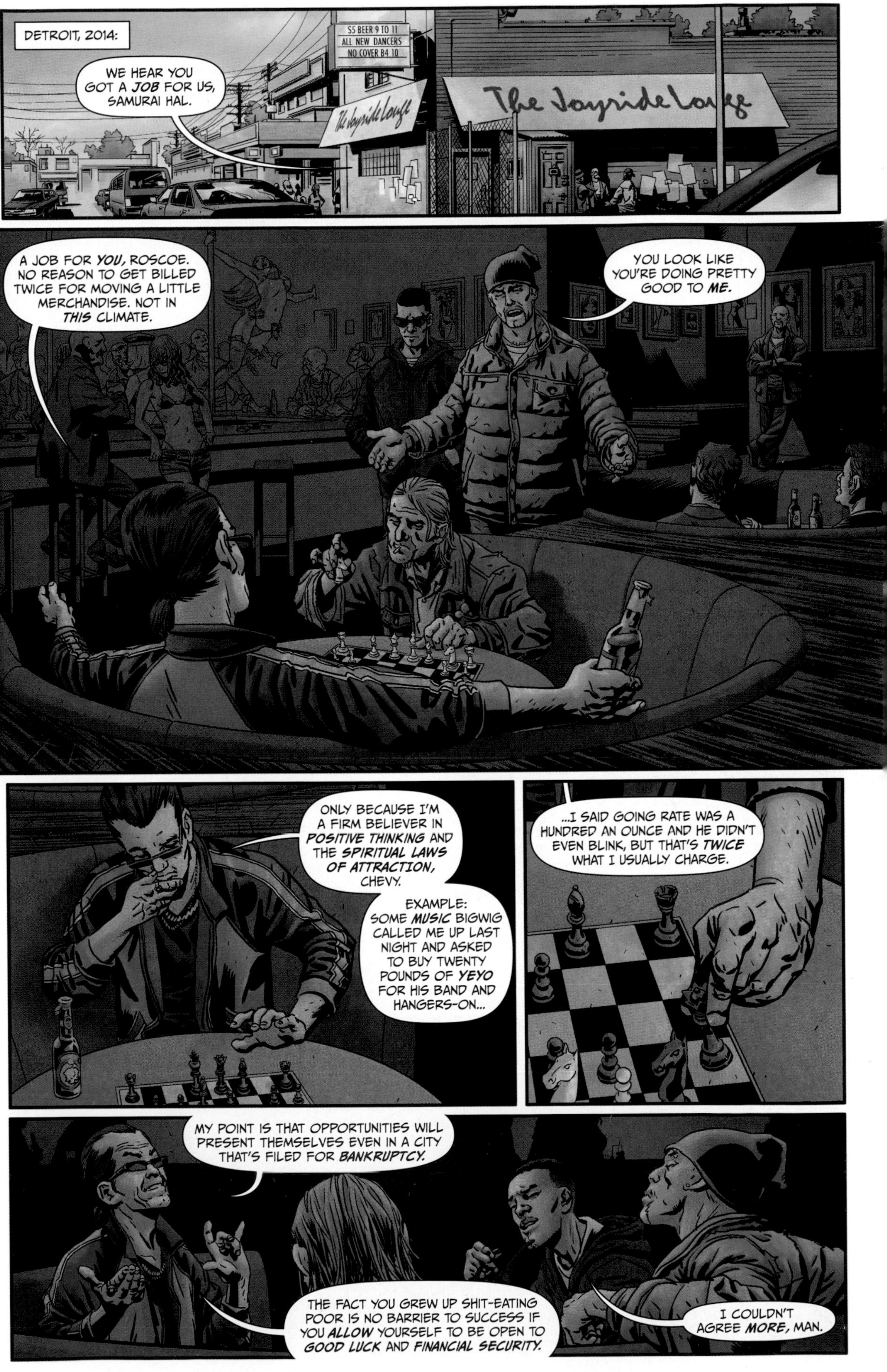
DETROIT, 2014:
$5 BEER 9 TO 11
ALL NEW DANCERS
NO COVER B4 10
The Joyride Lounge
The Joyride Lounge
WE HEAR YOU GOT A JOB FOR US, SAMURAI HAL.
A JOB FOR YOU, ROSCOE. NO REASON TO GET BILLED TWICE FOR MOVING A LITTLE MERCHANDISE. NOT IN THIS CLIMATE.
YOU LOOK LIKE YOU'RE DOING PRETTY GOOD TO ME.
ONLY BECAUSE I'M A FIRM BELIEVER IN POSITIVE THINKING AND THE SPIRITUAL LAWS OF ATTRACTION, CHEVY.
EXAMPLE: SOME MUSIC BIGWIG CALLED ME UP LAST NIGHT AND ASKED TO BUY TWENTY POUNDS OF YEYO FOR HIS BAND AND HANGERS-ON...
...I SAID GOING RATE WAS A HUNDRED AN OUNCE AND HE DIDN'T EVEN BLINK, BUT THAT'S TWICE WHAT I USUALLY CHARGE.
MY POINT IS THAT OPPORTUNITIES WILL PRESENT THEMSELVES EVEN IN A CITY THAT'S FILED FOR BANKRUPTCY.
THE FACT YOU GREW UP SHIT-EATING POOR IS NO BARRIER TO SUCCESS IF YOU ALLOW YOURSELF TO BE OPEN TO GOOD LUCK AND FINANCIAL SECURITY.
I COULDN'T AGREE MORE, MAN.

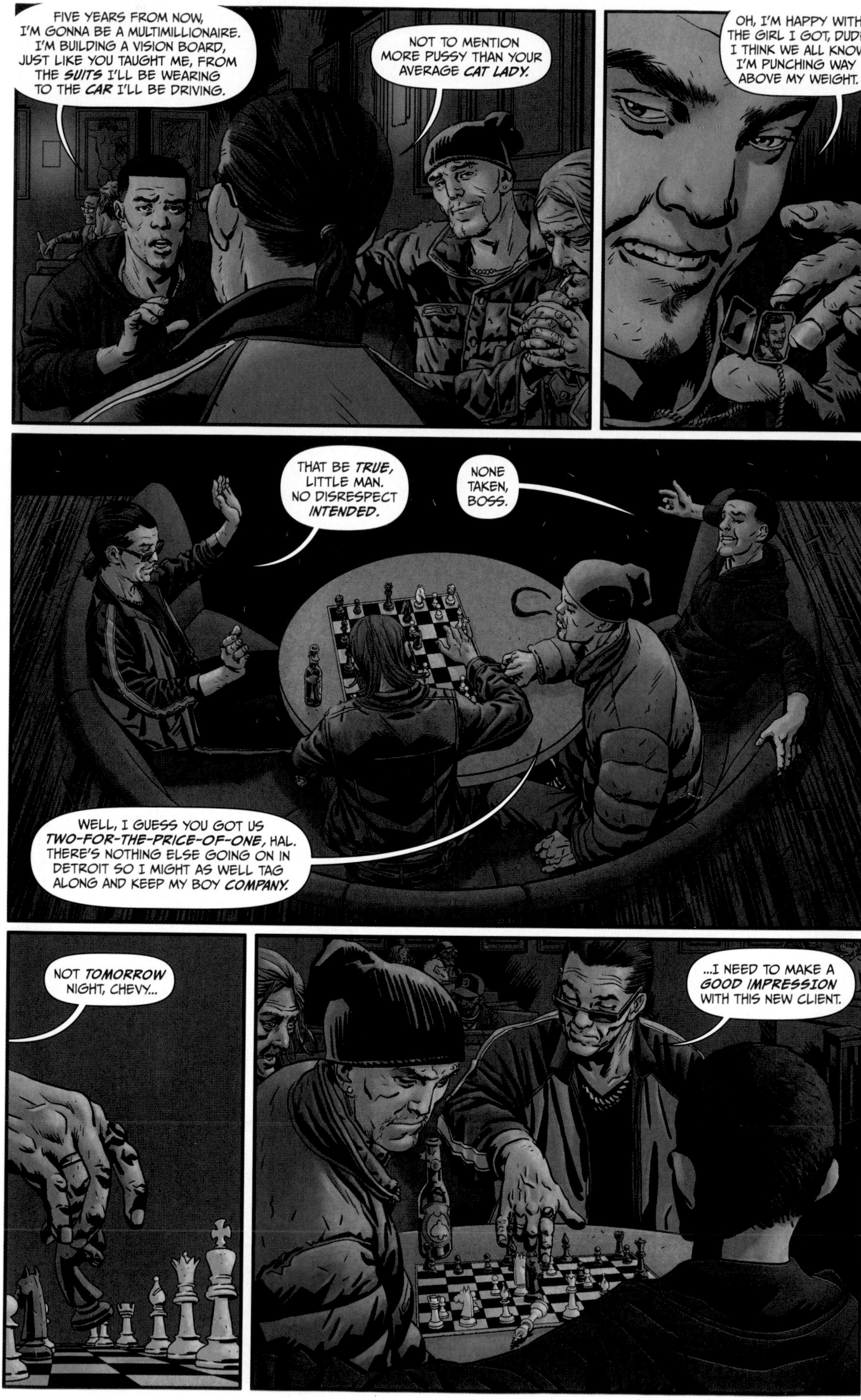
FIVE YEARS FROM NOW, I'M GONNA BE A MULTIMILLIONAIRE. I'M BUILDING A VISION BOARD, JUST LIKE YOU TAUGHT ME, FROM THE SUITS I'LL BE WEARING TO THE CAR I'LL BE DRIVING.
NOT TO MENTION MORE PUSSY THAN YOUR AVERAGE CAT LADY.
OH, I'M HAPPY WITH THE GIRL I GOT, DUDE. I THINK WE ALL KNOW I'M PUNCHING WAY ABOVE MY WEIGHT.
THAT BE TRUE, LITTLE MAN. NO DISRESPECT INTENDED.
NONE TAKEN, BOSS.
WELL, I GUESS YOU GOT US TWO-FOR-THE-PRICE-OF-ONE, HAL. THERE'S NOTHING ELSE GOING ON IN DETROIT SO I MIGHT AS WELL TAG ALONG AND KEEP MY BOY COMPANY.
NOT TOMORROW NIGHT, CHEVY...
...I NEED TO MAKE A GOOD IMPRESSION WITH THIS NEW CLIENT.

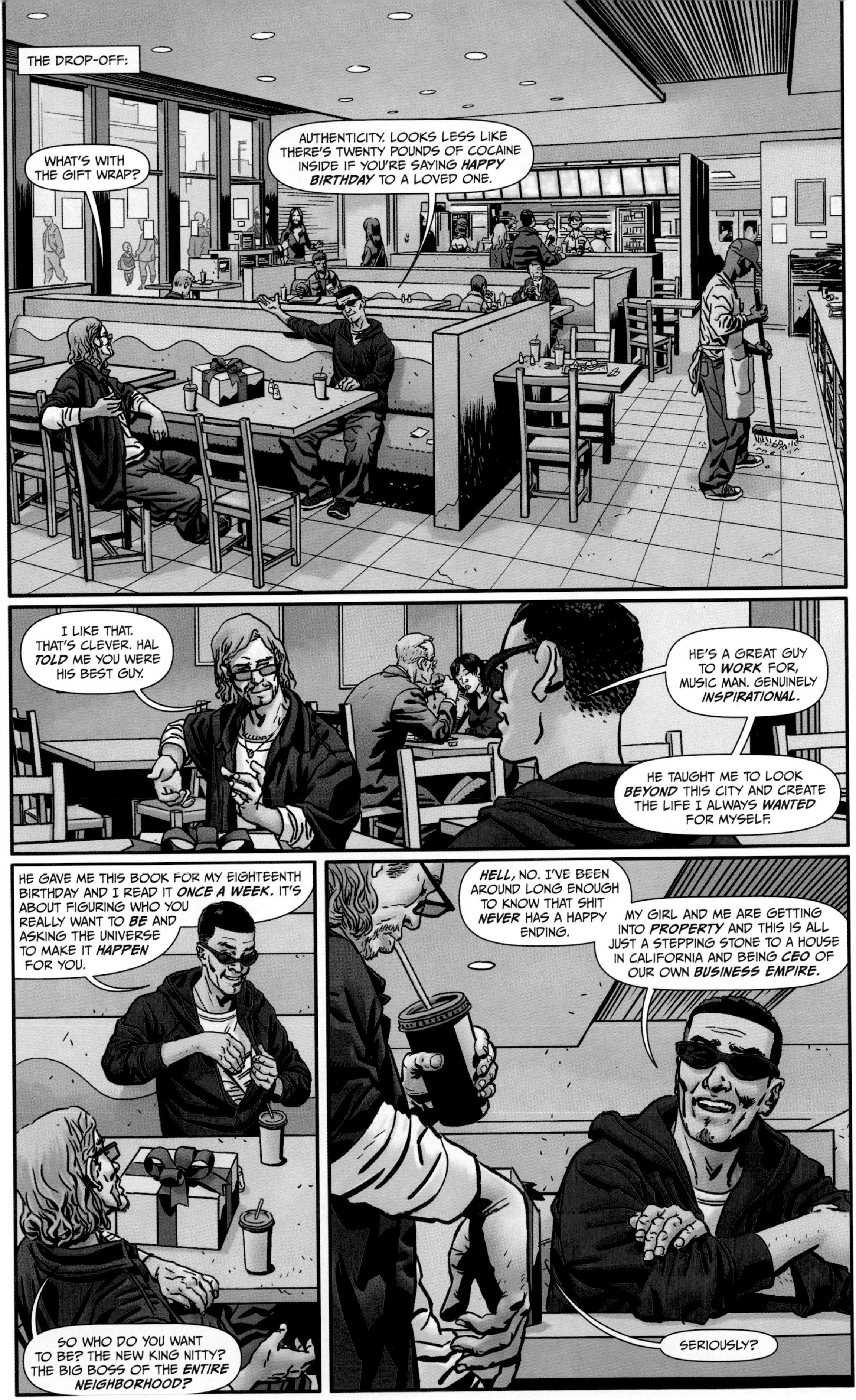
THE DROP-OFF:
WHAT'S WITH THE GIFT WRAP?
AUTHENTICITY. LOOKS LESS LIKE THERE'S TWENTY POUNDS OF COCAINE INSIDE IF YOU'RE SAYING *HAPPY BIRTHDAY* TO A LOVED ONE.
I LIKE THAT. THAT'S CLEVER. HAL *TOLD* ME YOU WERE HIS BEST GUY.
HE'S A GREAT GUY TO *WORK* FOR, MUSIC MAN. GENUINELY *INSPIRATIONAL.*
HE TAUGHT ME TO LOOK *BEYOND* THIS CITY AND CREATE THE LIFE I ALWAYS *WANTED* FOR MYSELF.
HE GAVE ME THIS BOOK FOR MY EIGHTEENTH BIRTHDAY AND I READ IT *ONCE A WEEK.* IT'S ABOUT FIGURING WHO YOU REALLY WANT TO *BE* AND ASKING THE UNIVERSE TO MAKE IT *HAPPEN* FOR YOU.
SO WHO DO YOU WANT TO BE? THE NEW KING NITTY? THE BIG BOSS OF THE *ENTIRE NEIGHBORHOOD?*
HELL, NO. I'VE BEEN AROUND LONG ENOUGH TO KNOW THAT SHIT *NEVER* HAS A HAPPY ENDING.
MY GIRL AND ME ARE GETTING INTO *PROPERTY* AND THIS IS ALL JUST A STEPPING STONE TO A HOUSE IN CALIFORNIA AND BEING *CEO* OF OUR OWN *BUSINESS EMPIRE.*
SERIOUSLY?

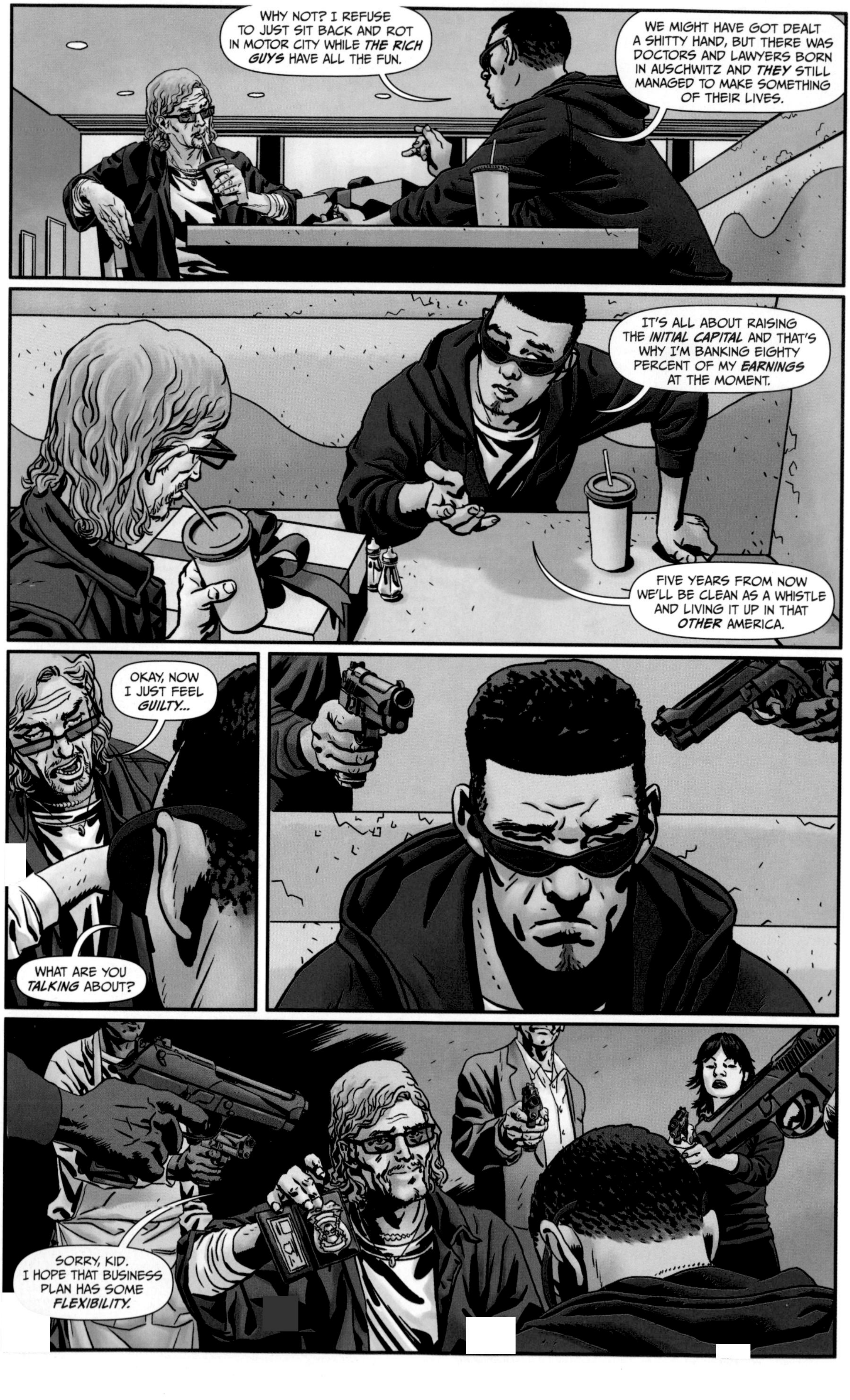
WHY NOT? I REFUSE TO JUST SIT BACK AND ROT IN MOTOR CITY WHILE THE RICH GUYS HAVE ALL THE FUN.
WE MIGHT HAVE GOT DEALT A SHITTY HAND, BUT THERE WAS DOCTORS AND LAWYERS BORN IN AUSCHWITZ AND THEY STILL MANAGED TO MAKE SOMETHING OF THEIR LIVES.
IT'S ALL ABOUT RAISING THE INITIAL CAPITAL AND THAT'S WHY I'M BANKING EIGHTY PERCENT OF MY EARNINGS AT THE MOMENT.
FIVE YEARS FROM NOW WE'LL BE CLEAN AS A WHISTLE AND LIVING IT UP IN THAT OTHER AMERICA.
OKAY, NOW I JUST FEEL GUILTY...
WHAT ARE YOU TALKING ABOUT?
SORRY, KID. I HOPE THAT BUSINESS PLAN HAS SOME FLEXIBILITY.

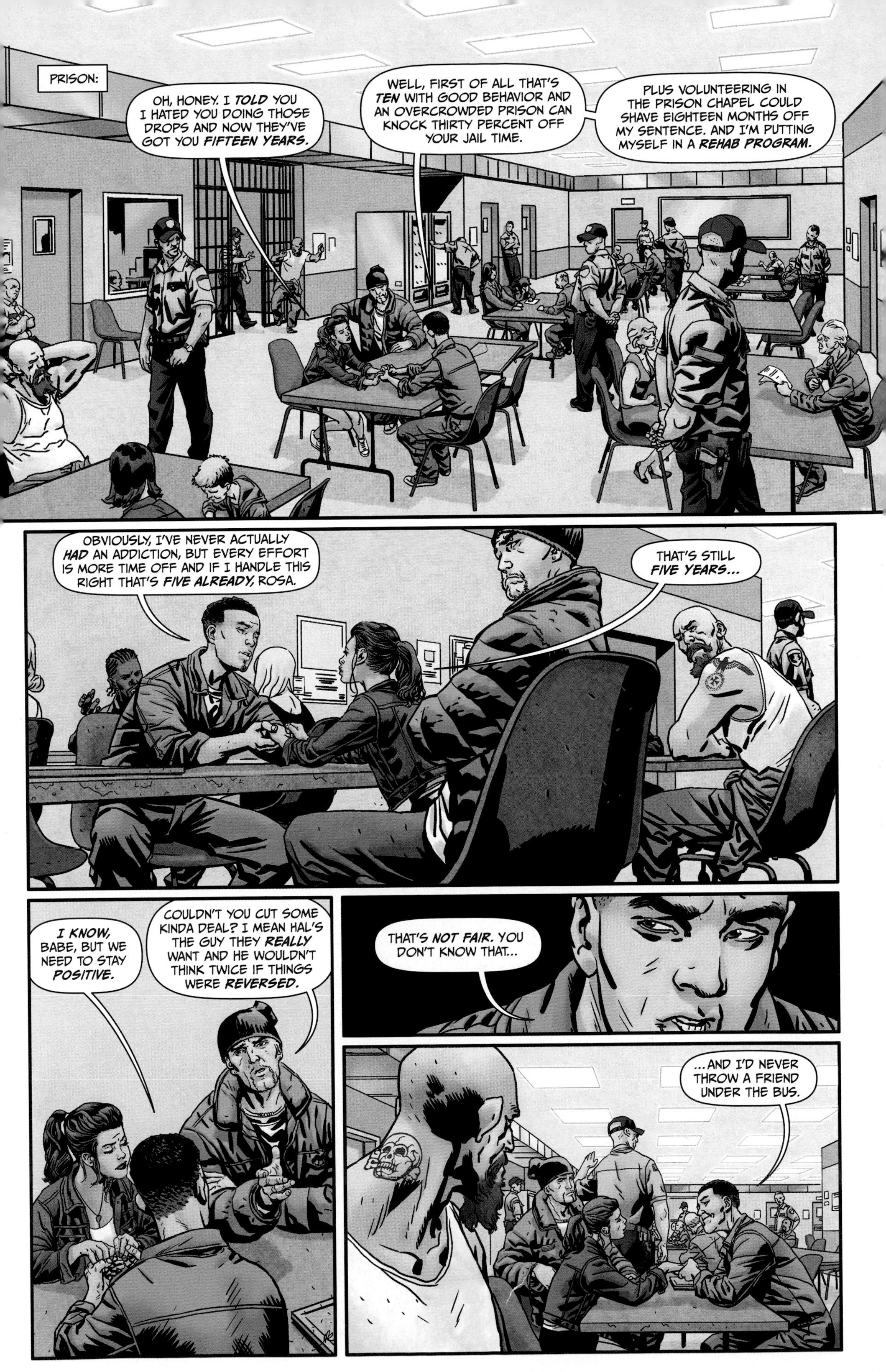
PRISON:
OH, HONEY. I TOLD YOU I HATED YOU DOING THOSE DROPS AND NOW THEY'VE GOT YOU FIFTEEN YEARS.
WELL, FIRST OF ALL THAT'S TEN WITH GOOD BEHAVIOR AND AN OVERCROWDED PRISON CAN KNOCK THIRTY PERCENT OFF YOUR JAIL TIME.
PLUS VOLUNTEERING IN THE PRISON CHAPEL COULD SHAVE EIGHTEEN MONTHS OFF MY SENTENCE. AND I'M PUTTING MYSELF IN A REHAB PROGRAM.
OBVIOUSLY, I'VE NEVER ACTUALLY HAD AN ADDICTION, BUT EVERY EFFORT IS MORE TIME OFF AND IF I HANDLE THIS RIGHT THAT'S FIVE ALREADY, ROSA.
THAT'S STILL FIVE YEARS...
I KNOW, BABE, BUT WE NEED TO STAY POSITIVE.
COULDN'T YOU CUT SOME KINDA DEAL? I MEAN HAL'S THE GUY THEY REALLY WANT AND HE WOULDN'T THINK TWICE IF THINGS WERE REVERSED.
THAT'S NOT FAIR. YOU DON'T KNOW THAT...
...AND I'D NEVER THROW A FRIEND UNDER THE BUS.

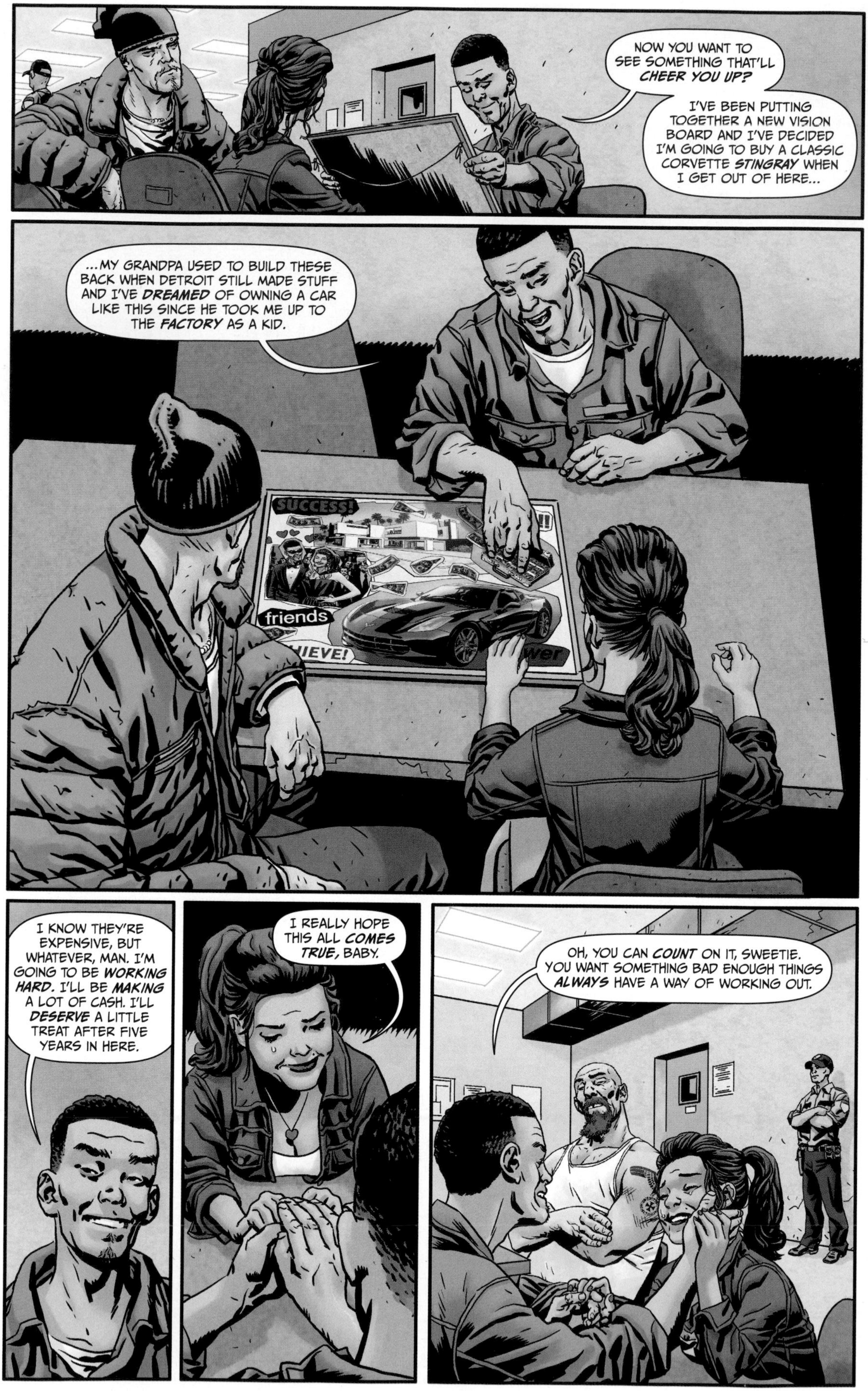
NOW YOU WANT TO SEE SOMETHING THAT'LL CHEER YOU UP?
I'VE BEEN PUTTING TOGETHER A NEW VISION BOARD AND I'VE DECIDED I'M GOING TO BUY A CLASSIC CORVETTE STINGRAY WHEN I GET OUT OF HERE...
...MY GRANDPA USED TO BUILD THESE BACK WHEN DETROIT STILL MADE STUFF AND I'VE DREAMED OF OWNING A CAR LIKE THIS SINCE HE TOOK ME UP TO THE FACTORY AS A KID.
SUCCESS!
friends
I KNOW THEY'RE EXPENSIVE, BUT WHATEVER, MAN. I'M GOING TO BE WORKING HARD. I'LL BE MAKING A LOT OF CASH. I'LL DESERVE A LITTLE TREAT AFTER FIVE YEARS IN HERE.
I REALLY HOPE THIS ALL COMES TRUE, BABY.
OH, YOU CAN COUNT ON IT, SWEETIE. YOU WANT SOMETHING BAD ENOUGH THINGS ALWAYS HAVE A WAY OF WORKING OUT.

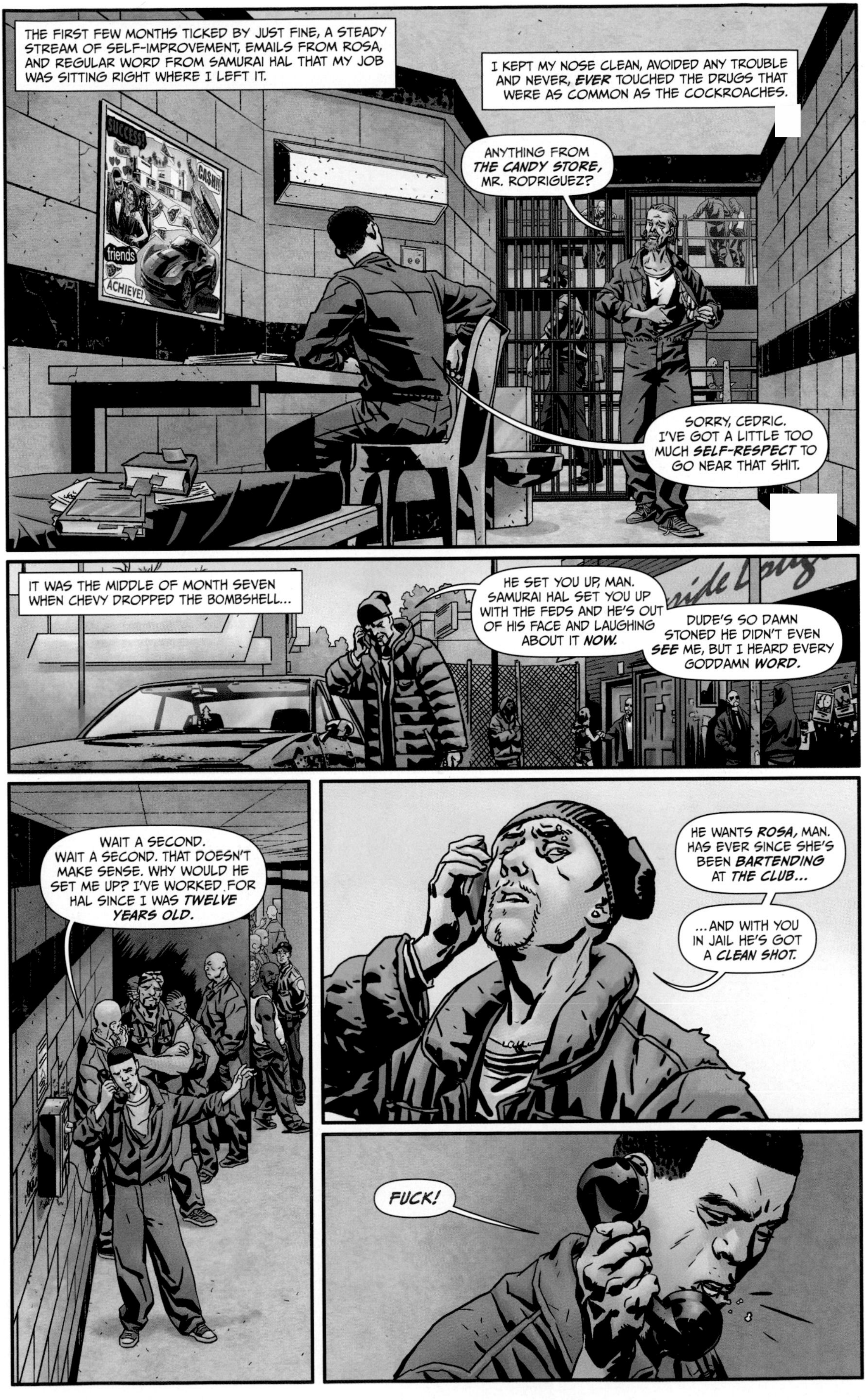
THE FIRST FEW MONTHS TICKED BY JUST FINE, A STEADY STREAM OF SELF-IMPROVEMENT, EMAILS FROM ROSA, AND REGULAR WORD FROM SAMURAI HAL THAT MY JOB WAS SITTING RIGHT WHERE I LEFT IT.
I KEPT MY NOSE CLEAN, AVOIDED ANY TROUBLE AND NEVER, EVER TOUCHED THE DRUGS THAT WERE AS COMMON AS THE COCKROACHES.
SUCCESS!
CASH!!
friends
ACHIEVE!
ANYTHING FROM THE CANDY STORE, MR. RODRIGUEZ?
SORRY, CEDRIC. I'VE GOT A LITTLE TOO MUCH SELF-RESPECT TO GO NEAR THAT SHIT.
IT WAS THE MIDDLE OF MONTH SEVEN WHEN CHEVY DROPPED THE BOMBSHELL...
HE SET YOU UP, MAN. SAMURAI HAL SET YOU UP WITH THE FEDS AND HE'S OUT OF HIS FACE AND LAUGHING ABOUT IT NOW.
DUDE'S SO DAMN STONED HE DIDN'T EVEN SEE ME, BUT I HEARD EVERY GODDAMN WORD.
WAIT A SECOND. WAIT A SECOND. THAT DOESN'T MAKE SENSE. WHY WOULD HE SET ME UP? I'VE WORKED FOR HAL SINCE I WAS TWELVE YEARS OLD.
HE WANTS ROSA, MAN. HAS EVER SINCE SHE'S BEEN BARTENDING AT THE CLUB...
...AND WITH YOU IN JAIL HE'S GOT A CLEAN SHOT.
FUCK!

I CALLED MY LAWYER TO SAY I'D CHANGED MY MIND AND I'D TAKE THE STAND TO DELIVER HAL'S HEAD.

BUT I WAS *TOO LATE.* HE FIGURED THEY WERE AFTER *BIGGER FISH* NOW AND HAVING HAL LOOSE WAS ALL JUST PART OF *CATCHING* THEM.

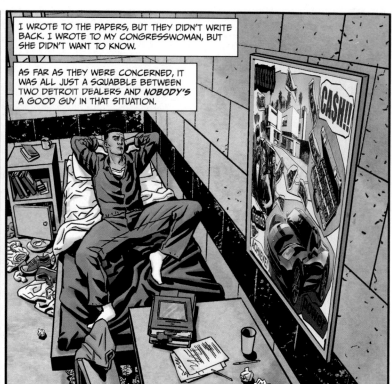

I WROTE TO THE PAPERS, BUT THEY DIDN'T WRITE BACK. I WROTE TO MY CONGRESSWOMAN, BUT SHE DIDN'T WANT TO KNOW.

AS FAR AS THEY WERE CONCERNED, IT WAS ALL JUST A SQUABBLE BETWEEN TWO DETROIT DEALERS AND *NOBODY'S* A GOOD GUY IN THAT SITUATION.

I QUIT THE CHURCH, FELL BEHIND ON MY STUDIES, AND STAYED UP NIGHTS TRYING TO RATIONALIZE *WHAT HAPPENED.*

I CAN ONLY BLAME *LACK OF SLEEP* FOR WHAT CAME NEXT...

HEY, ROSCOE. I HEAR YOUR PAL TURNED YOU OVER SO HE COULD HUMP YOUR *GIRLFRIEND.* IS IT WEIRD THAT YOU'RE SCRUBBING POTS AND PANS WHILE SHE'S PLAYING WITH HIS BALLS AND SUCKING HIM OFF?

YOU THINK HE FINISHES ON HER *TITS* OR HER *FACE?*

IF SHE'S THE ONE I SEEN DURING *VISITING HOURS* MY MONEY'S ON THOSE *TITTIES...*

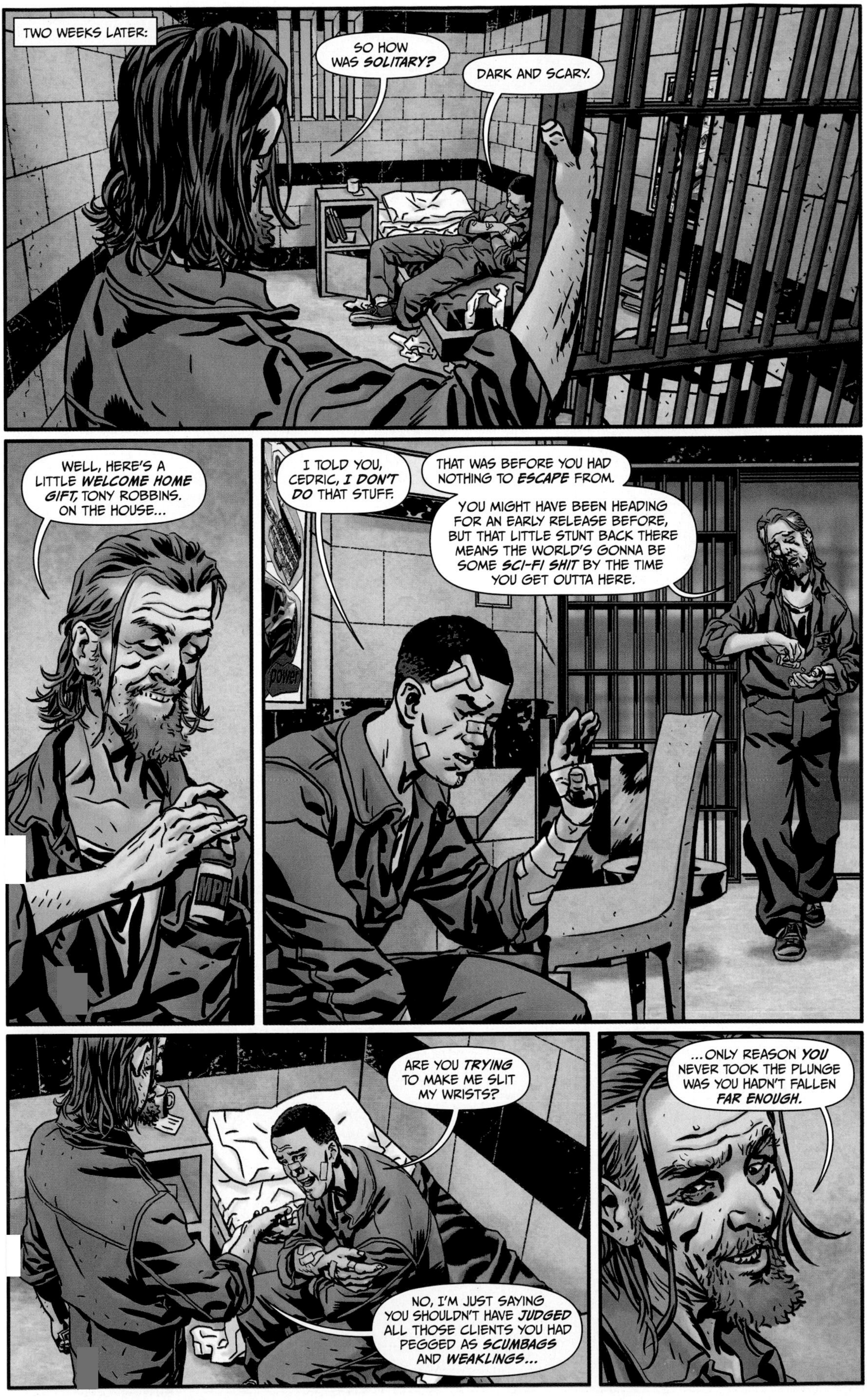
TWO WEEKS LATER:
SO HOW WAS SOLITARY?
DARK AND SCARY.
WELL, HERE'S A LITTLE WELCOME HOME GIFT, TONY ROBBINS. ON THE HOUSE...
I TOLD YOU, CEDRIC, I DON'T DO THAT STUFF.
THAT WAS BEFORE YOU HAD NOTHING TO ESCAPE FROM.
YOU MIGHT HAVE BEEN HEADING FOR AN EARLY RELEASE BEFORE, BUT THAT LITTLE STUNT BACK THERE MEANS THE WORLD'S GONNA BE SOME SCI-FI SHIT BY THE TIME YOU GET OUTTA HERE.
ARE YOU TRYING TO MAKE ME SLIT MY WRISTS?
NO, I'M JUST SAYING YOU SHOULDN'T HAVE JUDGED ALL THOSE CLIENTS YOU HAD PEGGED AS SCUMBAGS AND WEAKLINGS...
...ONLY REASON YOU NEVER TOOK THE PLUNGE WAS YOU HADN'T FALLEN FAR ENOUGH.

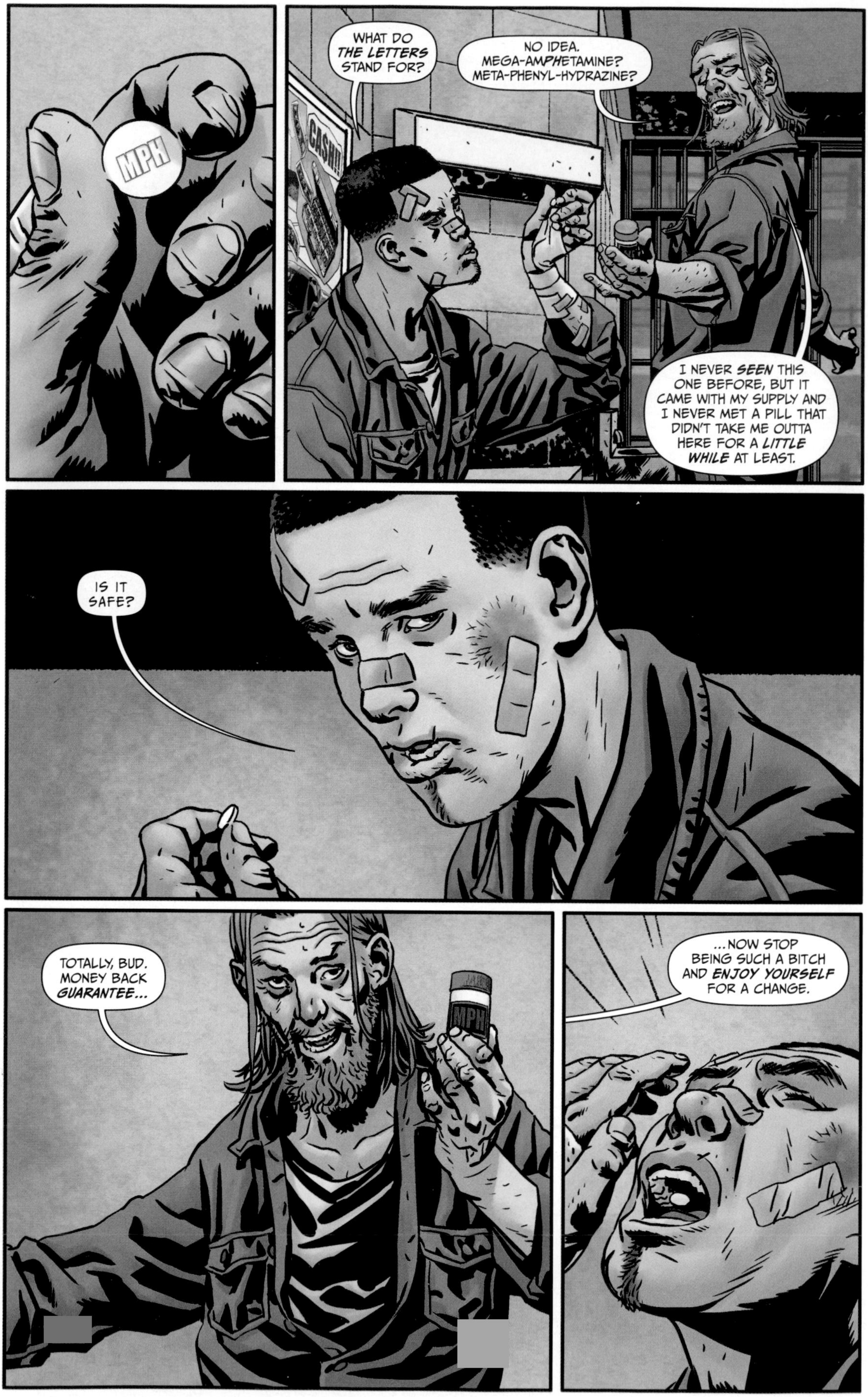
MPH
WHAT DO THE LETTERS STAND FOR?
NO IDEA. MEGA-AMPHETAMINE? META-PHENYL-HYDRAZINE?
CASH!!
I NEVER SEEN THIS ONE BEFORE, BUT IT CAME WITH MY SUPPLY AND I NEVER MET A PILL THAT DIDN'T TAKE ME OUTTA HERE FOR A LITTLE WHILE AT LEAST.
IS IT SAFE?
TOTALLY, BUD. MONEY BACK GUARANTEE...
MPH
...NOW STOP BEING SUCH A BITCH AND ENJOY YOURSELF FOR A CHANGE.

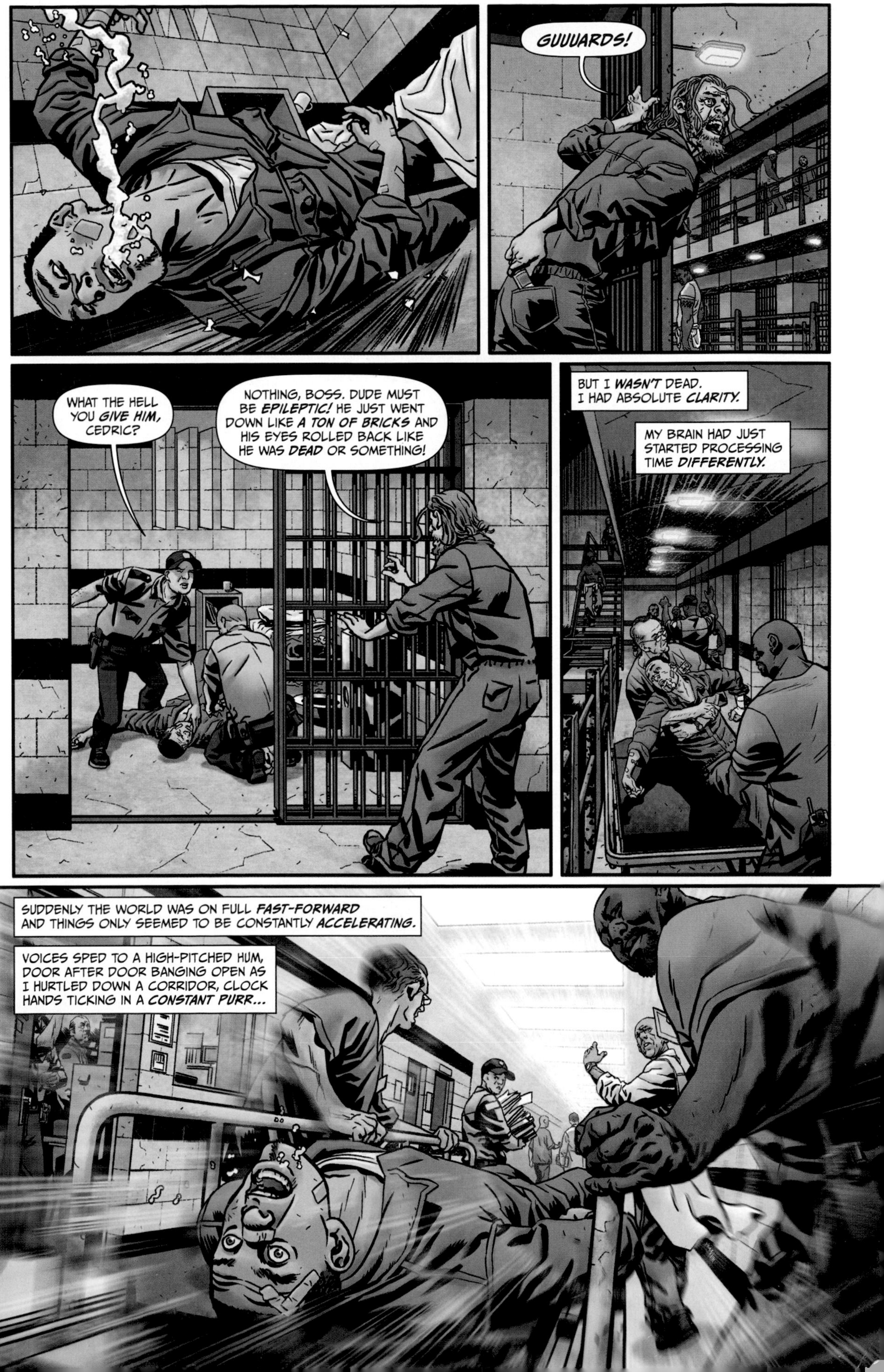
GUUUARDS!
WHAT THE HELL YOU GIVE HIM, CEDRIC?
NOTHING, BOSS. DUDE MUST BE EPILEPTIC! HE JUST WENT DOWN LIKE A TON OF BRICKS AND HIS EYES ROLLED BACK LIKE HE WAS DEAD OR SOMETHING!
BUT I WASN'T DEAD. I HAD ABSOLUTE CLARITY.
MY BRAIN HAD JUST STARTED PROCESSING TIME DIFFERENTLY.
SUDDENLY THE WORLD WAS ON FULL FAST-FORWARD AND THINGS ONLY SEEMED TO BE CONSTANTLY ACCELERATING.
VOICES SPED TO A HIGH-PITCHED HUM, DOOR AFTER DOOR BANGING OPEN AS I HURTLED DOWN A CORRIDOR, CLOCK HANDS TICKING IN A CONSTANT PURR...

MY CHEEKS BLEW BACK LIKE I WAS PILOTING A FIGHTER JET AND I KNEW I HAD TO *HIT THE BRAKES.*

I KNEW I HAD TO *CLOSE MY EYES* AND SNAP THINGS BACK TO *NORMAL...*

TICK

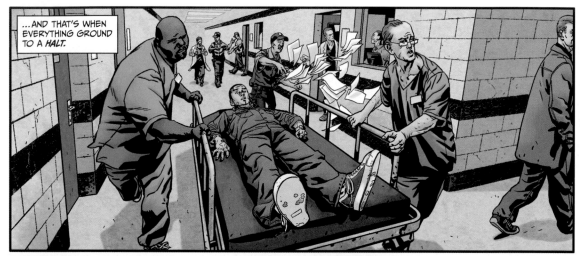

...AND THAT'S WHEN EVERYTHING GROUND TO A *HALT.*

UM, HELLO?

WHAT'S HAPPENING? WHY'S EVERYONE *STOPPED?*

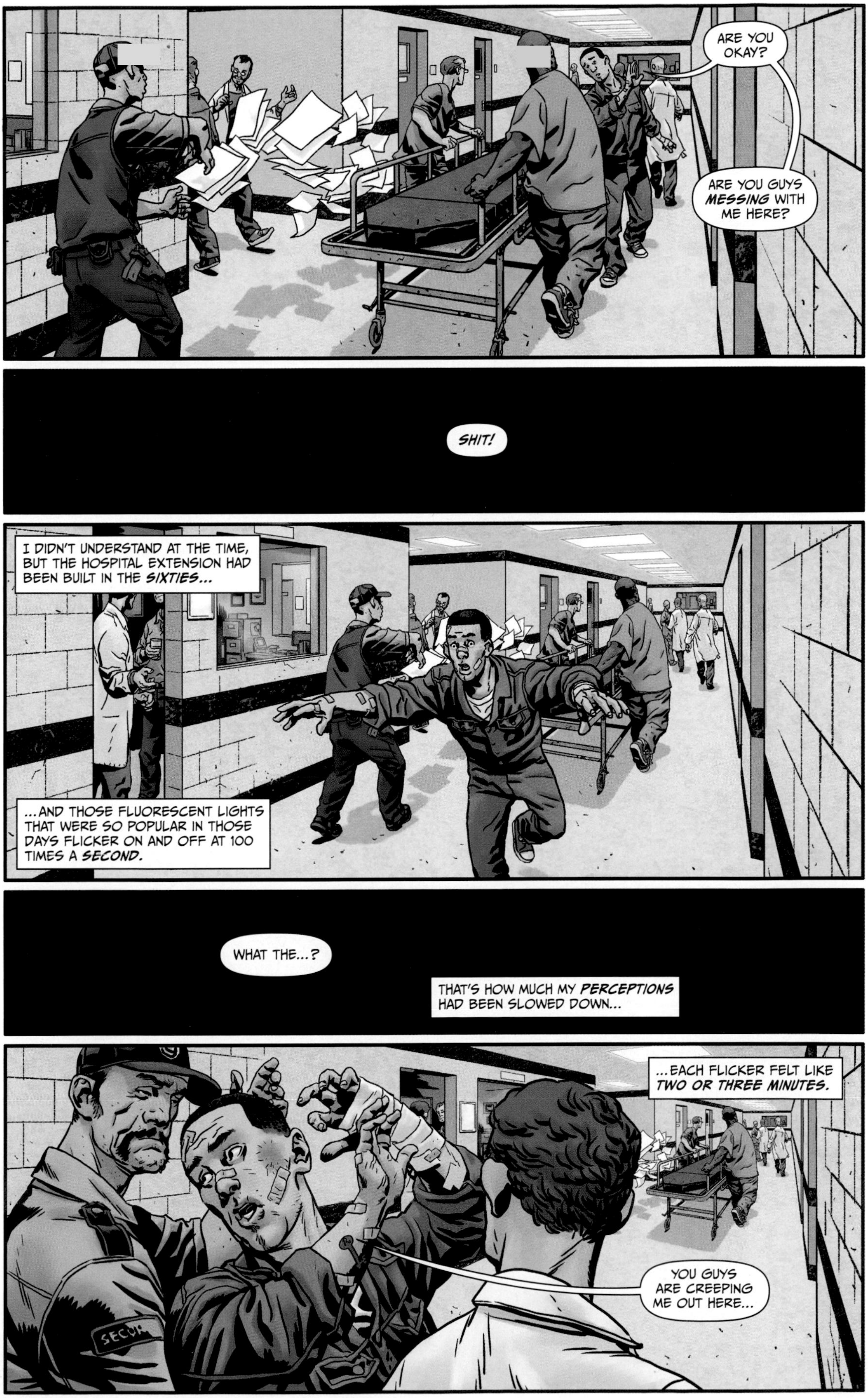
ARE YOU OKAY?
ARE YOU GUYS MESSING WITH ME HERE?
SHIT!
I DIDN'T UNDERSTAND AT THE TIME, BUT THE HOSPITAL EXTENSION HAD BEEN BUILT IN THE SIXTIES...
...AND THOSE FLUORESCENT LIGHTS THAT WERE SO POPULAR IN THOSE DAYS FLICKER ON AND OFF AT 100 TIMES A SECOND.
WHAT THE...?
THAT'S HOW MUCH MY PERCEPTIONS HAD BEEN SLOWED DOWN...
...EACH FLICKER FELT LIKE TWO OR THREE MINUTES.
YOU GUYS ARE CREEPING ME OUT HERE...
SECU

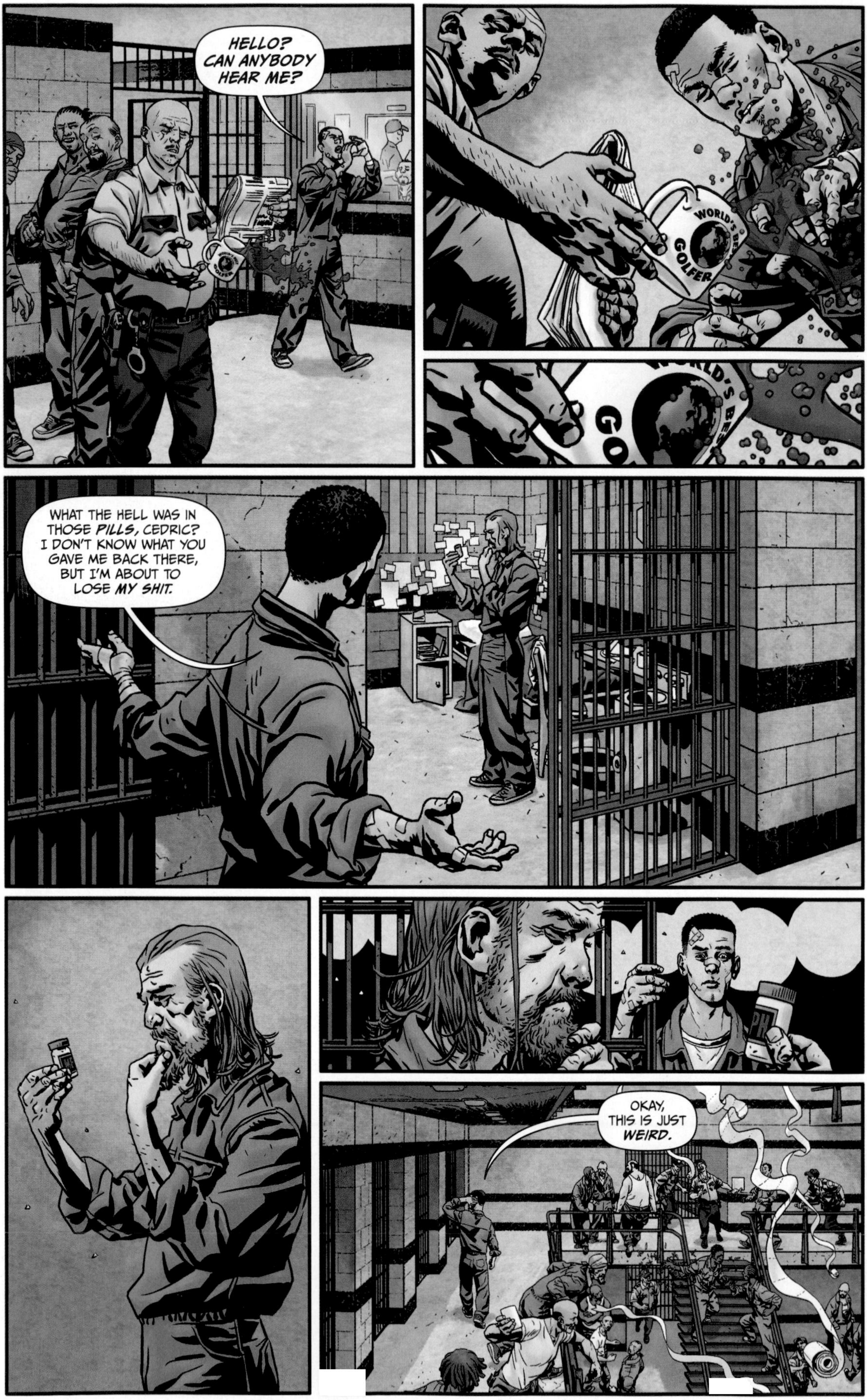
HELLO? CAN ANYBODY HEAR ME?
WORLD'S BEST GOLFER
WHAT THE HELL WAS IN THOSE PILLS, CEDRIC? I DON'T KNOW WHAT YOU GAVE ME BACK THERE, BUT I'M ABOUT TO LOSE MY SHIT.
OKAY, THIS IS JUST WEIRD.

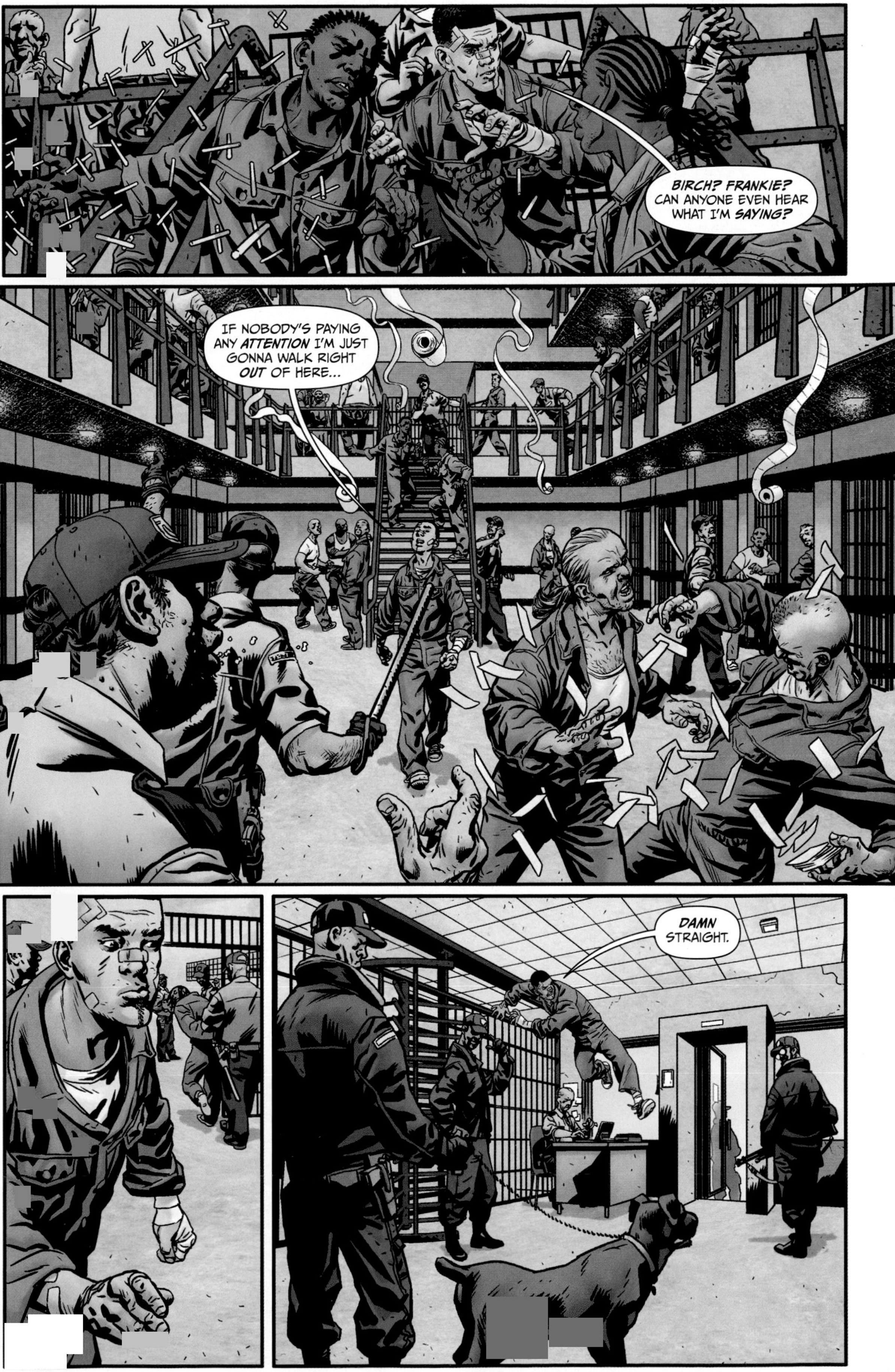
BIRCH? FRANKIE? CAN ANYONE EVEN HEAR WHAT I'M SAYING?
IF NOBODY'S PAYING ANY ATTENTION I'M JUST GONNA WALK RIGHT OUT OF HERE...
DAMN STRAIGHT.

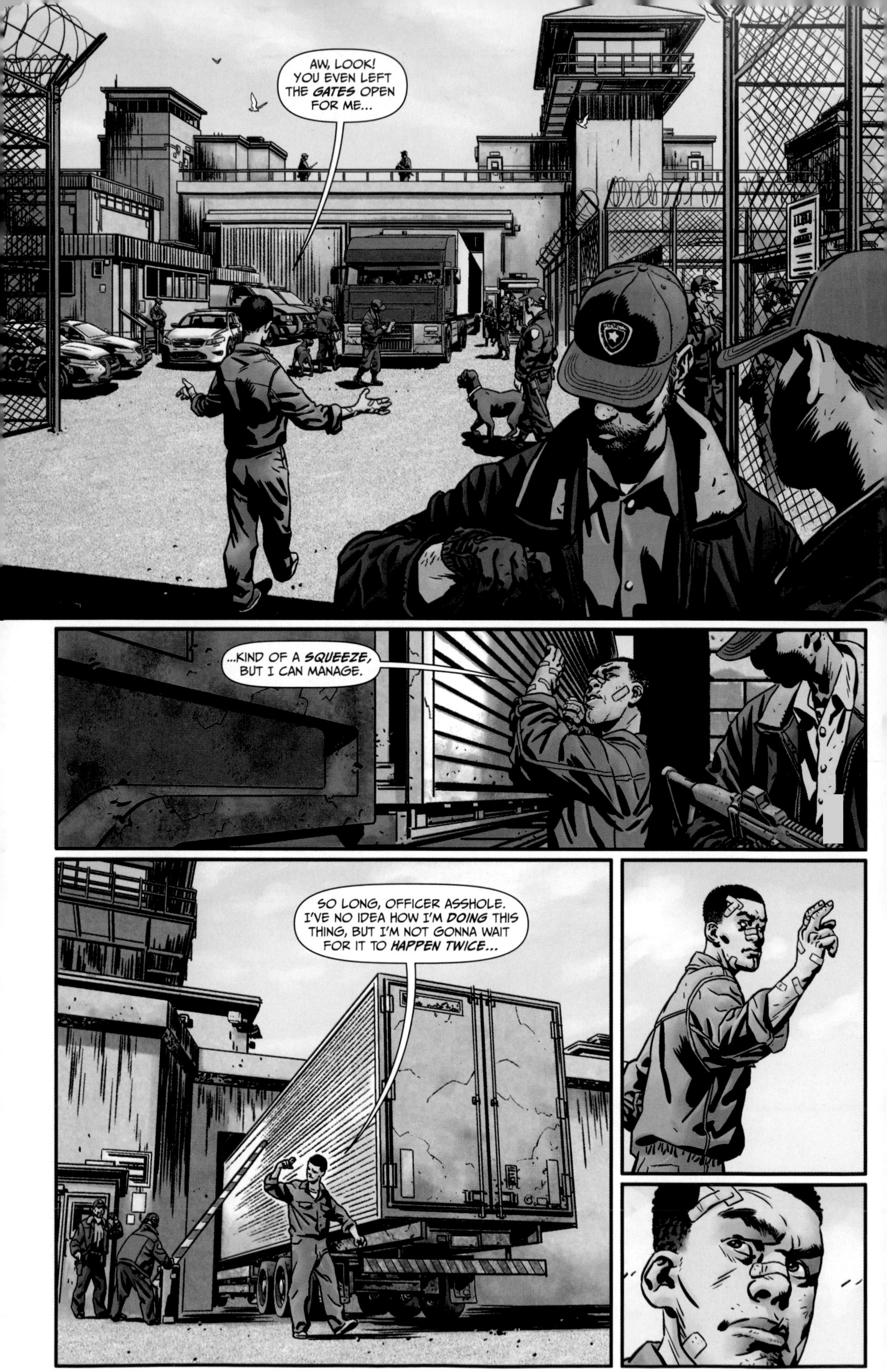
AW, LOOK! YOU EVEN LEFT THE GATES OPEN FOR ME...
...KIND OF A SQUEEZE, BUT I CAN MANAGE.
SO LONG, OFFICER ASSHOLE. I'VE NO IDEA HOW I'M DOING THIS THING, BUT I'M NOT GONNA WAIT FOR IT TO HAPPEN TWICE...

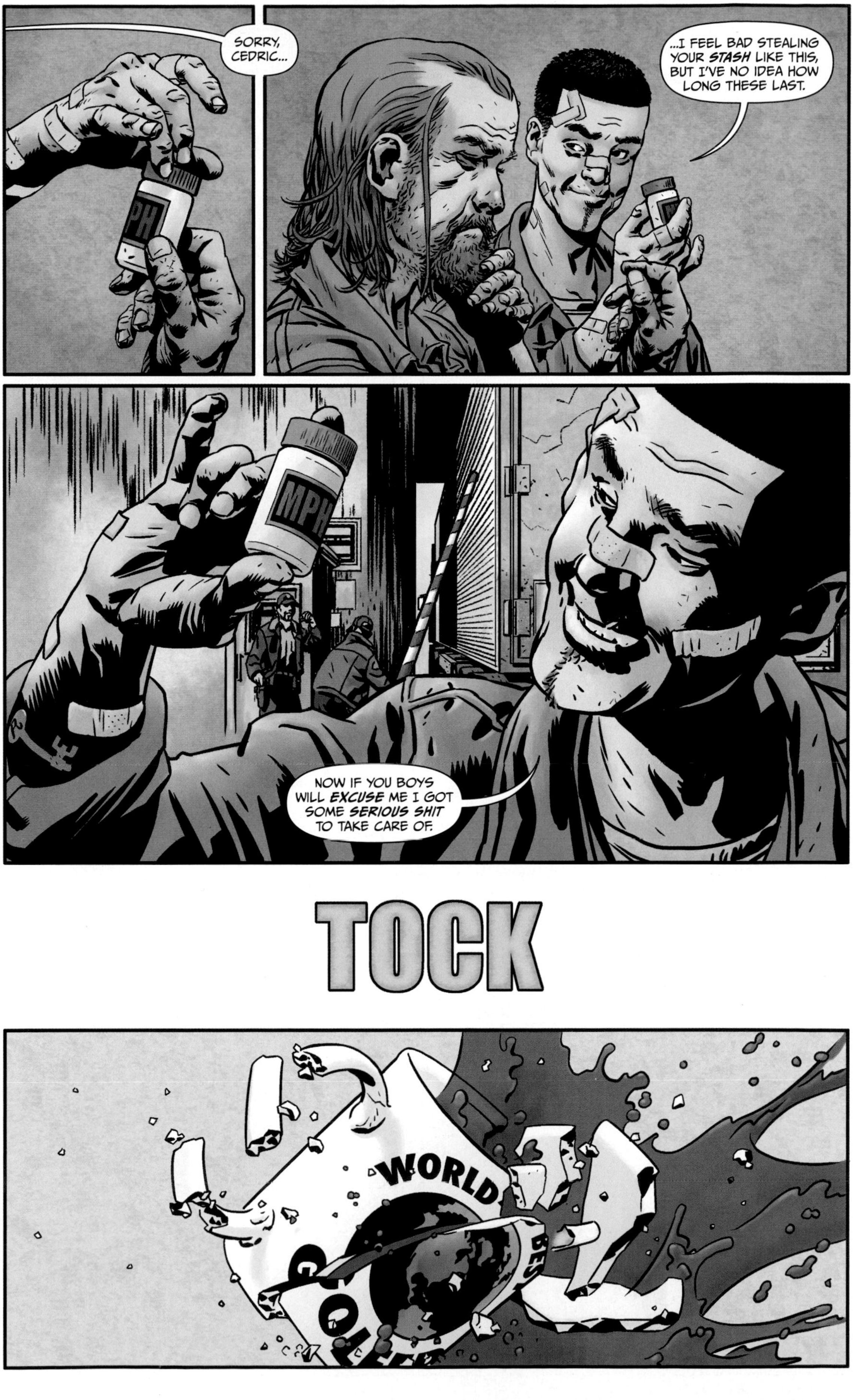
SORRY, CEDRIC...
...I FEEL BAD STEALING YOUR STASH LIKE THIS, BUT I'VE NO IDEA HOW LONG THESE LAST.
MPH
NOW IF YOU BOYS WILL EXCUSE ME I GOT SOME SERIOUS SHIT TO TAKE CARE OF.
TOCK
WORLD

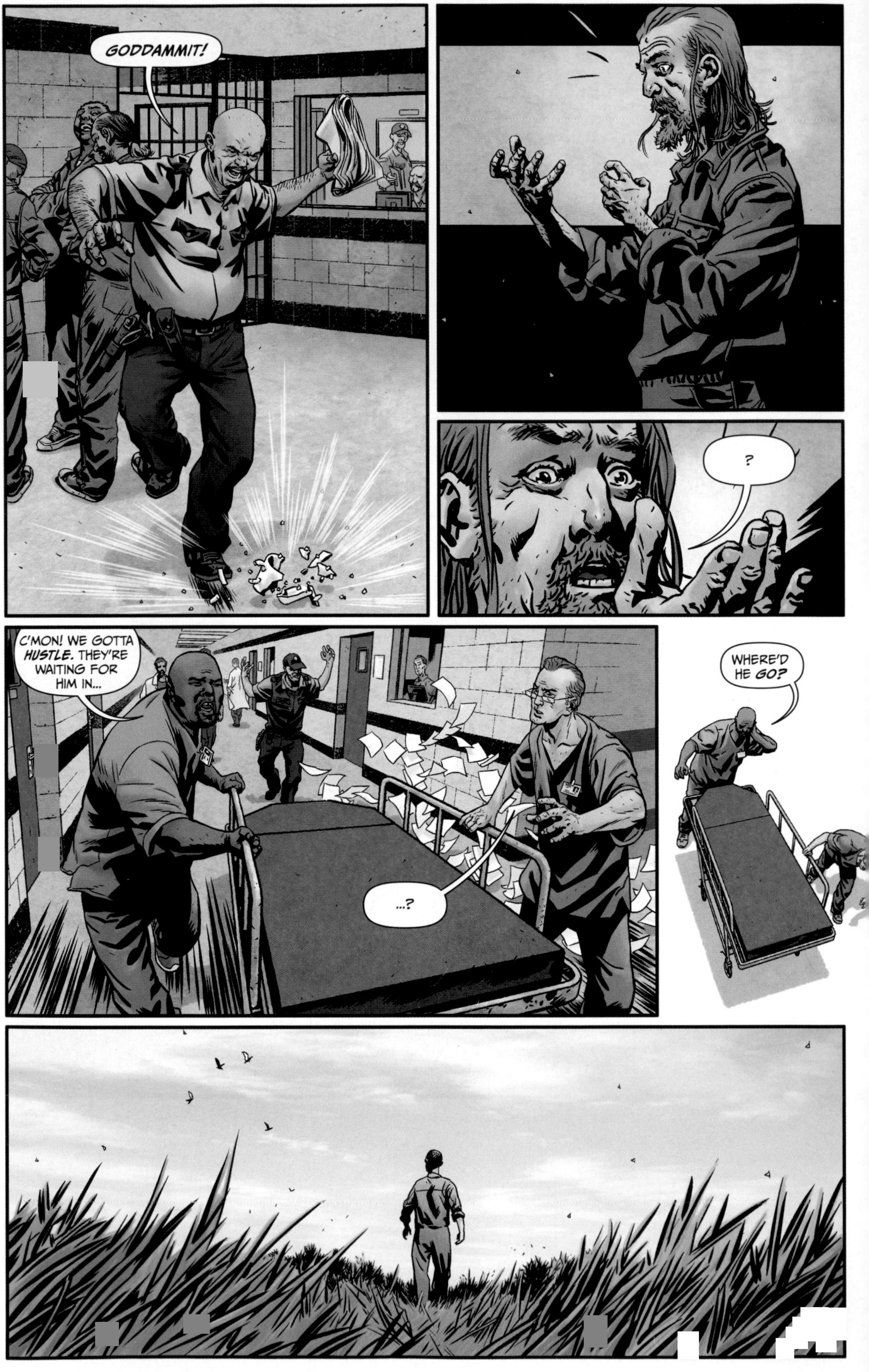
GODDAMMIT!
?
C'MON! WE GOTTA HUSTLE. THEY'RE WAITING FOR HIM IN...
...?
WHERE'D HE GO?

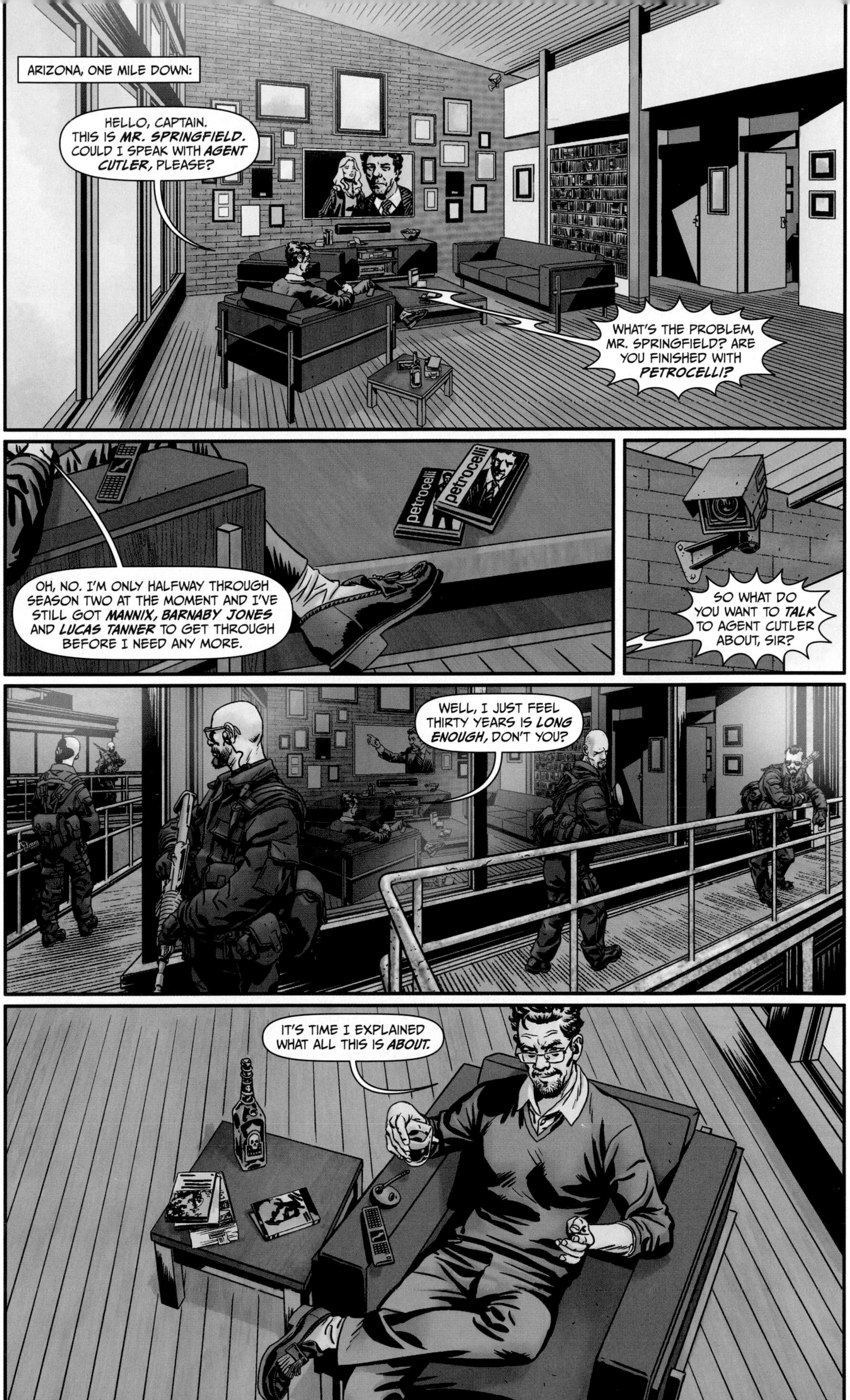
ARIZONA, ONE MILE DOWN:
HELLO, CAPTAIN. THIS IS MR. SPRINGFIELD. COULD I SPEAK WITH AGENT CUTLER, PLEASE?
WHAT'S THE PROBLEM, MR. SPRINGFIELD? ARE YOU FINISHED WITH PETROCELLI?
petrocelli
OH, NO. I'M ONLY HALFWAY THROUGH SEASON TWO AT THE MOMENT AND I'VE STILL GOT MANNIX, BARNABY JONES AND LUCAS TANNER TO GET THROUGH BEFORE I NEED ANY MORE.
SO WHAT DO YOU WANT TO TALK TO AGENT CUTLER ABOUT, SIR?
WELL, I JUST FEEL THIRTY YEARS IS LONG ENOUGH, DON'T YOU?
IT'S TIME I EXPLAINED WHAT ALL THIS IS ABOUT.

CHAPTER TWO

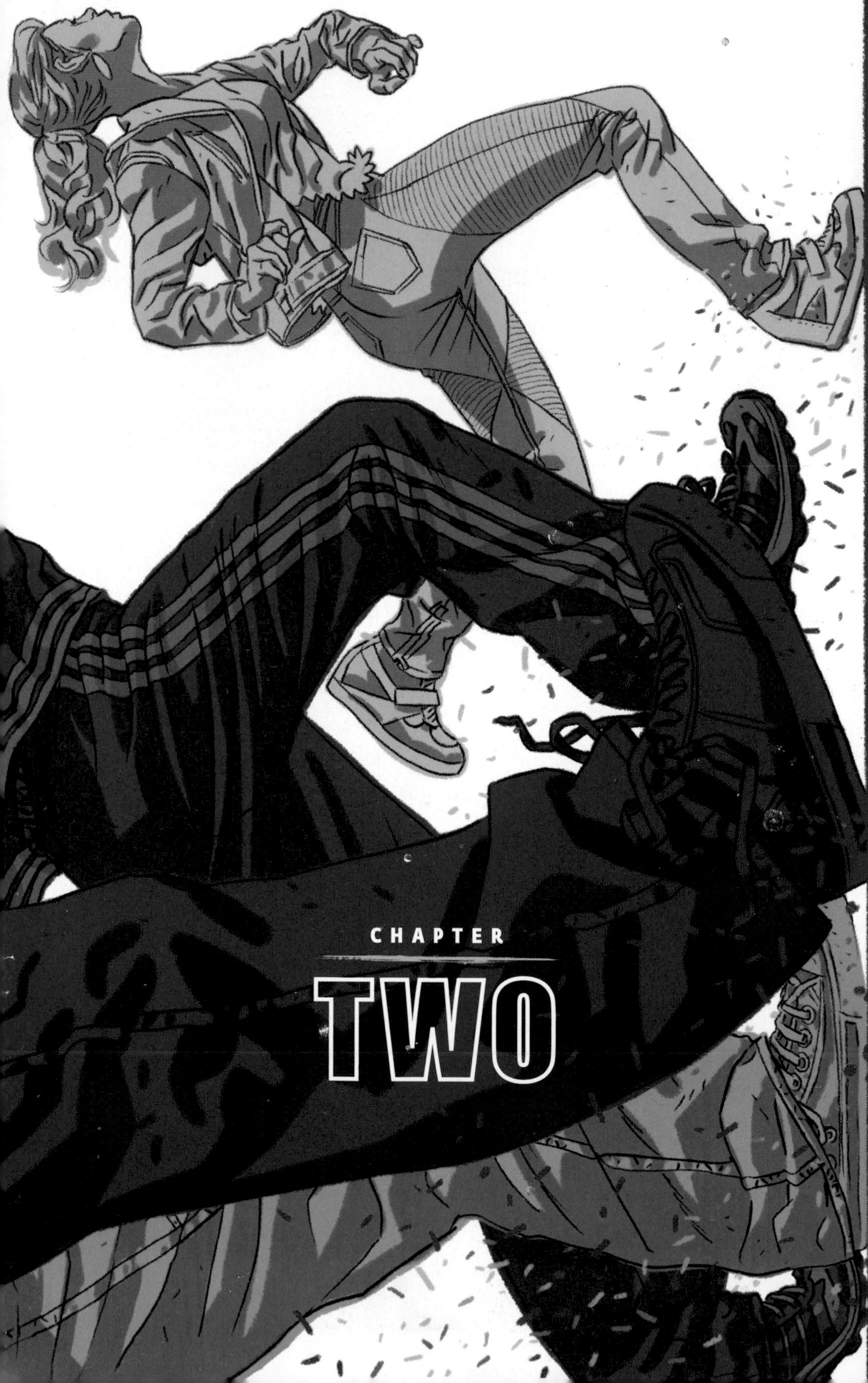

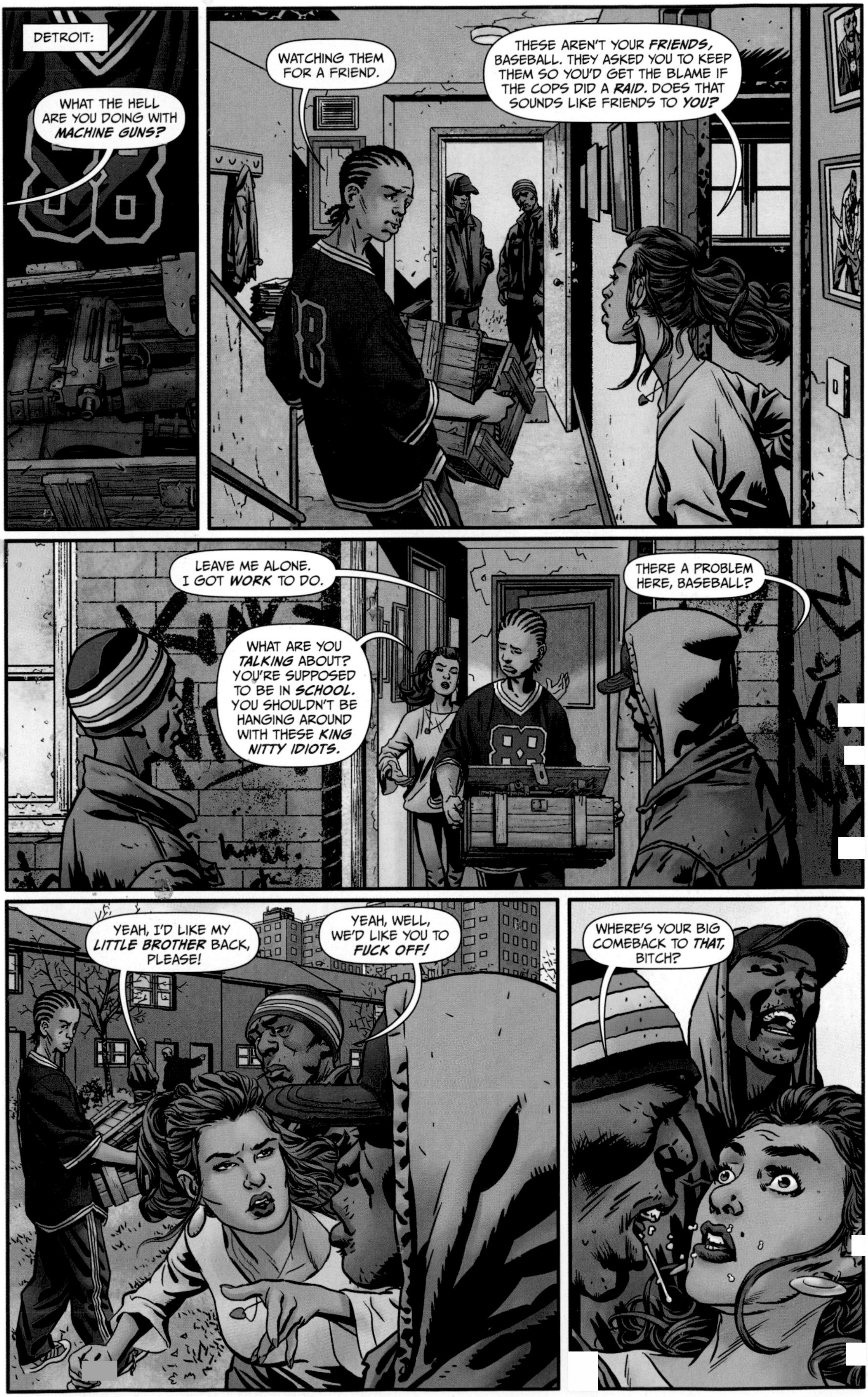
DETROIT:
WHAT THE HELL ARE YOU DOING WITH MACHINE GUNS?
WATCHING THEM FOR A FRIEND.
THESE AREN'T YOUR FRIENDS, BASEBALL. THEY ASKED YOU TO KEEP THEM SO YOU'D GET THE BLAME IF THE COPS DID A RAID. DOES THAT SOUNDS LIKE FRIENDS TO YOU?
LEAVE ME ALONE. I GOT WORK TO DO.
WHAT ARE YOU TALKING ABOUT? YOU'RE SUPPOSED TO BE IN SCHOOL. YOU SHOULDN'T BE HANGING AROUND WITH THESE KING NITTY IDIOTS.
THERE A PROBLEM HERE, BASEBALL?
YEAH, I'D LIKE MY LITTLE BROTHER BACK, PLEASE!
YEAH, WELL, WE'D LIKE YOU TO FUCK OFF!
WHERE'S YOUR BIG COMEBACK TO THAT, BITCH?

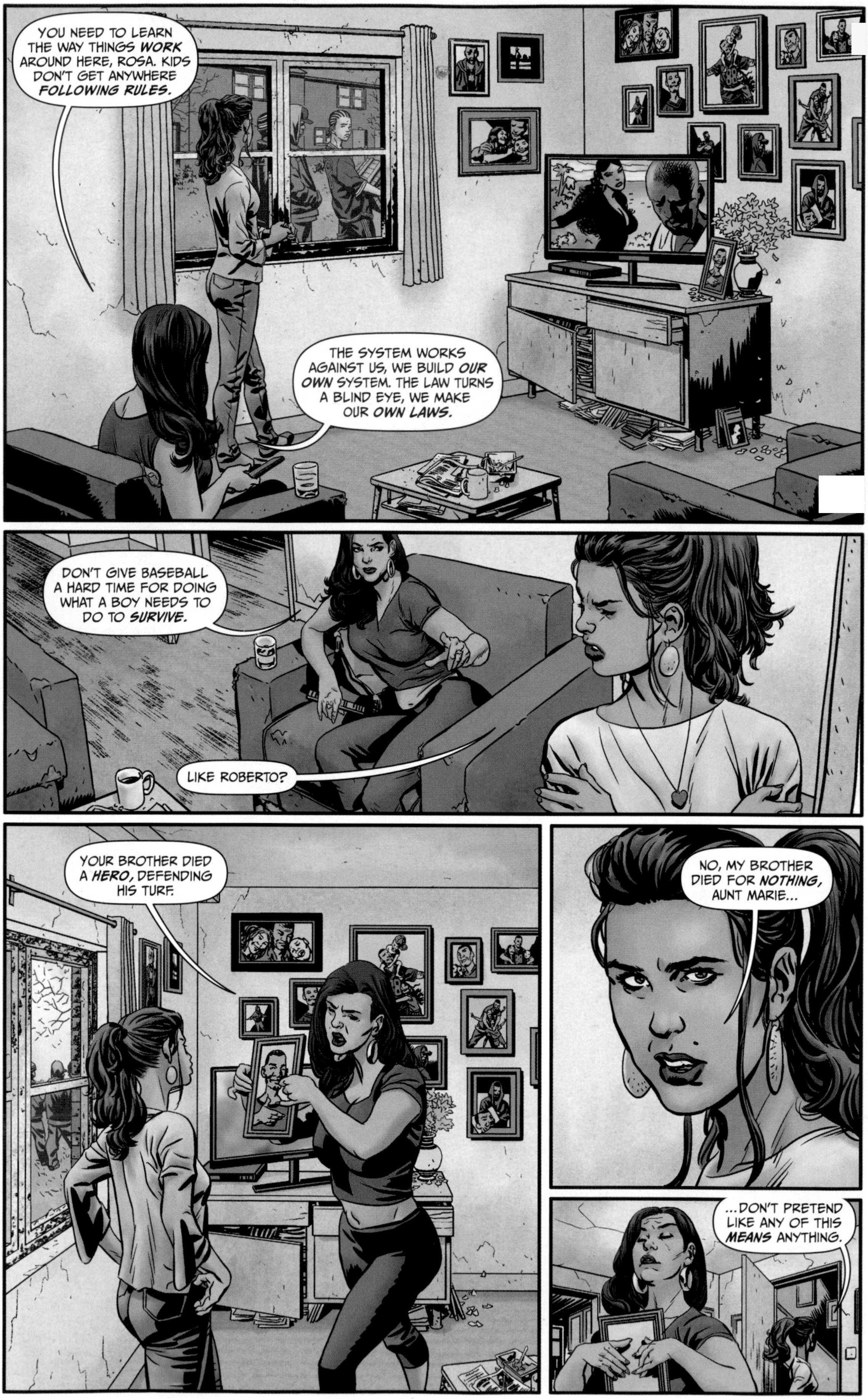
YOU NEED TO LEARN THE WAY THINGS WORK AROUND HERE, ROSA. KIDS DON'T GET ANYWHERE FOLLOWING RULES.
THE SYSTEM WORKS AGAINST US, WE BUILD OUR OWN SYSTEM. THE LAW TURNS A BLIND EYE, WE MAKE OUR OWN LAWS.
DON'T GIVE BASEBALL A HARD TIME FOR DOING WHAT A BOY NEEDS TO DO TO SURVIVE.
LIKE ROBERTO?
YOUR BROTHER DIED A HERO, DEFENDING HIS TURF.
NO, MY BROTHER DIED FOR NOTHING, AUNT MARIE...
...DON'T PRETEND LIKE ANY OF THIS MEANS ANYTHING.

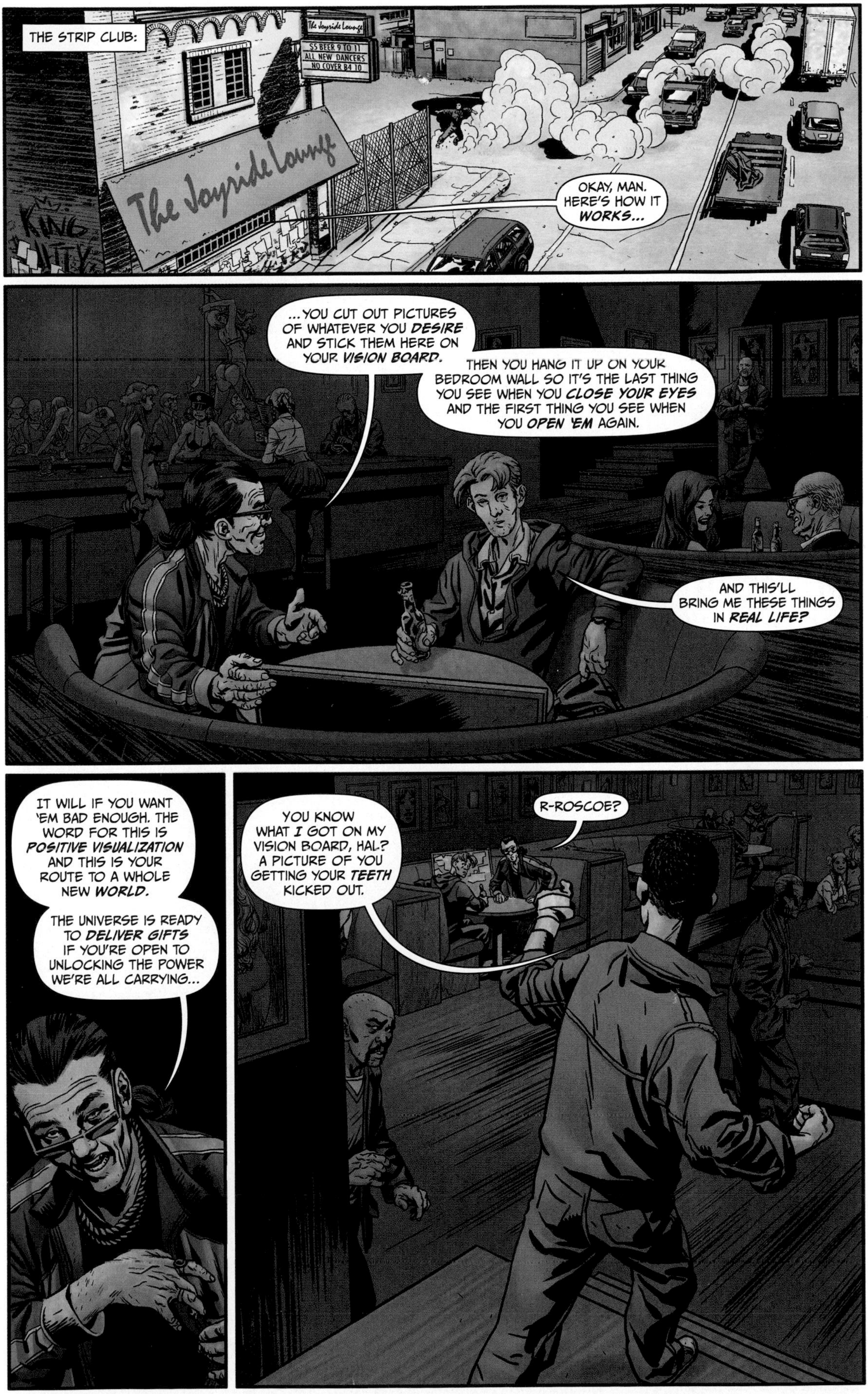

THE STRIP CLUB:
The Joyride Lounge
$5 BEER 9 TO 11
ALL NEW DANCERS
NO COVER B4 10
The Joyride Lounge
OKAY, MAN. HERE'S HOW IT WORKS...
...YOU CUT OUT PICTURES OF WHATEVER YOU DESIRE AND STICK THEM HERE ON YOUR VISION BOARD.
THEN YOU HANG IT UP ON YOUR BEDROOM WALL SO IT'S THE LAST THING YOU SEE WHEN YOU CLOSE YOUR EYES AND THE FIRST THING YOU SEE WHEN YOU OPEN 'EM AGAIN.
AND THIS'LL BRING ME THESE THINGS IN REAL LIFE?
IT WILL IF YOU WANT 'EM BAD ENOUGH. THE WORD FOR THIS IS POSITIVE VISUALIZATION AND THIS IS YOUR ROUTE TO A WHOLE NEW WORLD.
THE UNIVERSE IS READY TO DELIVER GIFTS IF YOU'RE OPEN TO UNLOCKING THE POWER WE'RE ALL CARRYING...
YOU KNOW WHAT I GOT ON MY VISION BOARD, HAL? A PICTURE OF YOU GETTING YOUR TEETH KICKED OUT.
R-ROSCOE?

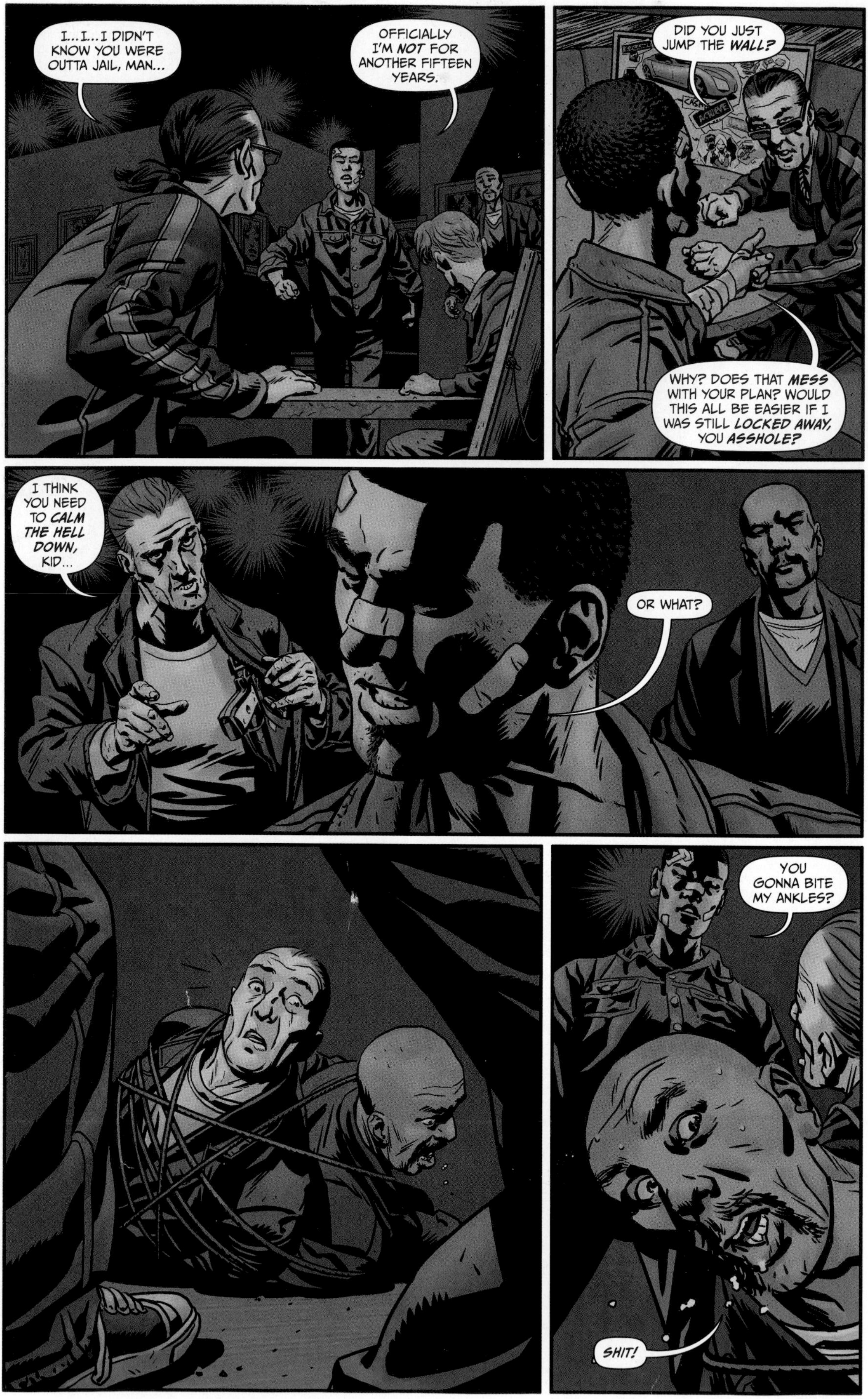
I...I...I DIDN'T KNOW YOU WERE OUTTA JAIL, MAN...
OFFICIALLY I'M NOT FOR ANOTHER FIFTEEN YEARS.
DID YOU JUST JUMP THE WALL?
WHY? DOES THAT MESS WITH YOUR PLAN? WOULD THIS ALL BE EASIER IF I WAS STILL LOCKED AWAY, YOU ASSHOLE?
I THINK YOU NEED TO CALM THE HELL DOWN, KID...
OR WHAT?
YOU GONNA BITE MY ANKLES?
SHIT!

I *TRUSTED* YOU AND YOU *SCREWED ME OVER.* I LOVED YOU LIKE A *BROTHER* AND YOU JUST *LAUGHED* BEHIND MY *BACK!*

GET AWAY FROM ME! I'M *SERIOUS!*

NO, YOU'RE NOT...

...OTHERWISE YOU WOULDN'T HAVE GOT STONED AND SPILLED THE BEANS TO MY BEST FRIEND! YOU THINK *CHEVY* WOULDN'T HAVE MY BACK?

HUH?

THESE *BILLS* FLOATING AROUND IS ALL THE CASH YOU GOT *LEFT,* MAN...

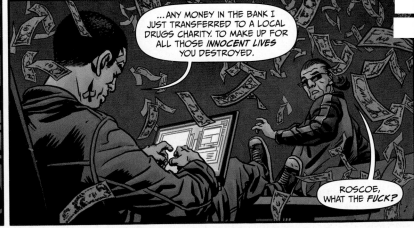

...ANY MONEY IN THE BANK I JUST TRANSFERRED TO A LOCAL DRUGS CHARITY. TO MAKE UP FOR ALL THOSE *INNOCENT LIVES* YOU DESTROYED.

ROSCOE, WHAT THE *FUCK?*

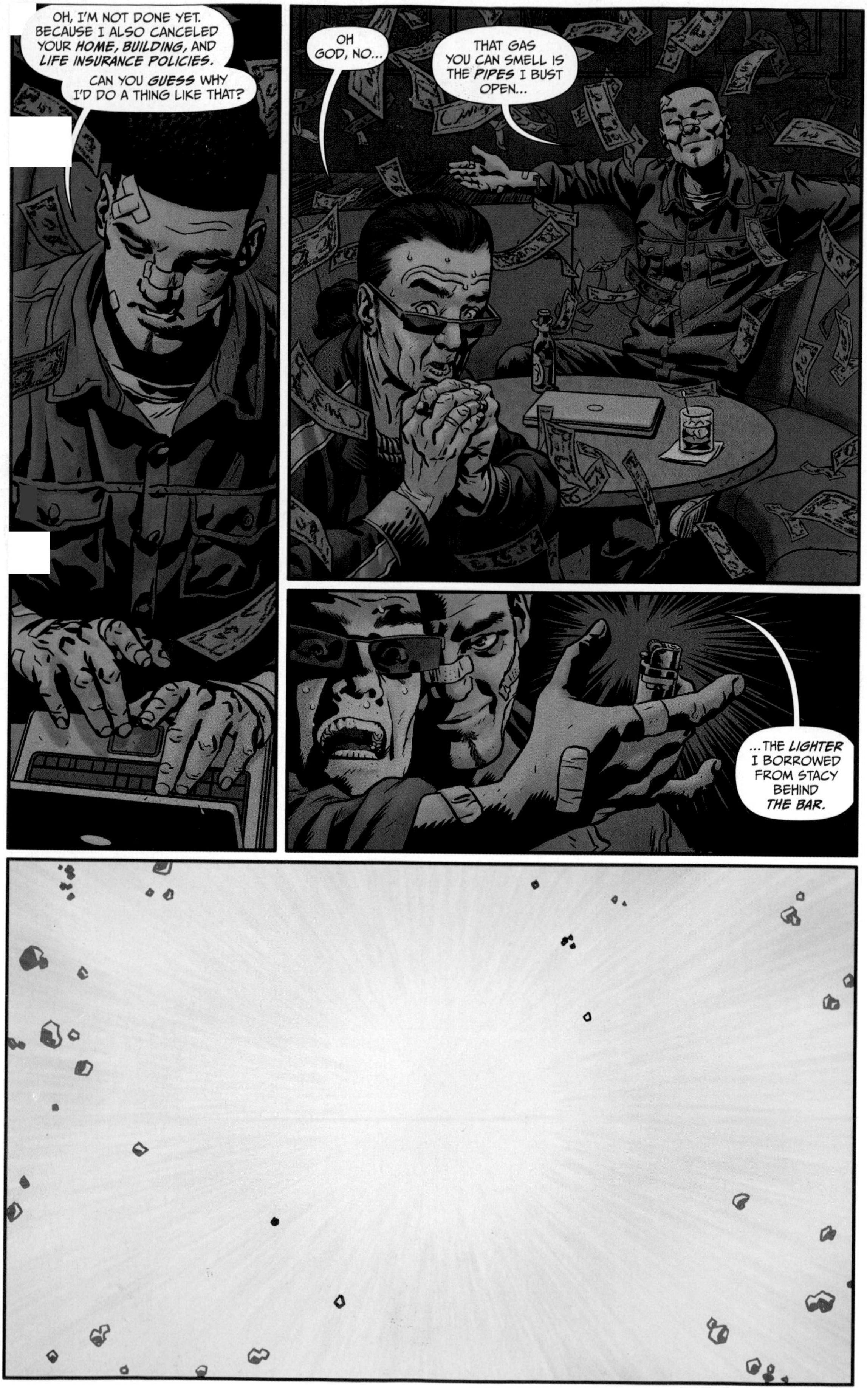
OH, I'M NOT DONE YET. BECAUSE I ALSO CANCELED YOUR HOME, BUILDING, AND LIFE INSURANCE POLICIES.
CAN YOU GUESS WHY I'D DO A THING LIKE THAT?
OH GOD, NO...
THAT GAS YOU CAN SMELL IS THE PIPES I BUST OPEN...
...THE LIGHTER I BORROWED FROM STACY BEHIND THE BAR.

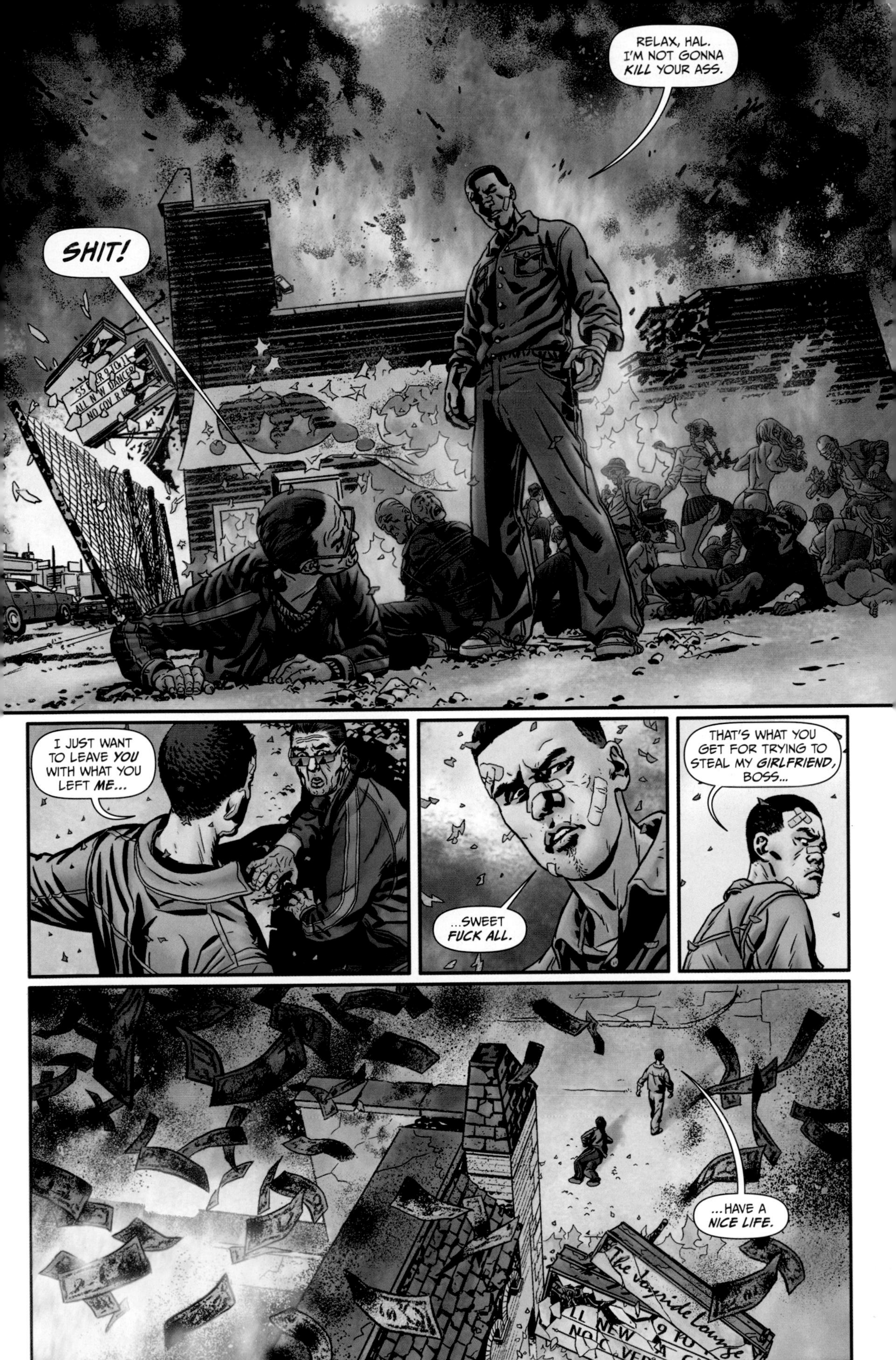
RELAX, HAL. I'M NOT GONNA KILL YOUR ASS.
SHIT!
I JUST WANT TO LEAVE YOU WITH WHAT YOU LEFT ME...
...SWEET FUCK ALL.
THAT'S WHAT YOU GET FOR TRYING TO STEAL MY GIRLFRIEND, BOSS...
...HAVE A NICE LIFE.
The Joyride Lounge

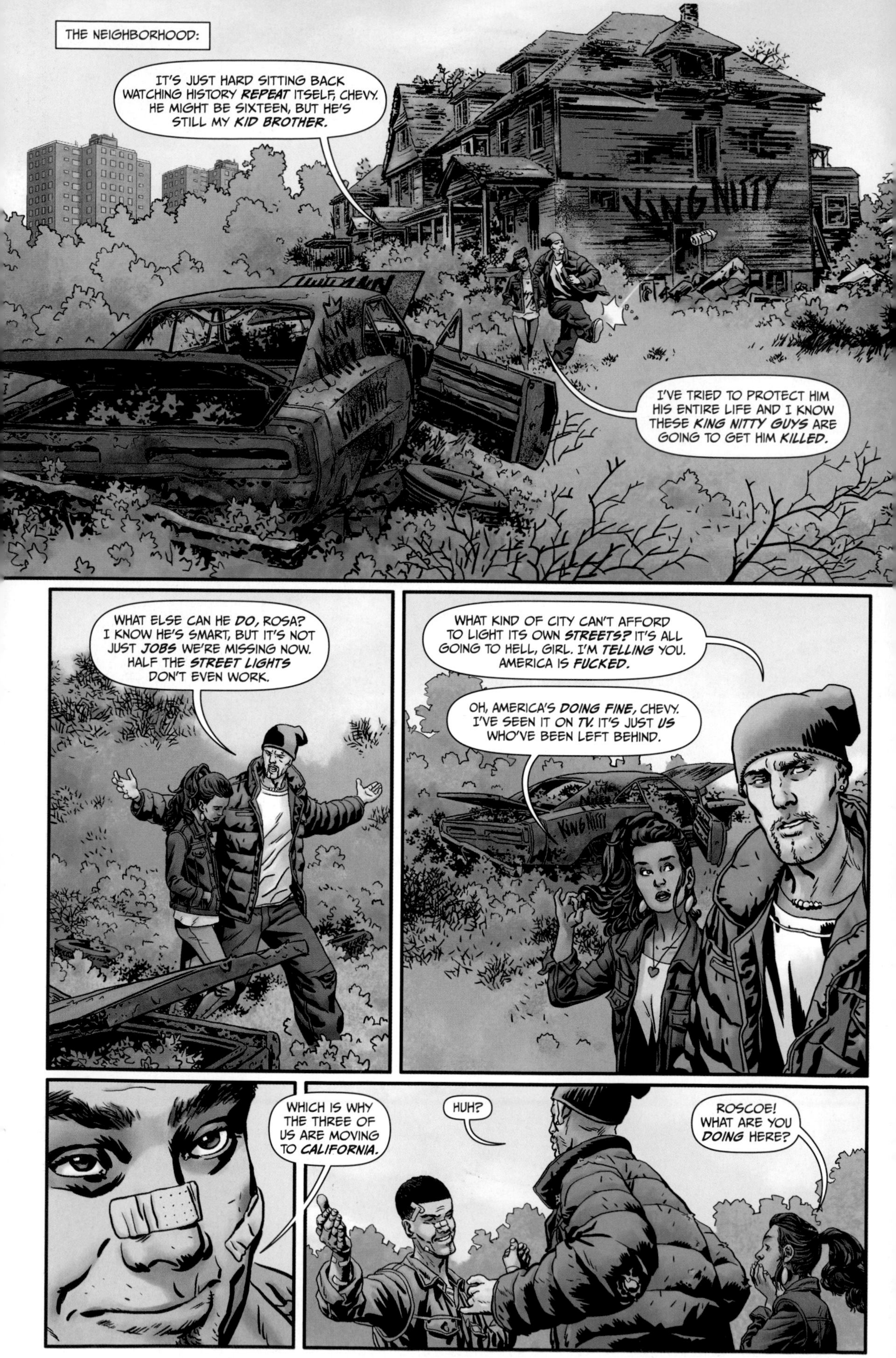
THE NEIGHBORHOOD:
IT'S JUST HARD SITTING BACK WATCHING HISTORY REPEAT ITSELF, CHEVY. HE MIGHT BE SIXTEEN, BUT HE'S STILL MY KID BROTHER.
KING NITTY
I'VE TRIED TO PROTECT HIM HIS ENTIRE LIFE AND I KNOW THESE KING NITTY GUYS ARE GOING TO GET HIM KILLED.
WHAT ELSE CAN HE DO, ROSA? I KNOW HE'S SMART, BUT IT'S NOT JUST JOBS WE'RE MISSING NOW. HALF THE STREET LIGHTS DON'T EVEN WORK.
WHAT KIND OF CITY CAN'T AFFORD TO LIGHT ITS OWN STREETS? IT'S ALL GOING TO HELL, GIRL. I'M TELLING YOU. AMERICA IS FUCKED.
OH, AMERICA'S DOING FINE, CHEVY. I'VE SEEN IT ON TV. IT'S JUST US WHO'VE BEEN LEFT BEHIND.
WHICH IS WHY THE THREE OF US ARE MOVING TO CALIFORNIA.
HUH?
ROSCOE! WHAT ARE YOU DOING HERE?

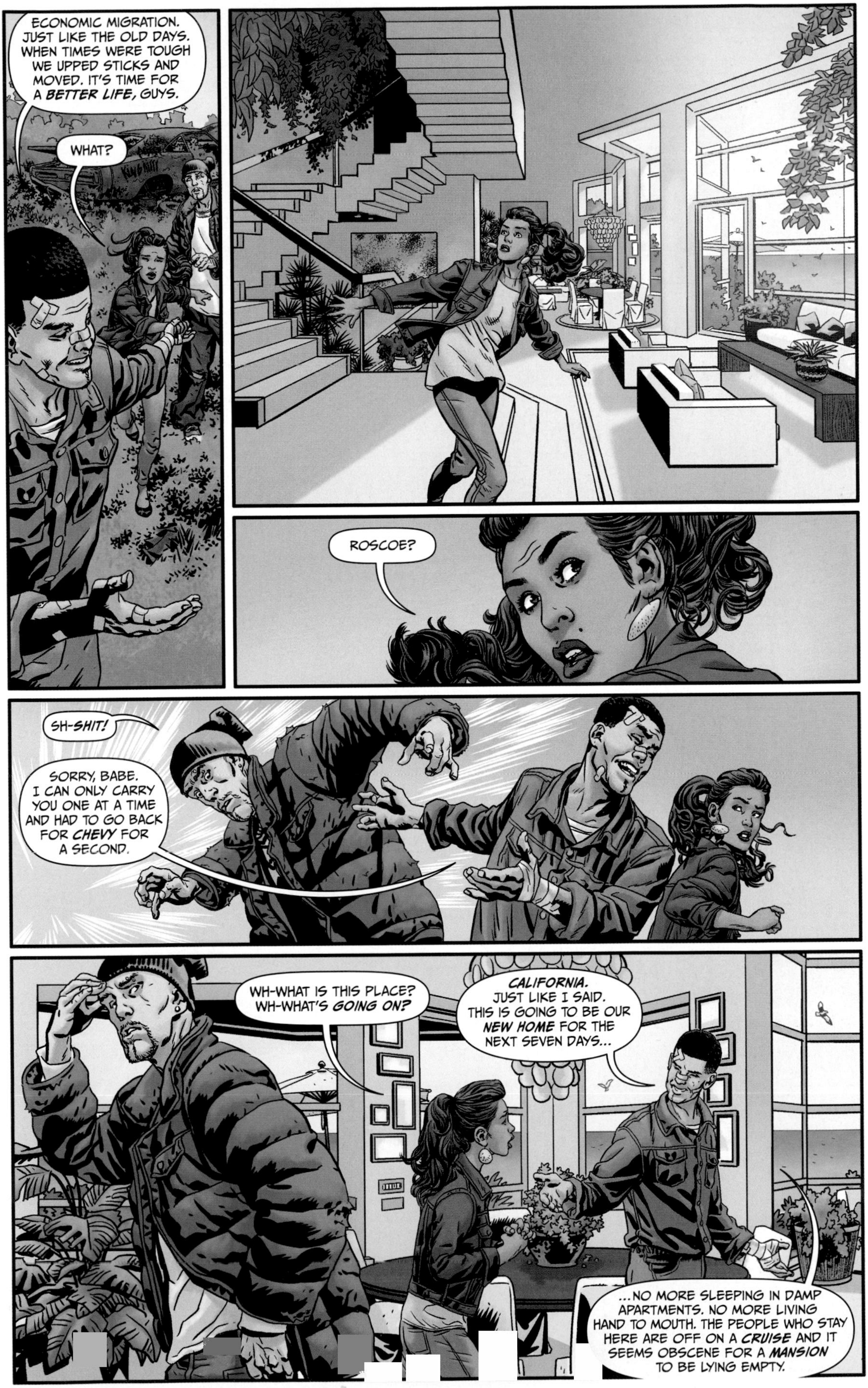
ECONOMIC MIGRATION. JUST LIKE THE OLD DAYS. WHEN TIMES WERE TOUGH WE UPPED STICKS AND MOVED. IT'S TIME FOR A BETTER LIFE, GUYS.
WHAT?
ROSCOE?
SH-SHIT!
SORRY, BABE. I CAN ONLY CARRY YOU ONE AT A TIME AND HAD TO GO BACK FOR CHEVY FOR A SECOND.
WH-WHAT IS THIS PLACE? WH-WHAT'S GOING ON?
CALIFORNIA. JUST LIKE I SAID. THIS IS GOING TO BE OUR NEW HOME FOR THE NEXT SEVEN DAYS...
...NO MORE SLEEPING IN DAMP APARTMENTS. NO MORE LIVING HAND TO MOUTH. THE PEOPLE WHO STAY HERE ARE OFF ON A CRUISE AND IT SEEMS OBSCENE FOR A MANSION TO BE LYING EMPTY.

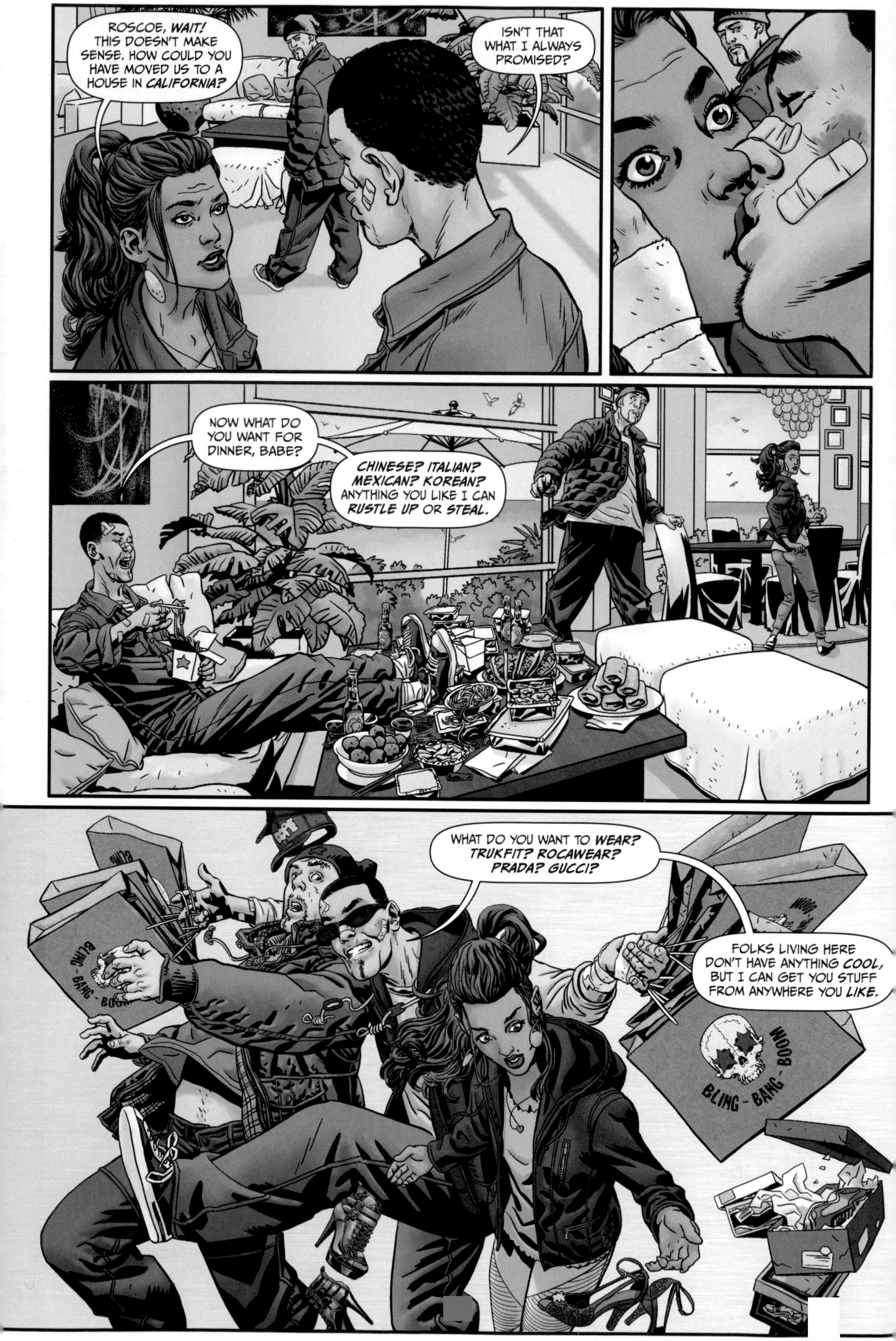
ROSCOE, WAIT! THIS DOESN'T MAKE SENSE. HOW COULD YOU HAVE MOVED US TO A HOUSE IN CALIFORNIA?
ISN'T THAT WHAT I ALWAYS PROMISED?
NOW WHAT DO YOU WANT FOR DINNER, BABE?
CHINESE? ITALIAN? MEXICAN? KOREAN? ANYTHING YOU LIKE I CAN RUSTLE UP OR STEAL.
WHAT DO YOU WANT TO WEAR? TRUKFIT? ROCAWEAR? PRADA? GUCCI?
FOLKS LIVING HERE DON'T HAVE ANYTHING COOL, BUT I CAN GET YOU STUFF FROM ANYWHERE YOU LIKE.
BLING - BANG - BOOM
BLING - BANG - BOOM

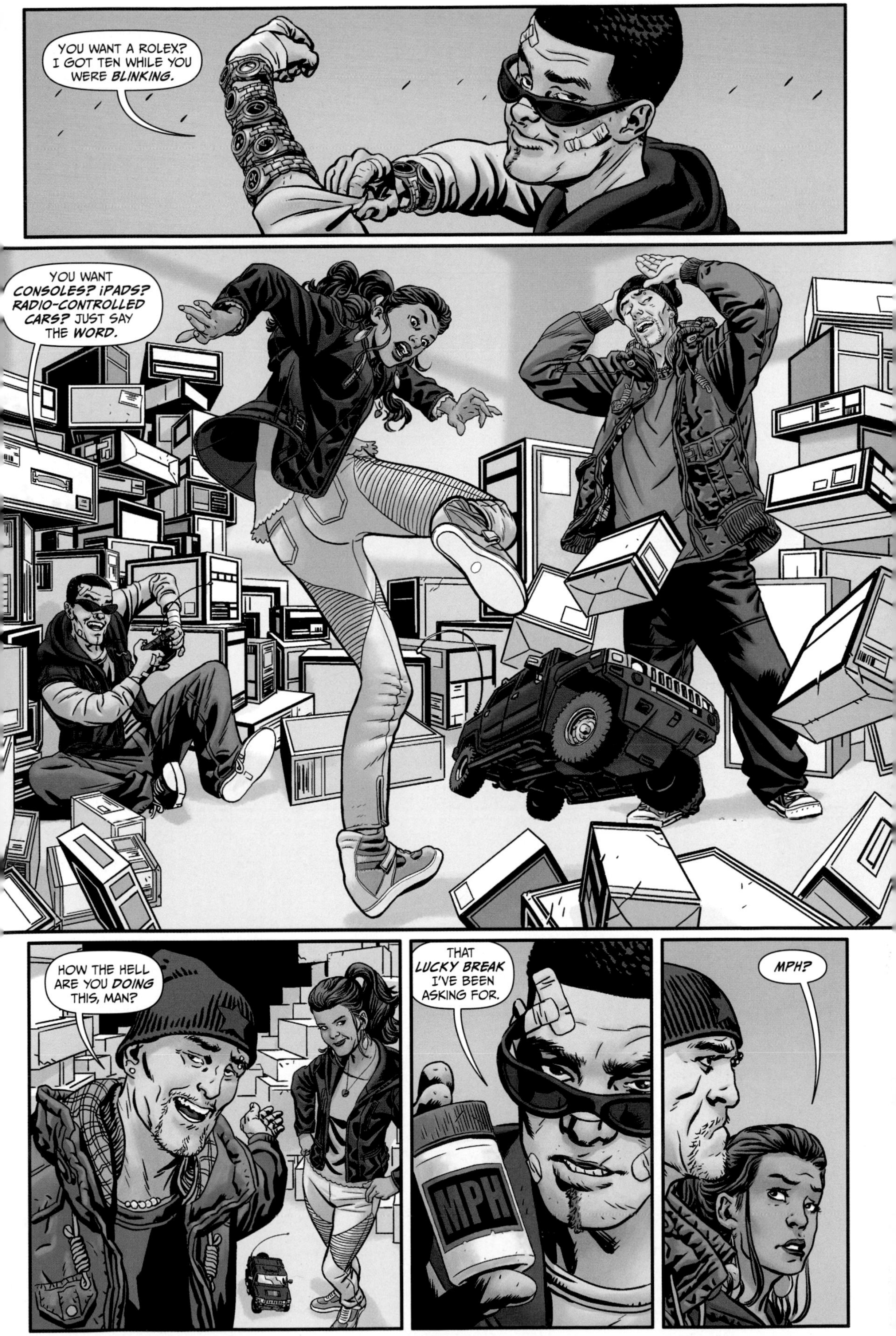
YOU WANT A ROLEX? I GOT TEN WHILE YOU WERE BLINKING.
YOU WANT CONSOLES? iPADS? RADIO-CONTROLLED CARS? JUST SAY THE WORD.
HOW THE HELL ARE YOU DOING THIS, MAN?
THAT LUCKY BREAK I'VE BEEN ASKING FOR.
MPH
MPH?

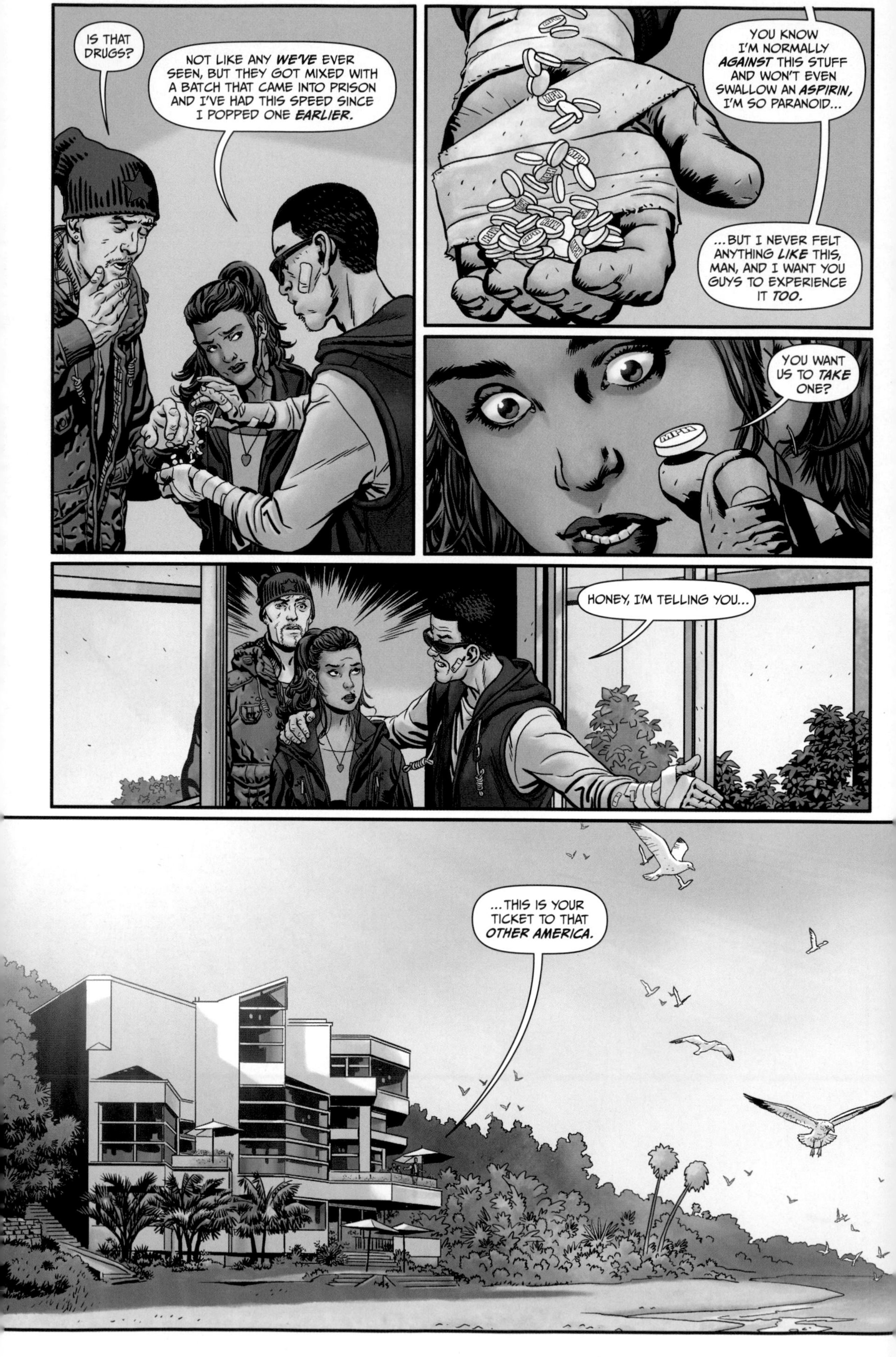
IS THAT DRUGS?
NOT LIKE ANY WE'VE EVER SEEN, BUT THEY GOT MIXED WITH A BATCH THAT CAME INTO PRISON AND I'VE HAD THIS SPEED SINCE I POPPED ONE EARLIER.
YOU KNOW I'M NORMALLY AGAINST THIS STUFF AND WON'T EVEN SWALLOW AN ASPIRIN, I'M SO PARANOID...
...BUT I NEVER FELT ANYTHING LIKE THIS, MAN, AND I WANT YOU GUYS TO EXPERIENCE IT TOO.
YOU WANT US TO TAKE ONE?
HONEY, I'M TELLING YOU...
...THIS IS YOUR TICKET TO THAT OTHER AMERICA.

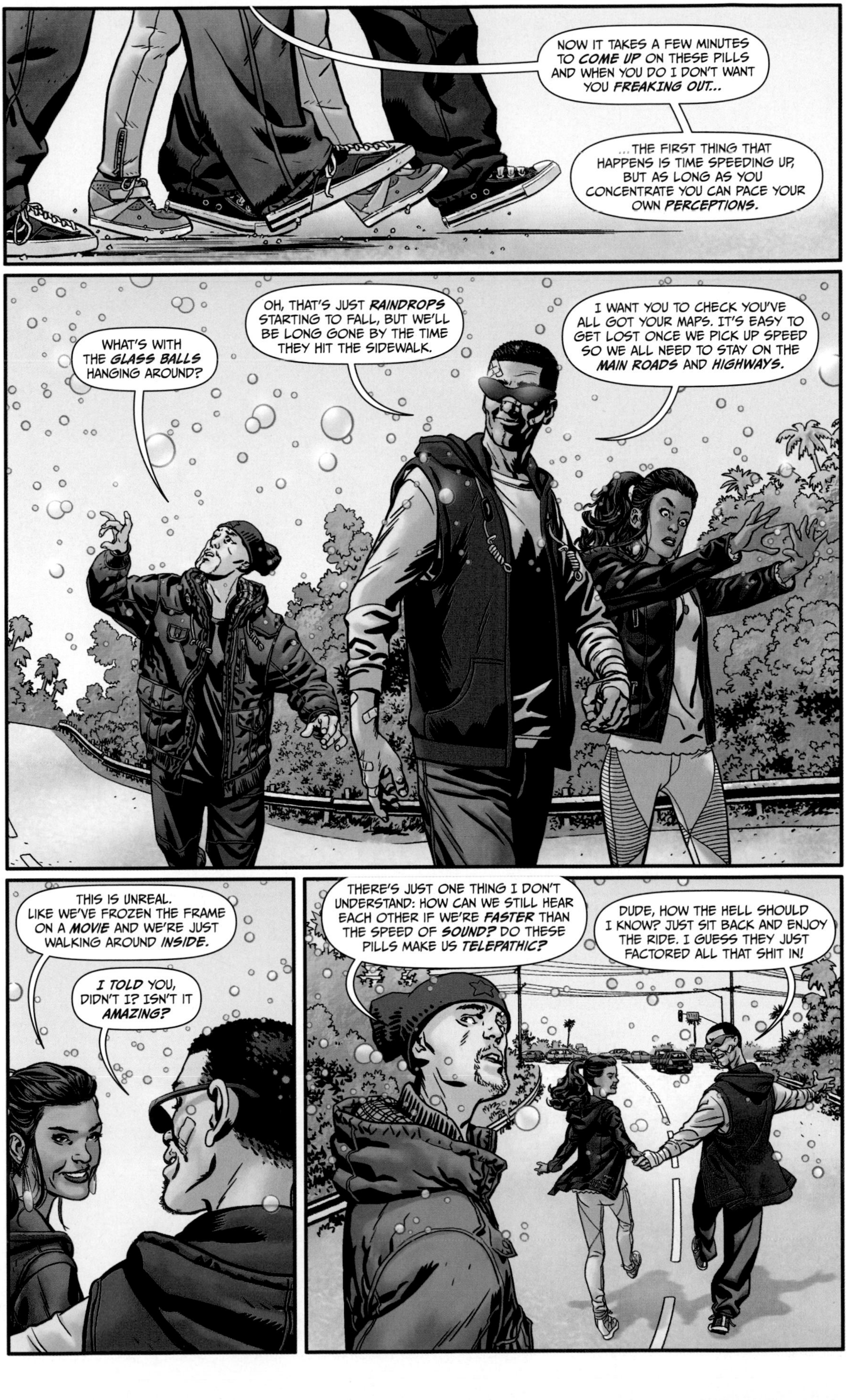
NOW IT TAKES A FEW MINUTES TO COME UP ON THESE PILLS AND WHEN YOU DO I DON'T WANT YOU FREAKING OUT...
...THE FIRST THING THAT HAPPENS IS TIME SPEEDING UP, BUT AS LONG AS YOU CONCENTRATE YOU CAN PACE YOUR OWN PERCEPTIONS.
WHAT'S WITH THE GLASS BALLS HANGING AROUND?
OH, THAT'S JUST RAINDROPS STARTING TO FALL, BUT WE'LL BE LONG GONE BY THE TIME THEY HIT THE SIDEWALK.
I WANT YOU TO CHECK YOU'VE ALL GOT YOUR MAPS. IT'S EASY TO GET LOST ONCE WE PICK UP SPEED SO WE ALL NEED TO STAY ON THE MAIN ROADS AND HIGHWAYS.
THIS IS UNREAL. LIKE WE'VE FROZEN THE FRAME ON A MOVIE AND WE'RE JUST WALKING AROUND INSIDE.
I TOLD YOU, DIDN'T I? ISN'T IT AMAZING?
THERE'S JUST ONE THING I DON'T UNDERSTAND: HOW CAN WE STILL HEAR EACH OTHER IF WE'RE FASTER THAN THE SPEED OF SOUND? DO THESE PILLS MAKE US TELEPATHIC?
DUDE, HOW THE HELL SHOULD I KNOW? JUST SIT BACK AND ENJOY THE RIDE. I GUESS THEY JUST FACTORED ALL THAT SHIT IN!

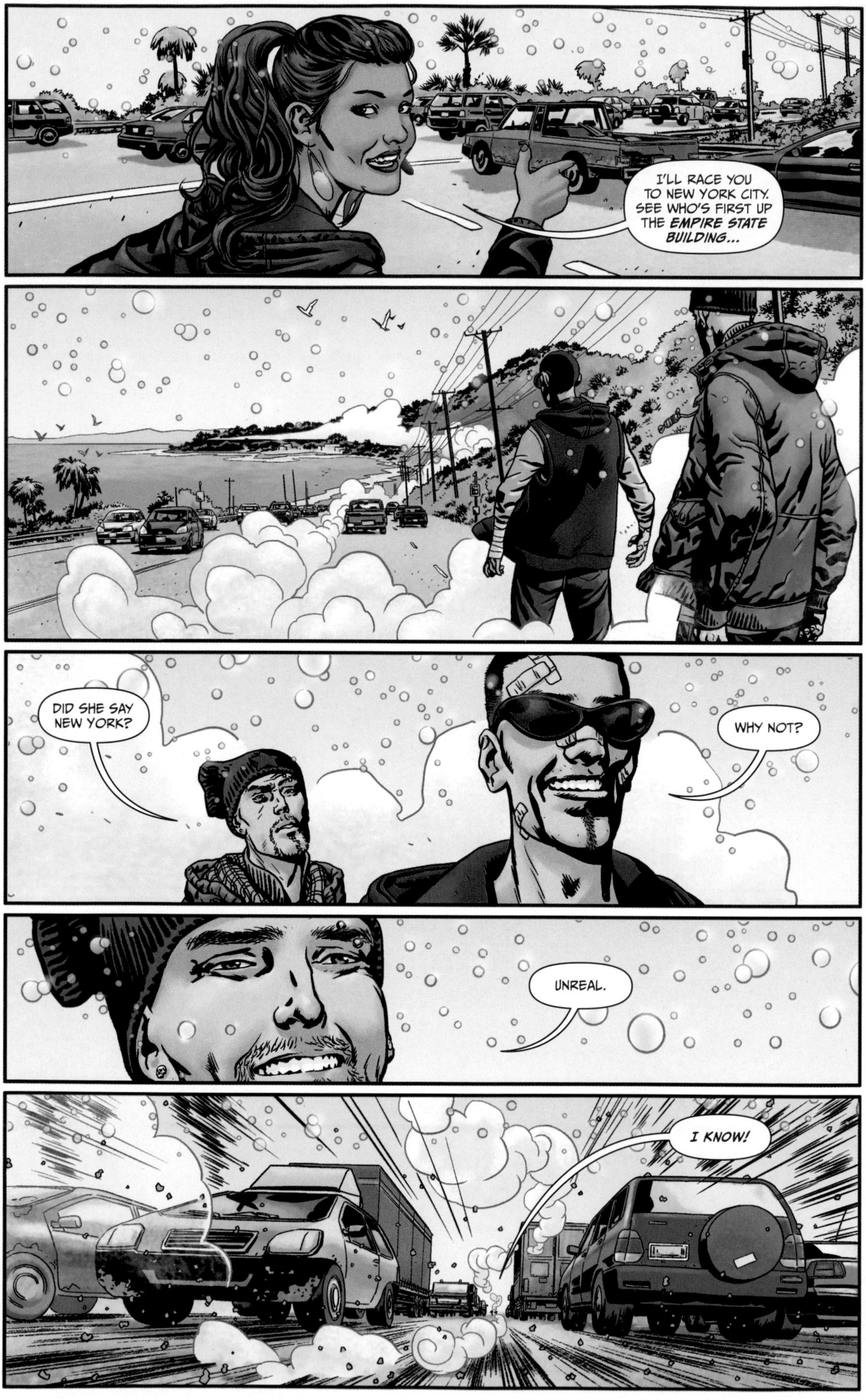
I'LL RACE YOU TO NEW YORK CITY. SEE WHO'S FIRST UP THE EMPIRE STATE BUILDING...
DID SHE SAY NEW YORK?
WHY NOT?
UNREAL.
I KNOW!

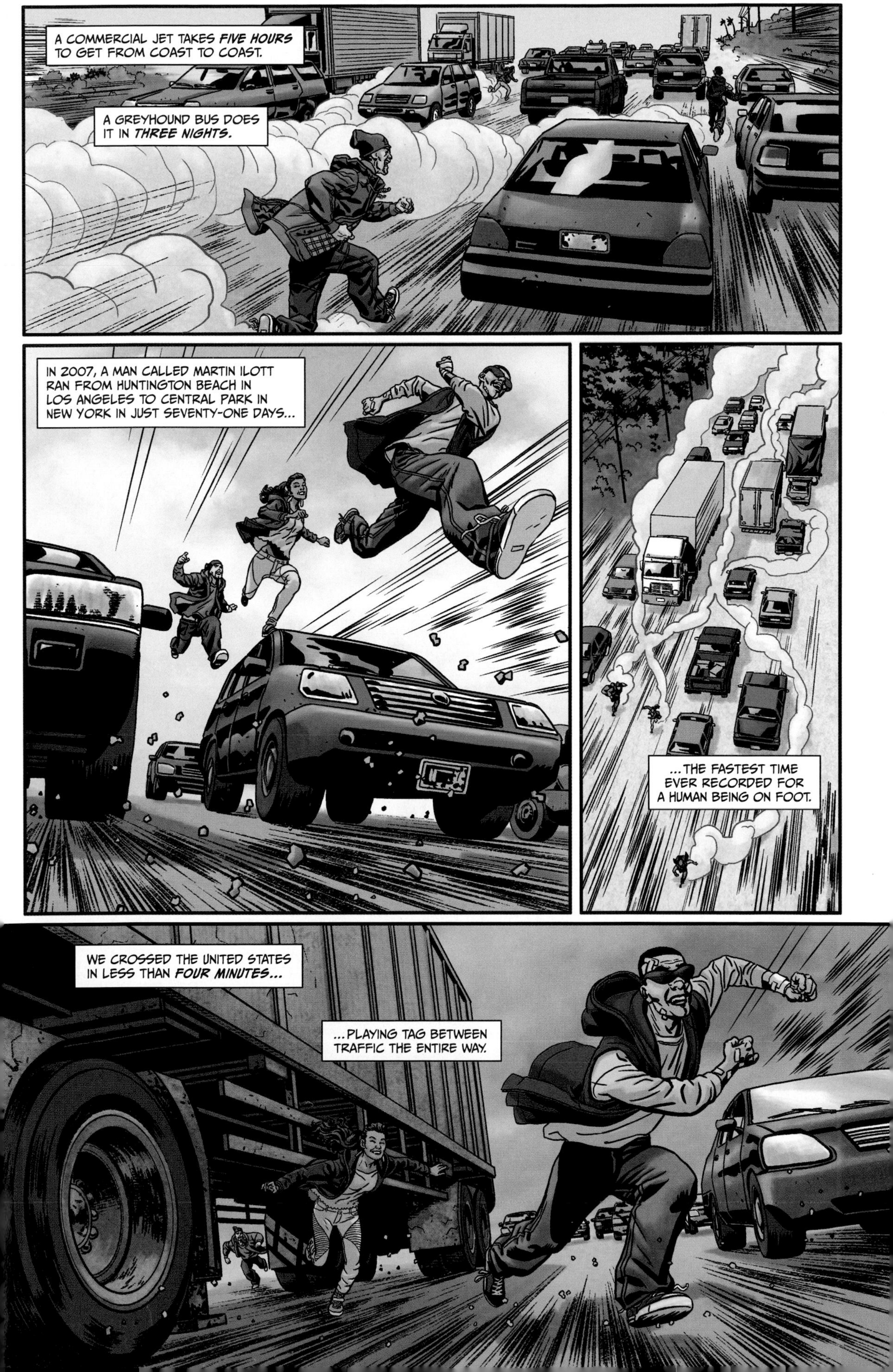
A COMMERCIAL JET TAKES FIVE HOURS TO GET FROM COAST TO COAST.
A GREYHOUND BUS DOES IT IN THREE NIGHTS.
IN 2007, A MAN CALLED MARTIN ILOTT RAN FROM HUNTINGTON BEACH IN LOS ANGELES TO CENTRAL PARK IN NEW YORK IN JUST SEVENTY-ONE DAYS...
...THE FASTEST TIME EVER RECORDED FOR A HUMAN BEING ON FOOT.
WE CROSSED THE UNITED STATES IN LESS THAN FOUR MINUTES...
...PLAYING TAG BETWEEN TRAFFIC THE ENTIRE WAY.

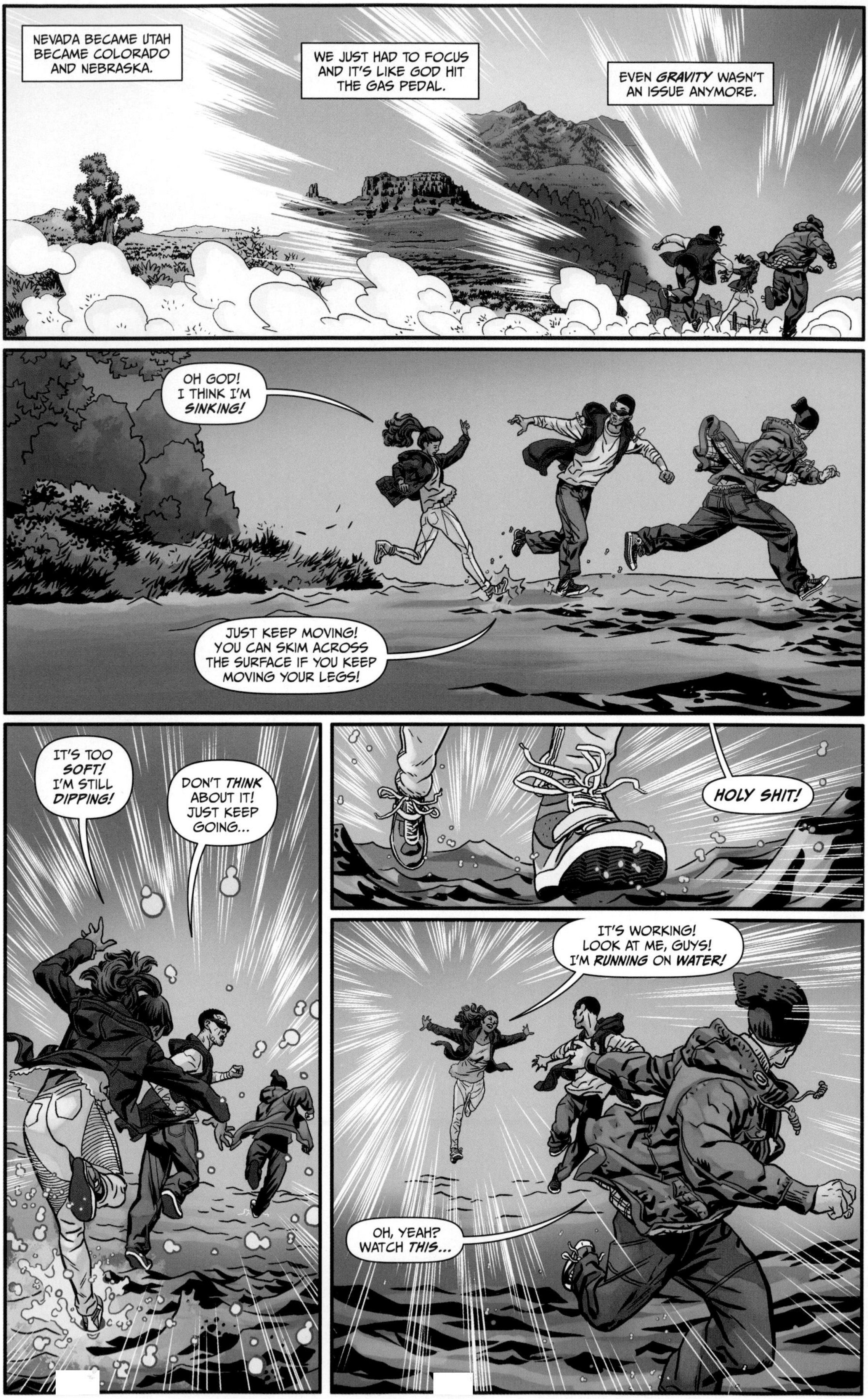

NEVADA BECAME UTAH BECAME COLORADO AND NEBRASKA.
WE JUST HAD TO FOCUS AND IT'S LIKE GOD HIT THE GAS PEDAL.
EVEN *GRAVITY* WASN'T AN ISSUE ANYMORE.
OH GOD! I THINK I'M *SINKING!*
JUST KEEP MOVING! YOU CAN SKIM ACROSS THE SURFACE IF YOU KEEP MOVING YOUR LEGS!
IT'S TOO *SOFT!* I'M STILL *DIPPING!*
DON'T *THINK* ABOUT IT! JUST KEEP GOING...
HOLY SHIT!
IT'S WORKING! LOOK AT ME, GUYS! I'M *RUNNING* ON *WATER!*
OH, YEAH? WATCH *THIS...*

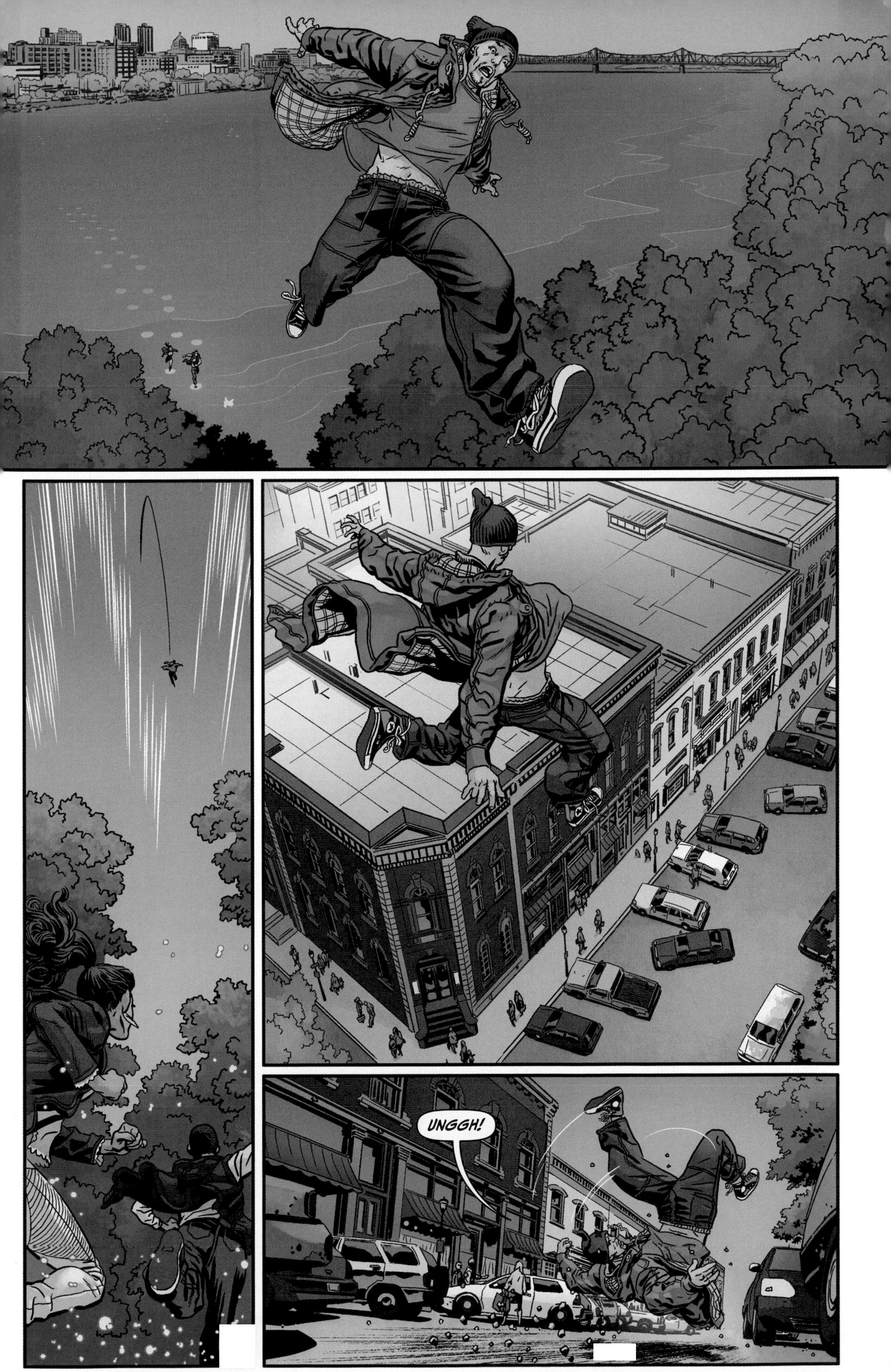
UNGGH!

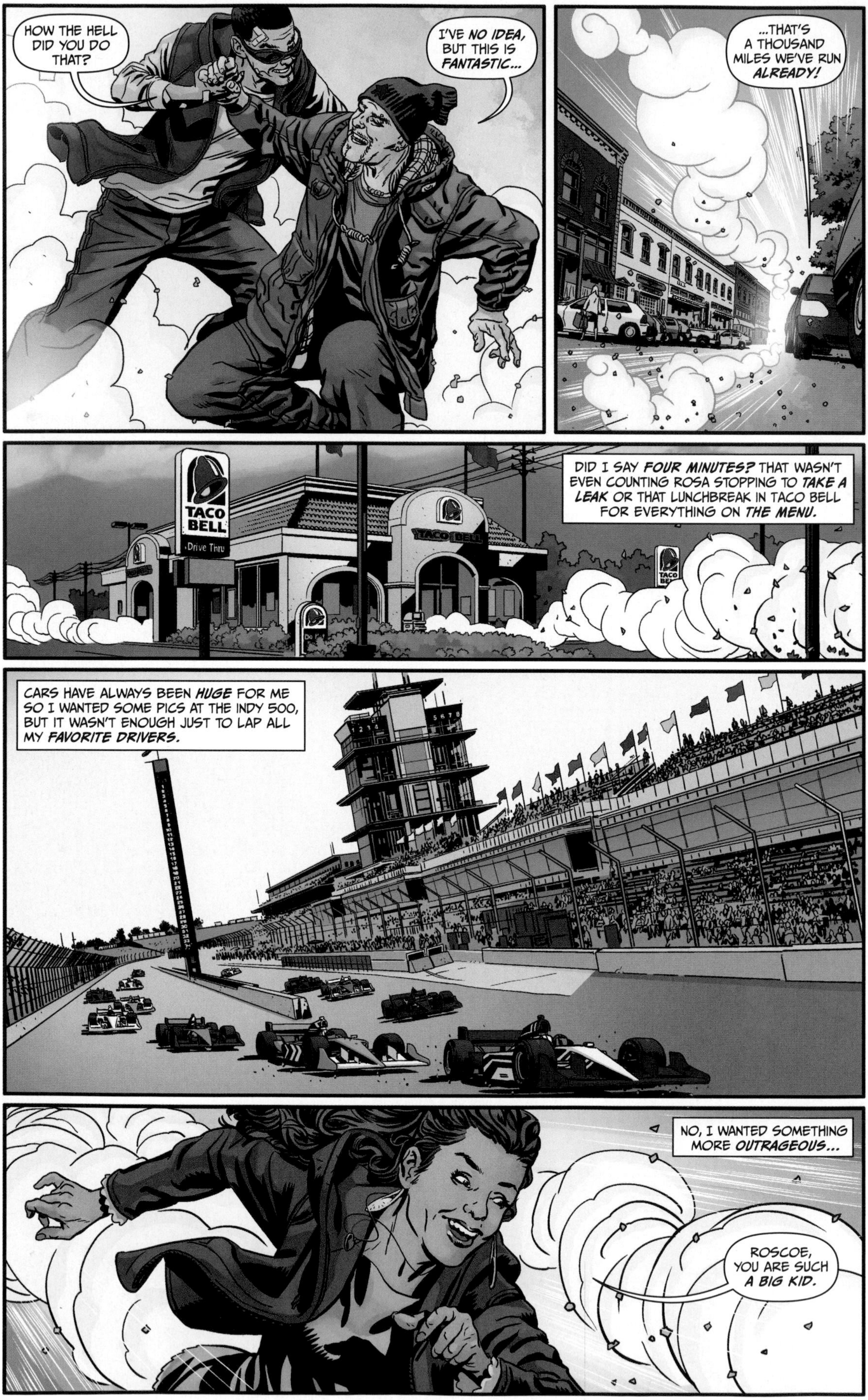
HOW THE HELL DID YOU DO THAT?
I'VE NO IDEA, BUT THIS IS FANTASTIC...
...THAT'S A THOUSAND MILES WE'VE RUN ALREADY!
DID I SAY FOUR MINUTES? THAT WASN'T EVEN COUNTING ROSA STOPPING TO TAKE A LEAK OR THAT LUNCHBREAK IN TACO BELL FOR EVERYTHING ON THE MENU.
TACO BELL
Drive Thru
TACO BELL
CARS HAVE ALWAYS BEEN HUGE FOR ME SO I WANTED SOME PICS AT THE INDY 500, BUT IT WASN'T ENOUGH JUST TO LAP ALL MY FAVORITE DRIVERS.
NO, I WANTED SOMETHING MORE OUTRAGEOUS...
ROSCOE, YOU ARE SUCH A BIG KID.

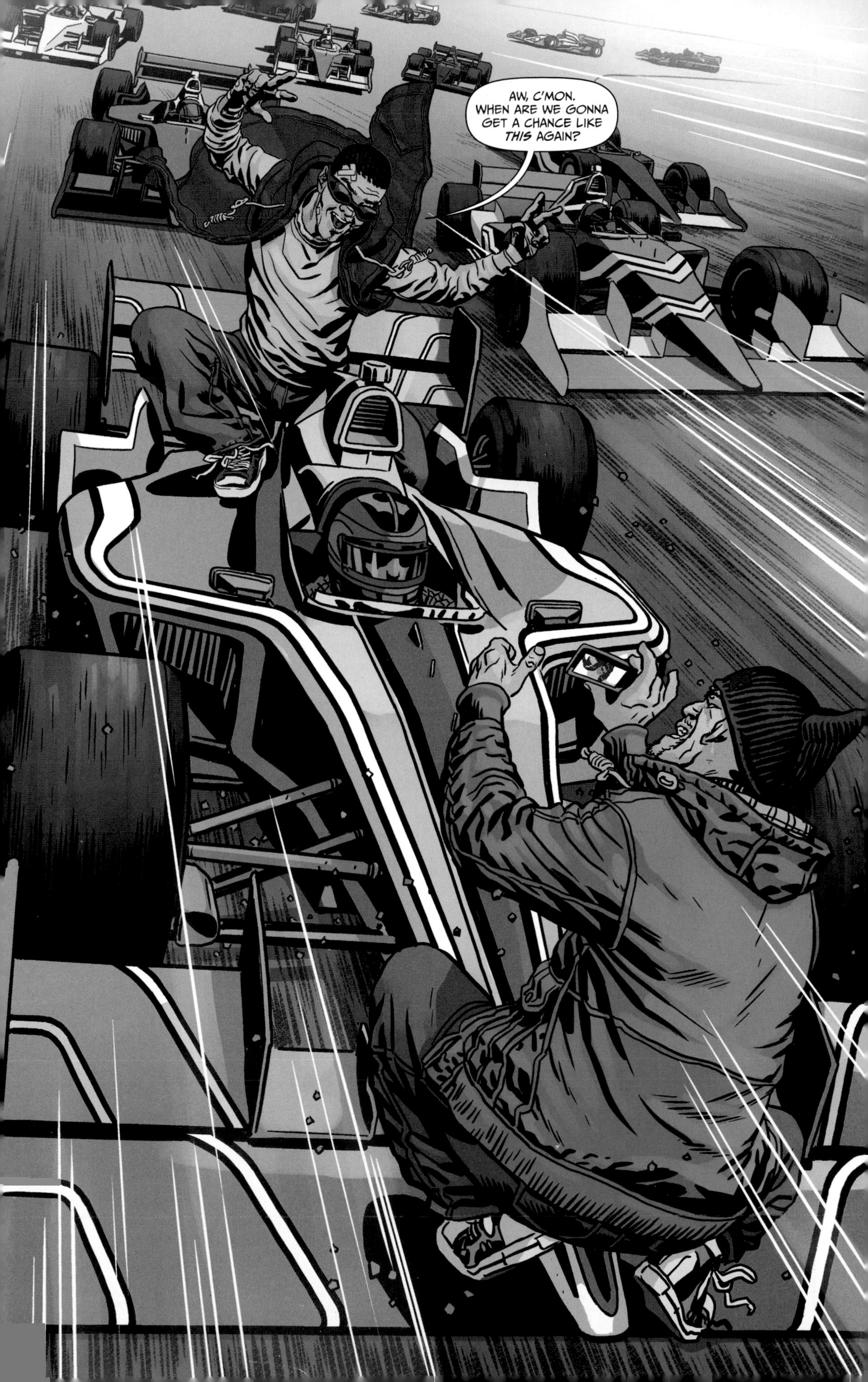
AW, C'MON. WHEN ARE WE GONNA GET A CHANCE LIKE *THIS* AGAIN?

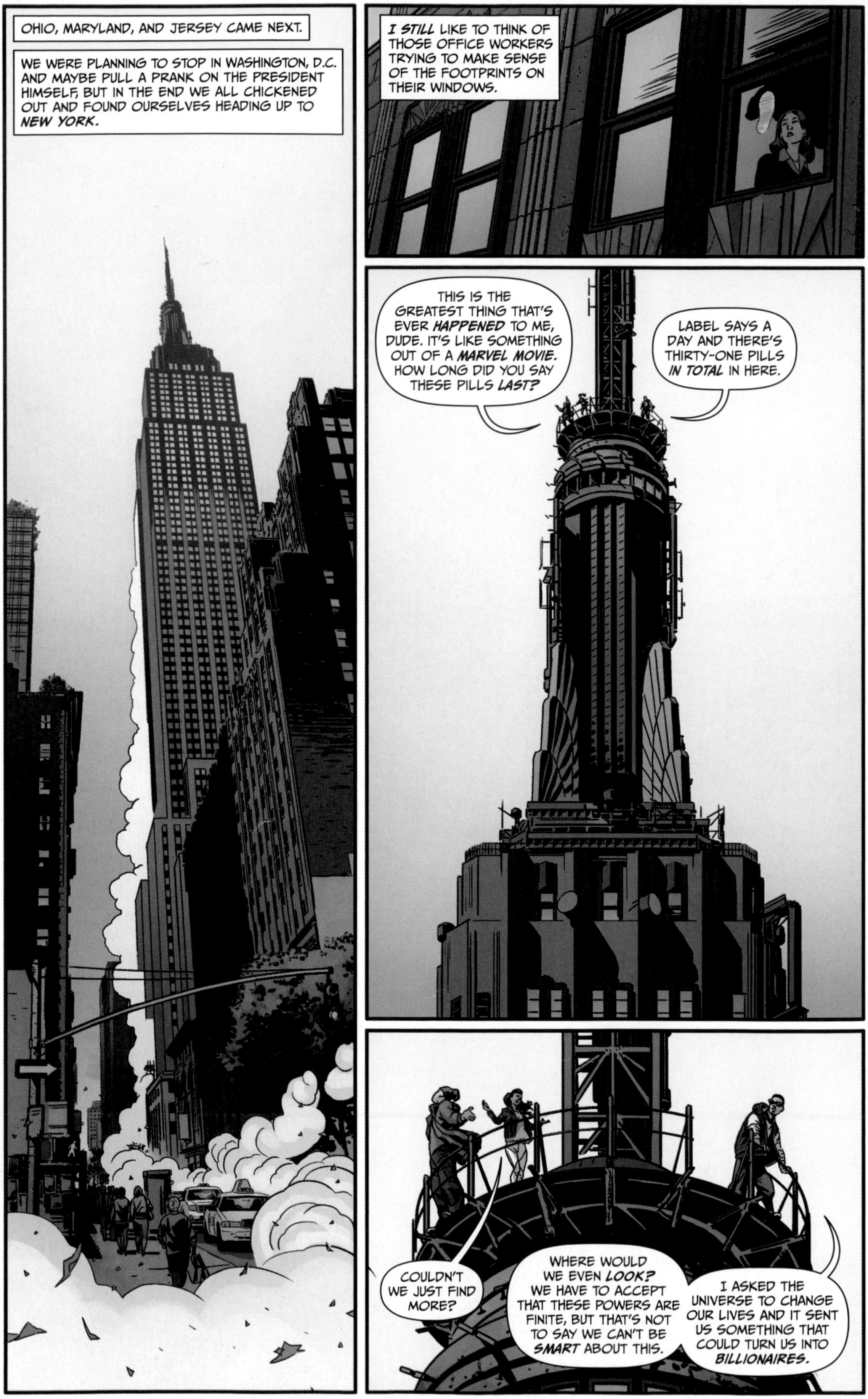
OHIO, MARYLAND, AND JERSEY CAME NEXT.
WE WERE PLANNING TO STOP IN WASHINGTON, D.C. AND MAYBE PULL A PRANK ON THE PRESIDENT HIMSELF, BUT IN THE END WE ALL CHICKENED OUT AND FOUND OURSELVES HEADING UP TO NEW YORK.
I STILL LIKE TO THINK OF THOSE OFFICE WORKERS TRYING TO MAKE SENSE OF THE FOOTPRINTS ON THEIR WINDOWS.
THIS IS THE GREATEST THING THAT'S EVER HAPPENED TO ME, DUDE. IT'S LIKE SOMETHING OUT OF A MARVEL MOVIE. HOW LONG DID YOU SAY THESE PILLS LAST?
LABEL SAYS A DAY AND THERE'S THIRTY-ONE PILLS IN TOTAL IN HERE.
COULDN'T WE JUST FIND MORE?
WHERE WOULD WE EVEN LOOK? WE HAVE TO ACCEPT THAT THESE POWERS ARE FINITE, BUT THAT'S NOT TO SAY WE CAN'T BE SMART ABOUT THIS.
I ASKED THE UNIVERSE TO CHANGE OUR LIVES AND IT SENT US SOMETHING THAT COULD TURN US INTO BILLIONAIRES.

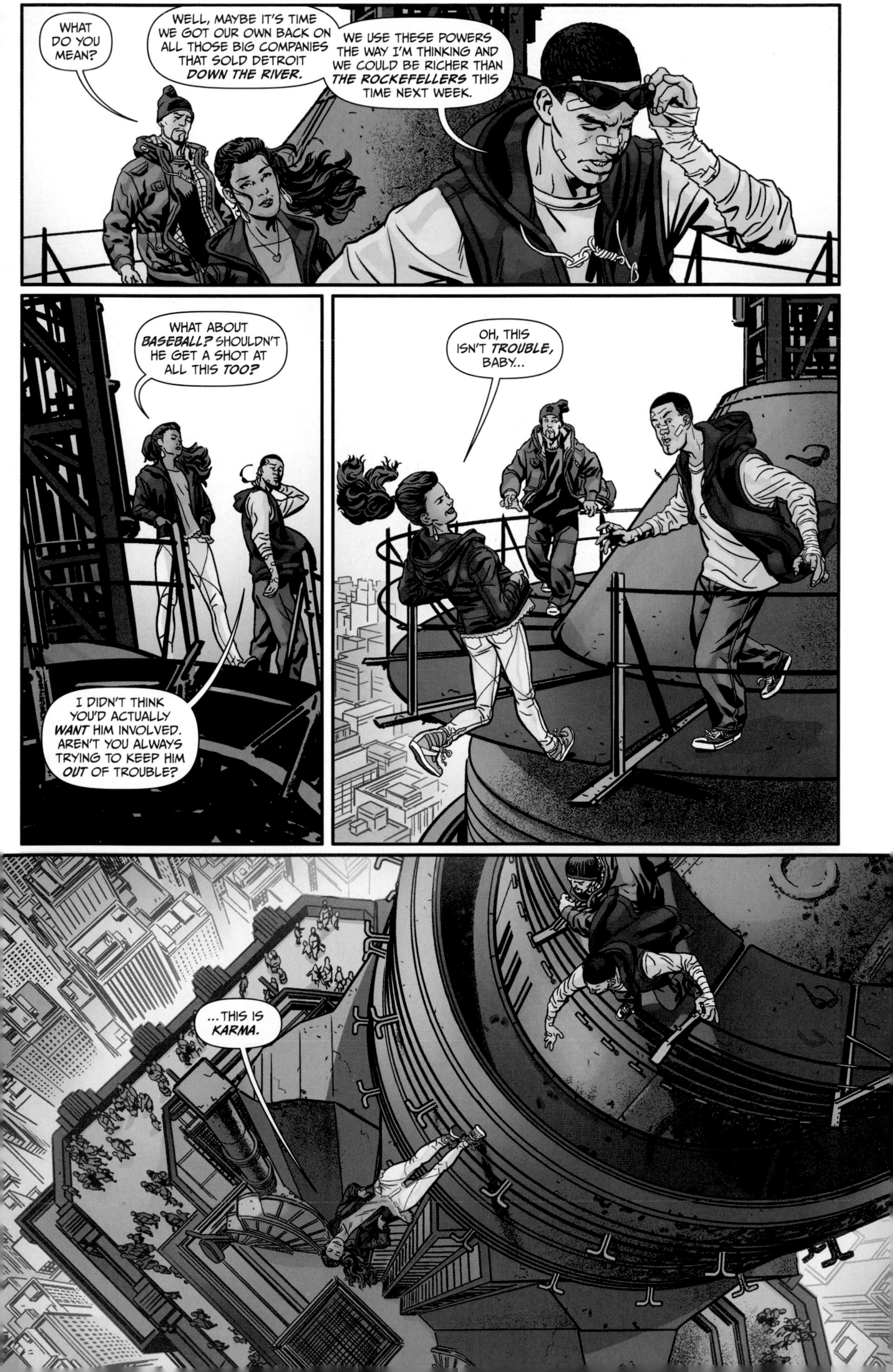
WHAT DO YOU MEAN?
WELL, MAYBE IT'S TIME WE GOT OUR OWN BACK ON ALL THOSE BIG COMPANIES THAT SOLD DETROIT *DOWN THE RIVER.*
WE USE THESE POWERS THE WAY I'M THINKING AND WE COULD BE RICHER THAN *THE ROCKEFELLERS* THIS TIME NEXT WEEK.
WHAT ABOUT *BASEBALL?* SHOULDN'T HE GET A SHOT AT ALL THIS *TOO?*
I DIDN'T THINK YOU'D ACTUALLY *WANT* HIM INVOLVED. AREN'T YOU ALWAYS TRYING TO KEEP HIM *OUT* OF TROUBLE?
OH, THIS ISN'T *TROUBLE,* BABY...
...THIS IS *KARMA.*

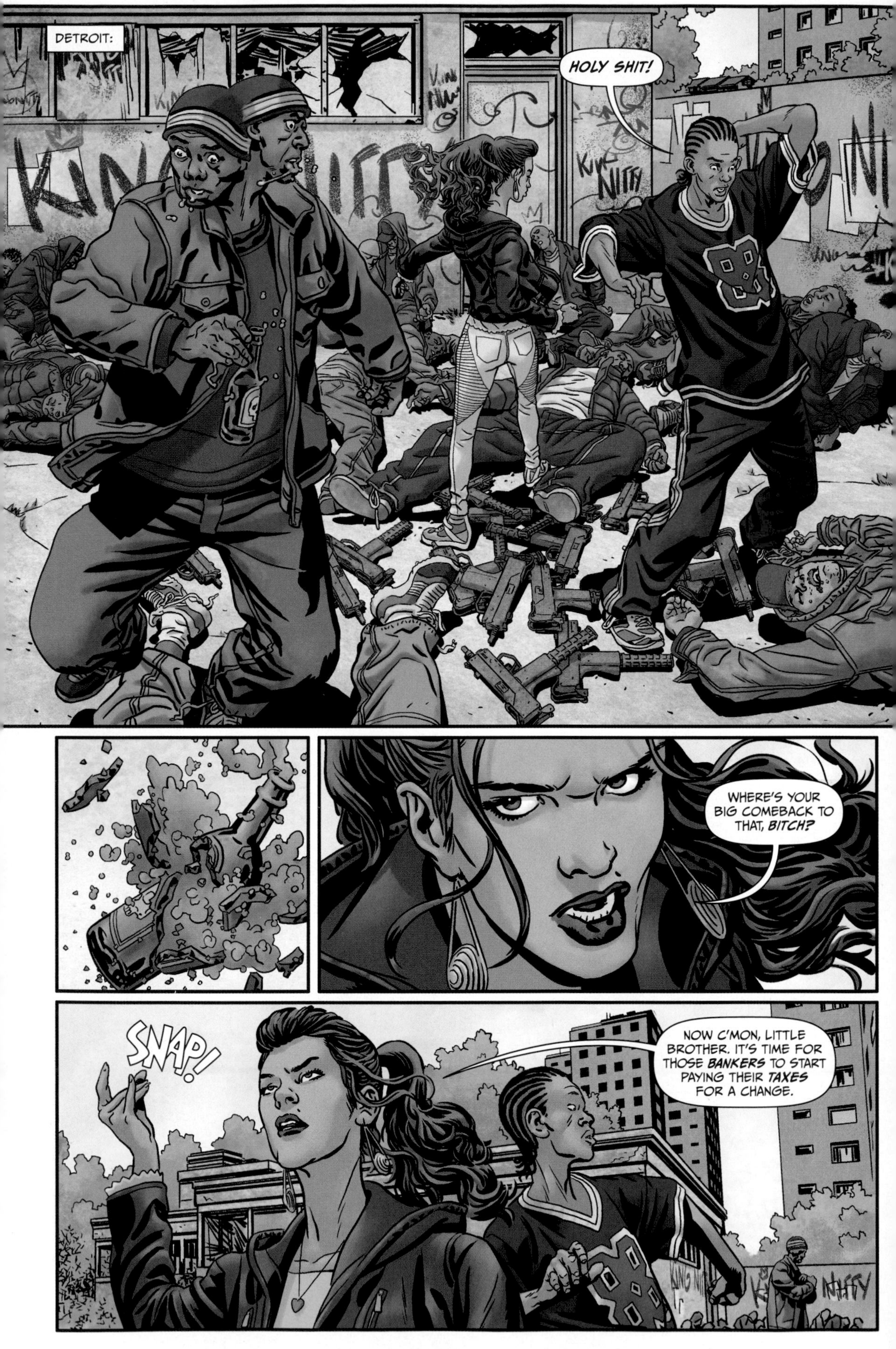
DETROIT:
HOLY SHIT!
WHERE'S YOUR BIG COMEBACK TO THAT, BITCH?
SNAP!
NOW C'MON, LITTLE BROTHER. IT'S TIME FOR THOSE BANKERS TO START PAYING THEIR TAXES FOR A CHANGE.

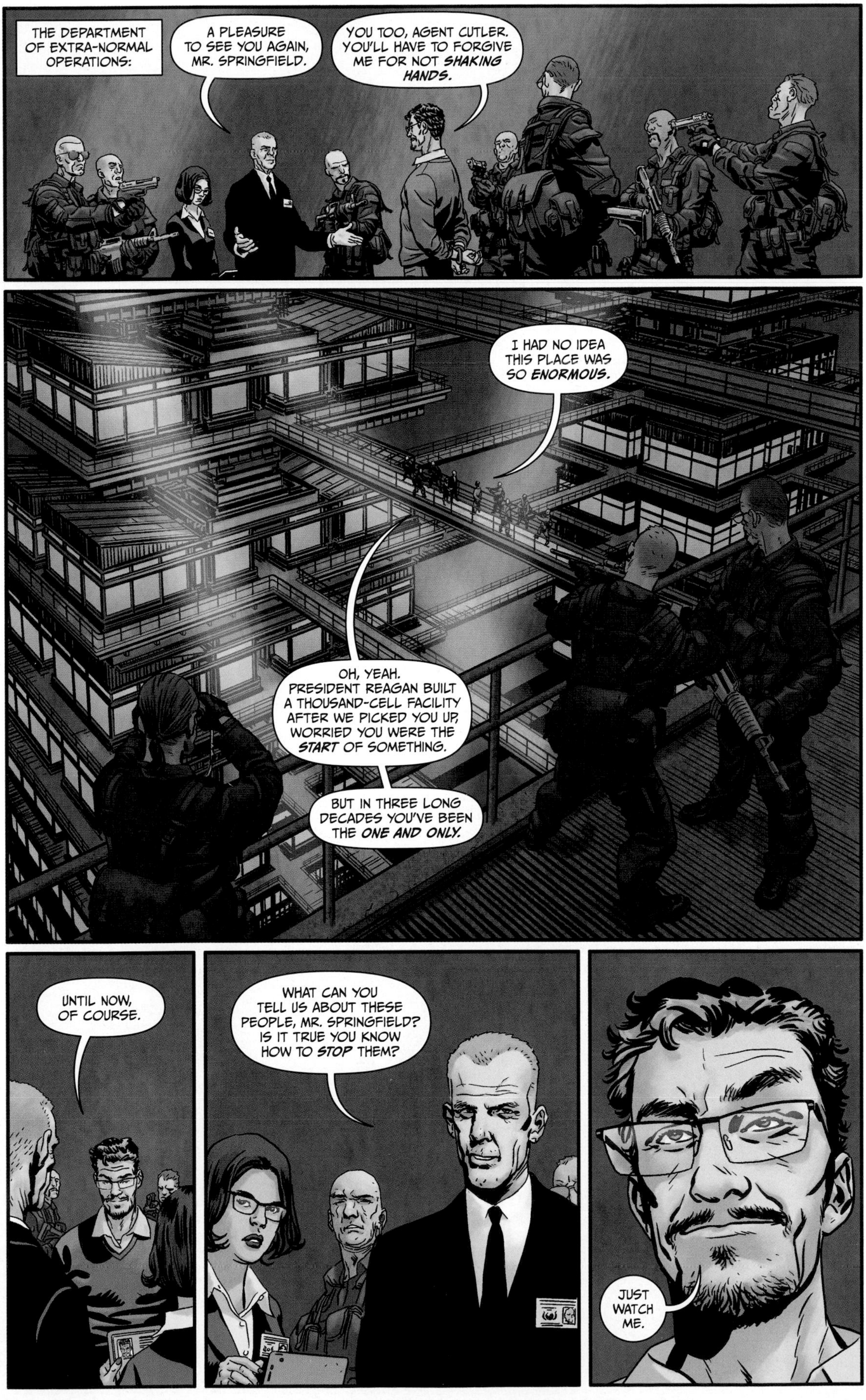
THE DEPARTMENT OF EXTRA-NORMAL OPERATIONS:
A PLEASURE TO SEE YOU AGAIN, MR. SPRINGFIELD.
YOU TOO, AGENT CUTLER. YOU'LL HAVE TO FORGIVE ME FOR NOT SHAKING HANDS.
I HAD NO IDEA THIS PLACE WAS SO ENORMOUS.
OH, YEAH. PRESIDENT REAGAN BUILT A THOUSAND-CELL FACILITY AFTER WE PICKED YOU UP, WORRIED YOU WERE THE START OF SOMETHING.
BUT IN THREE LONG DECADES YOU'VE BEEN THE ONE AND ONLY.
UNTIL NOW, OF COURSE.
WHAT CAN YOU TELL US ABOUT THESE PEOPLE, MR. SPRINGFIELD? IS IT TRUE YOU KNOW HOW TO STOP THEM?
JUST WATCH ME.

CHAPTER THREE

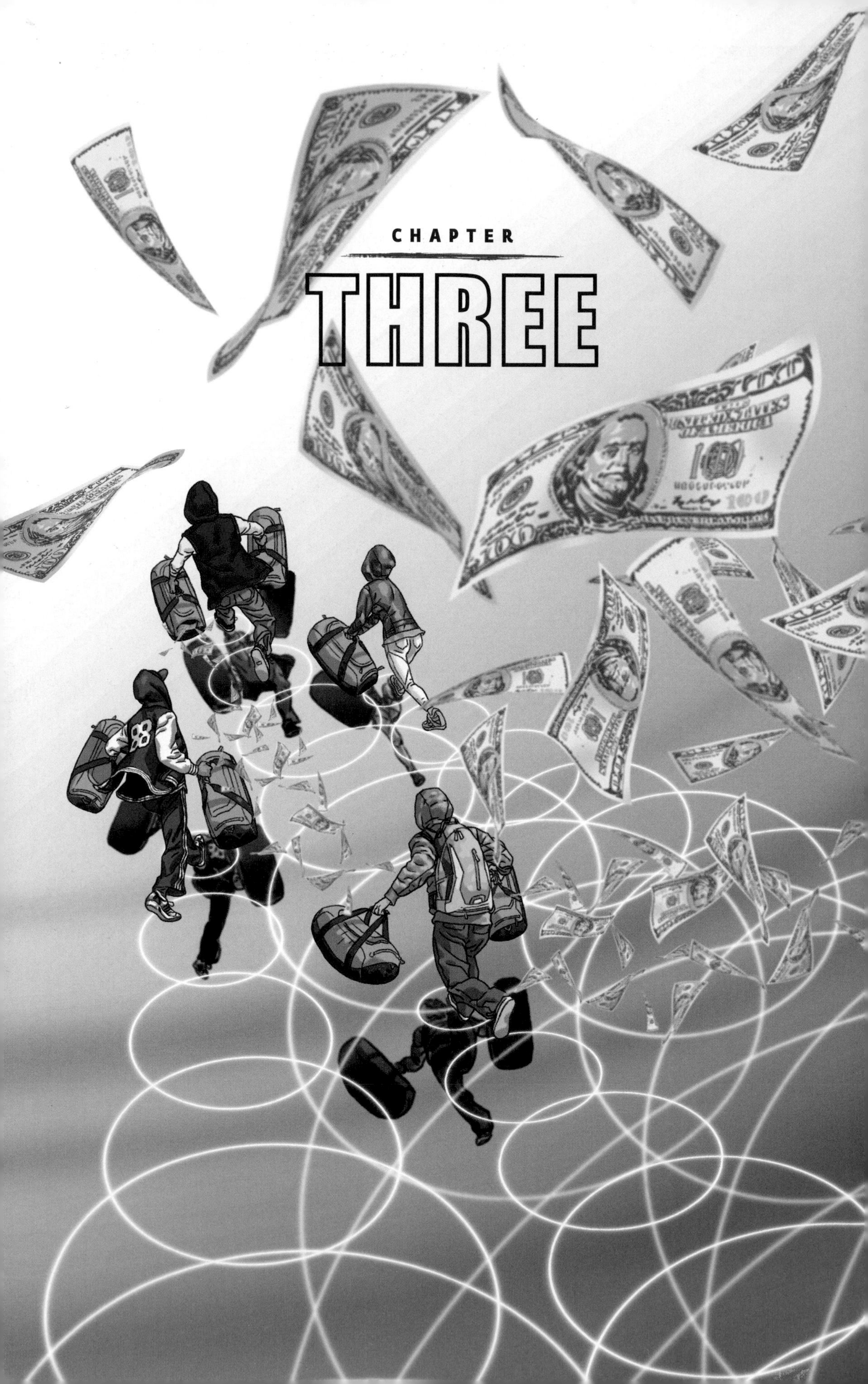

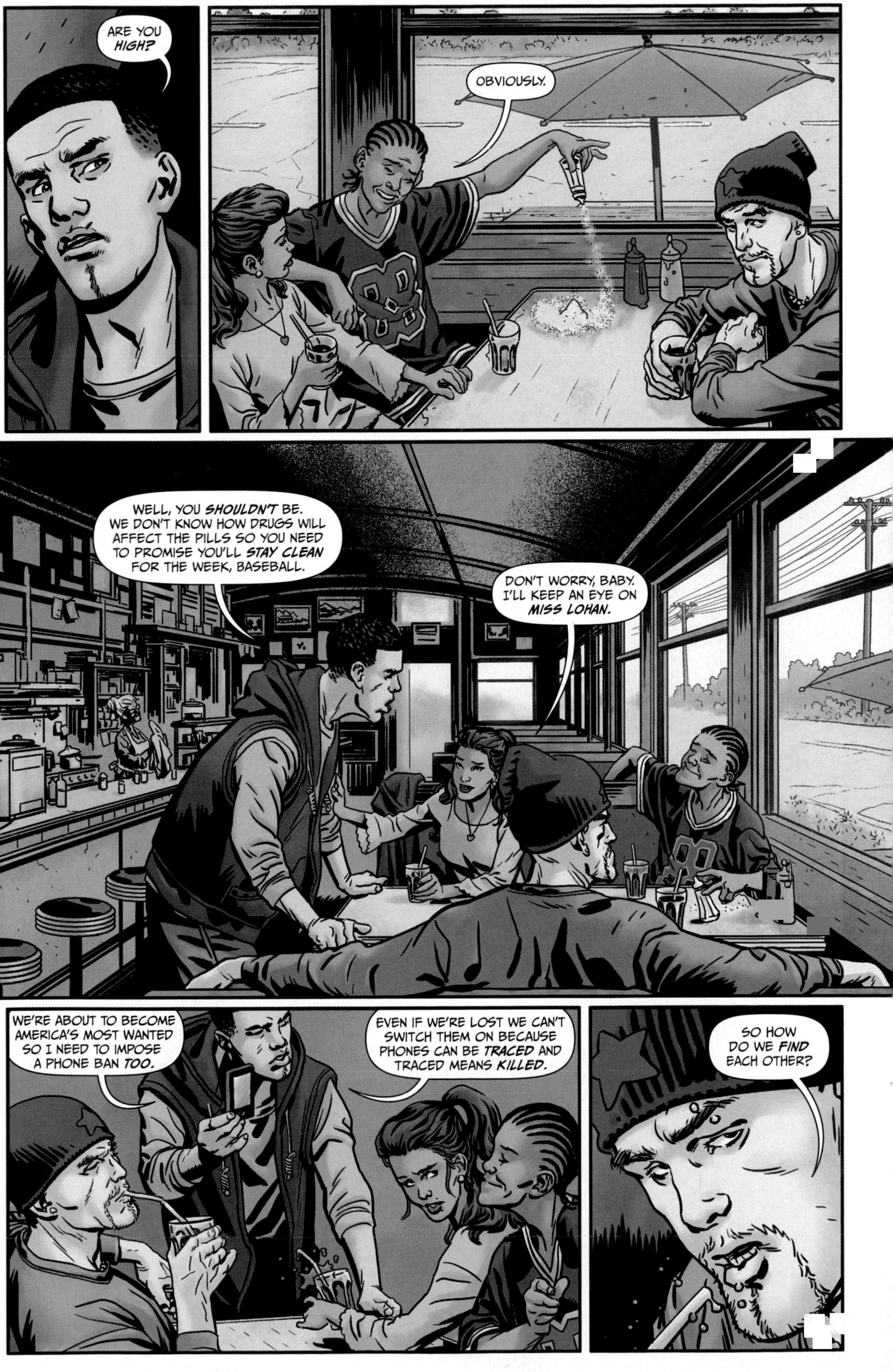
ARE YOU HIGH?
OBVIOUSLY.
WELL, YOU SHOULDN'T BE. WE DON'T KNOW HOW DRUGS WILL AFFECT THE PILLS SO YOU NEED TO PROMISE YOU'LL STAY CLEAN FOR THE WEEK, BASEBALL.
DON'T WORRY, BABY. I'LL KEEP AN EYE ON MISS LOHAN.
WE'RE ABOUT TO BECOME AMERICA'S MOST WANTED SO I NEED TO IMPOSE A PHONE BAN TOO.
EVEN IF WE'RE LOST WE CAN'T SWITCH THEM ON BECAUSE PHONES CAN BE TRACED AND TRACED MEANS KILLED.
SO HOW DO WE FIND EACH OTHER?

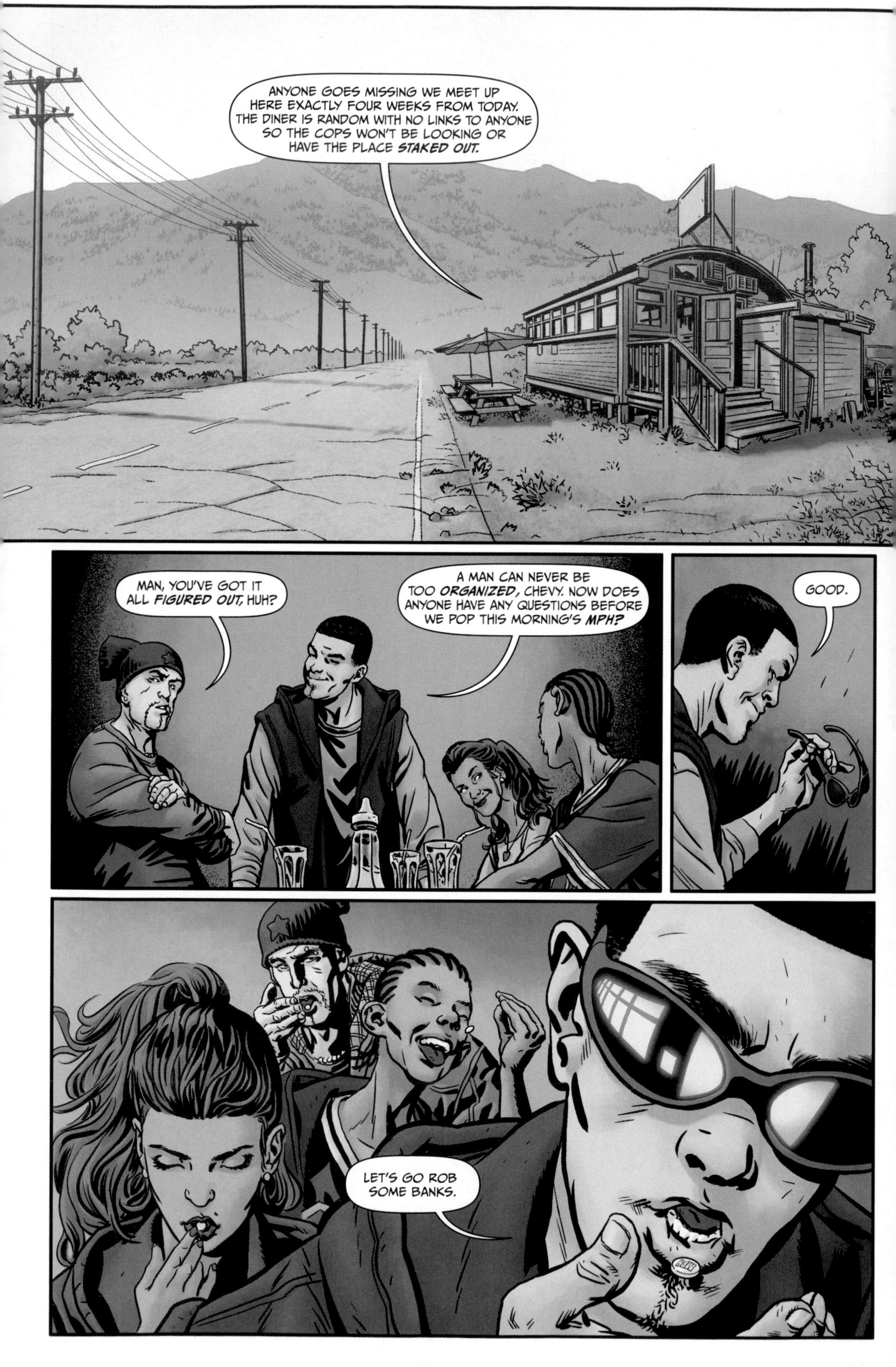
ANYONE GOES MISSING WE MEET UP HERE EXACTLY FOUR WEEKS FROM TODAY. THE DINER IS RANDOM WITH NO LINKS TO ANYONE SO THE COPS WON'T BE LOOKING OR HAVE THE PLACE STAKED OUT.
MAN, YOU'VE GOT IT ALL FIGURED OUT, HUH?
A MAN CAN NEVER BE TOO ORGANIZED, CHEVY. NOW DOES ANYONE HAVE ANY QUESTIONS BEFORE WE POP THIS MORNING'S MPH?
GOOD.
LET'S GO ROB SOME BANKS.

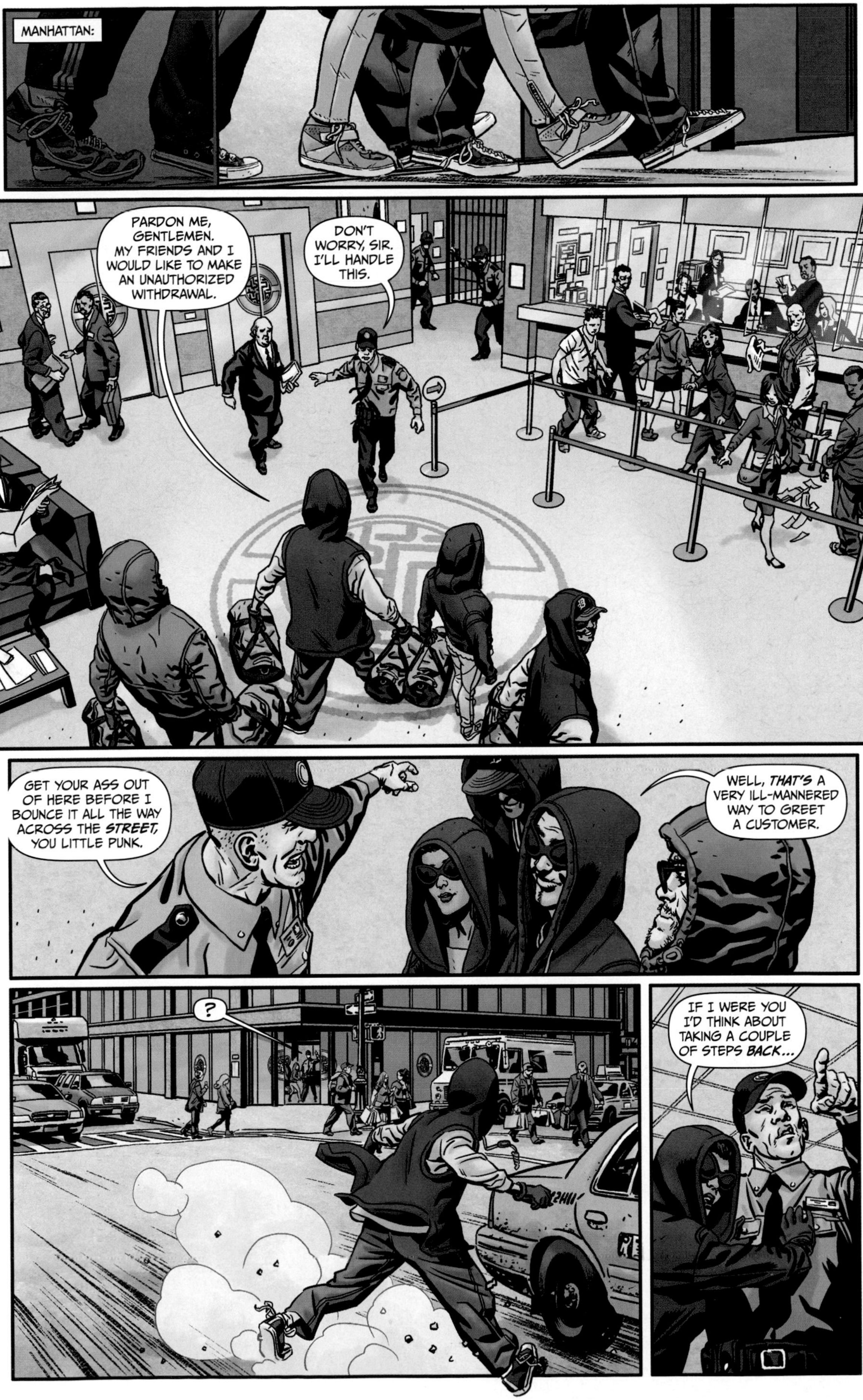
MANHATTAN:
PARDON ME, GENTLEMEN. MY FRIENDS AND I WOULD LIKE TO MAKE AN UNAUTHORIZED WITHDRAWAL.
DON'T WORRY, SIR. I'LL HANDLE THIS.
GET YOUR ASS OUT OF HERE BEFORE I BOUNCE IT ALL THE WAY ACROSS THE STREET, YOU LITTLE PUNK.
WELL, THAT'S A VERY ILL-MANNERED WAY TO GREET A CUSTOMER.
IF I WERE YOU I'D THINK ABOUT TAKING A COUPLE OF STEPS BACK...
?

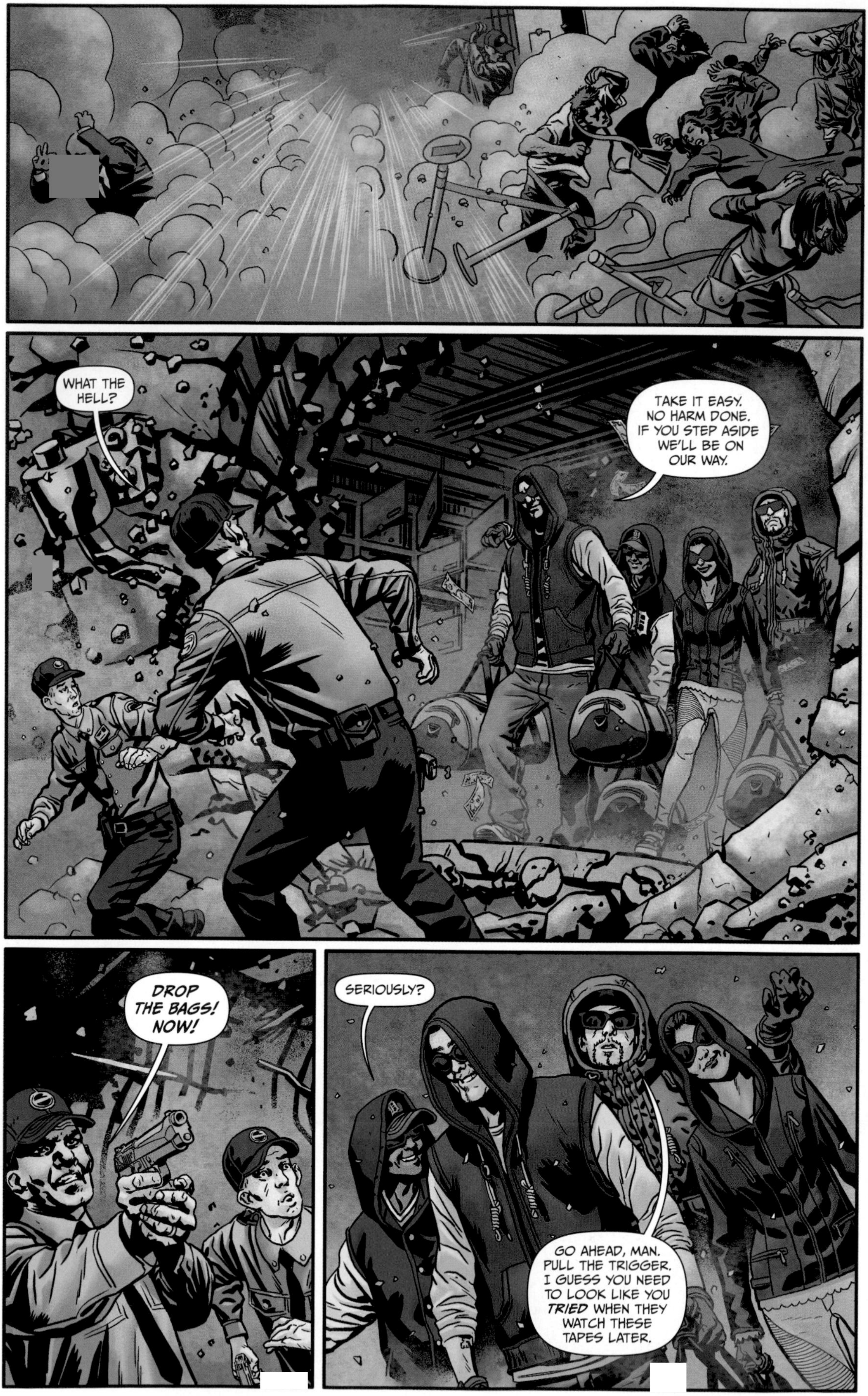
WHAT THE HELL?
TAKE IT EASY. NO HARM DONE. IF YOU STEP ASIDE WE'LL BE ON OUR WAY.
DROP THE BAGS! NOW!
SERIOUSLY?
GO AHEAD, MAN. PULL THE TRIGGER. I GUESS YOU NEED TO LOOK LIKE YOU TRIED WHEN THEY WATCH THESE TAPES LATER.

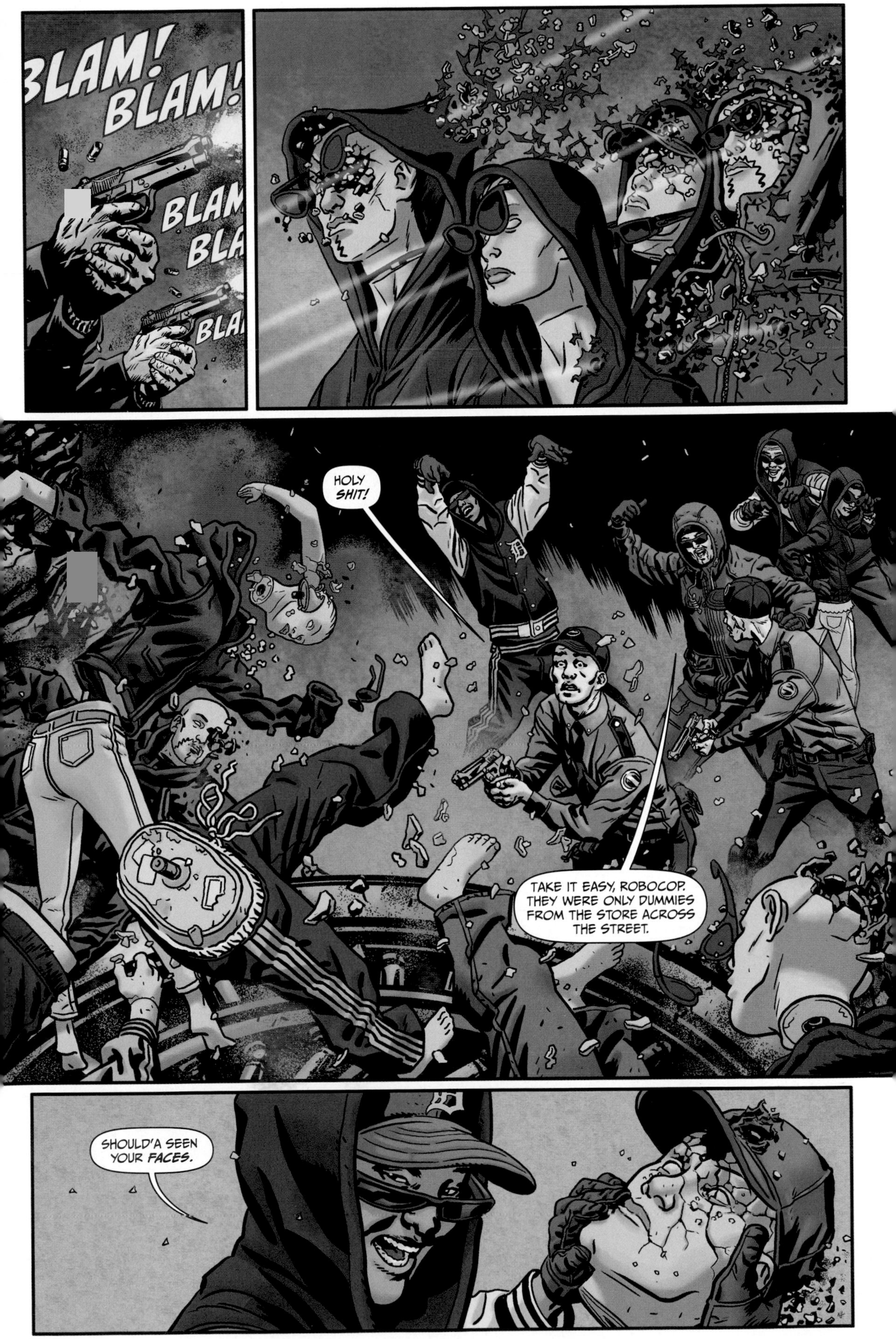
BLAM!
BLAM!
BLAM
BLA
BLA
HOLY SHIT!
TAKE IT EASY, ROBOCOP. THEY WERE ONLY DUMMIES FROM THE STORE ACROSS THE STREET.
SHOULD'A SEEN YOUR FACES.

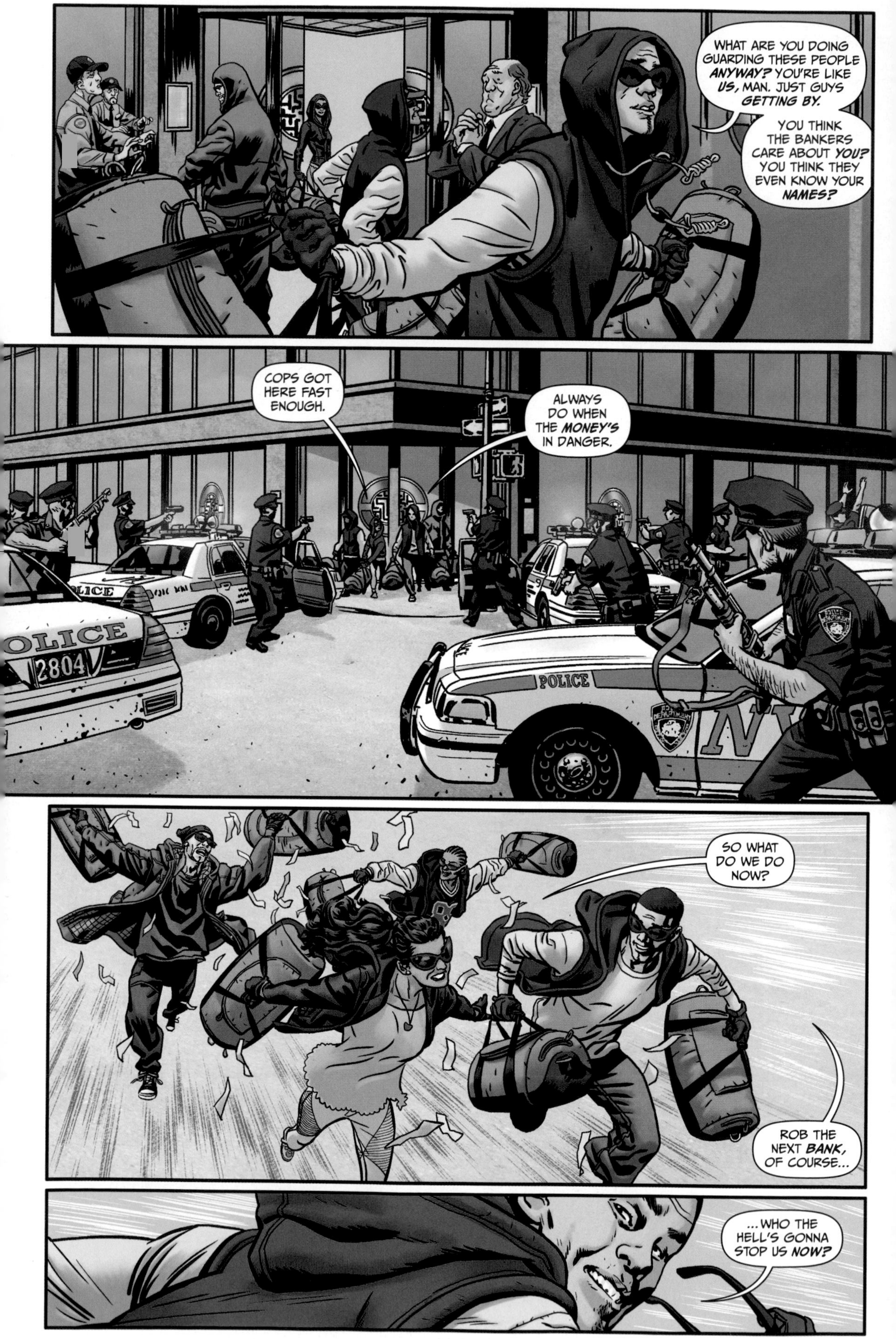
WHAT ARE YOU DOING GUARDING THESE PEOPLE ANYWAY? YOU'RE LIKE US, MAN. JUST GUYS GETTING BY.
YOU THINK THE BANKERS CARE ABOUT YOU? YOU THINK THEY EVEN KNOW YOUR NAMES?
COPS GOT HERE FAST ENOUGH.
ALWAYS DO WHEN THE MONEY'S IN DANGER.
POLICE
2804
POLICE
SO WHAT DO WE DO NOW?
ROB THE NEXT BANK, OF COURSE...
...WHO THE HELL'S GONNA STOP US NOW?

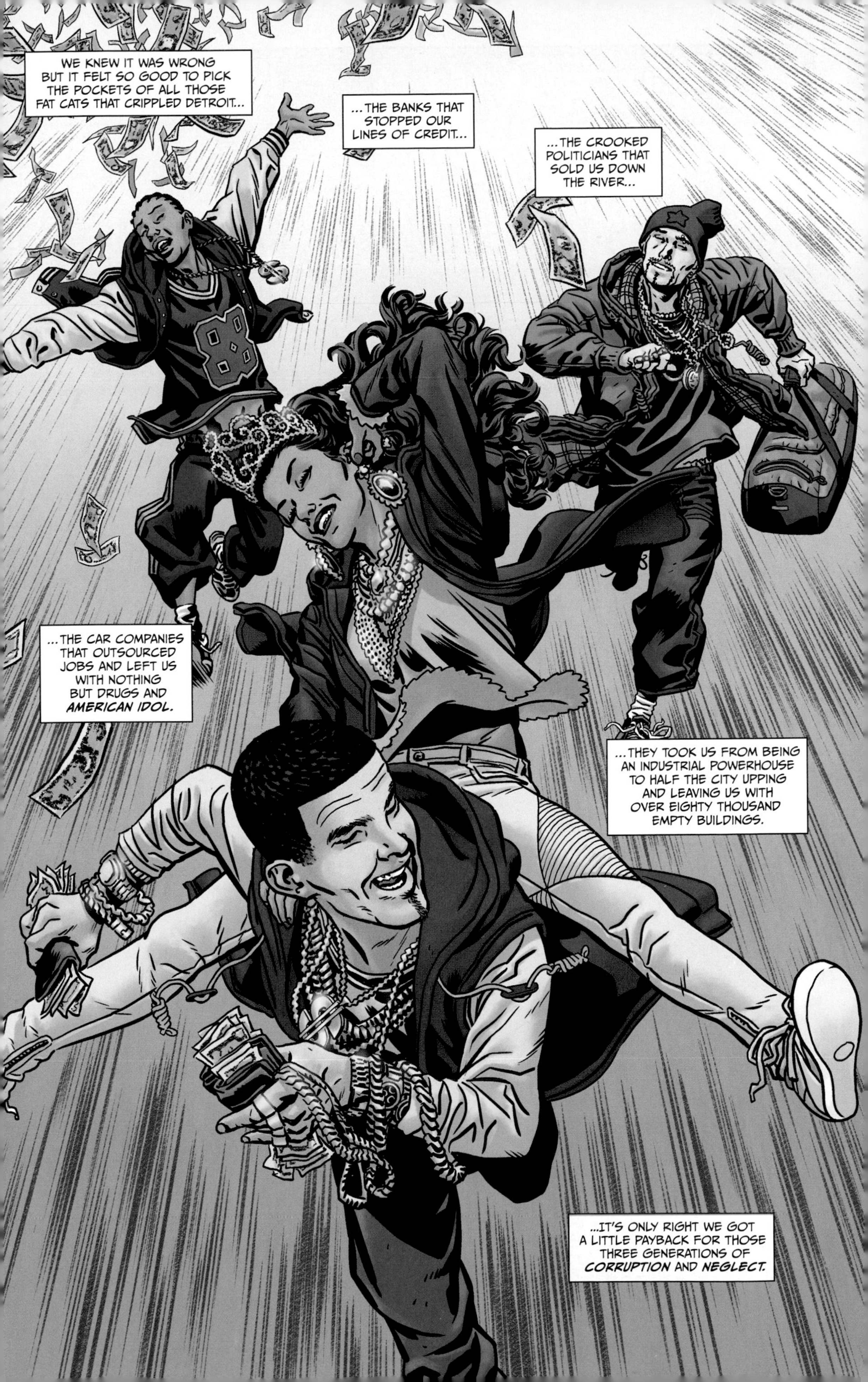
WE KNEW IT WAS WRONG BUT IT FELT SO GOOD TO PICK THE POCKETS OF ALL THOSE FAT CATS THAT CRIPPLED DETROIT...
...THE BANKS THAT STOPPED OUR LINES OF CREDIT...
...THE CROOKED POLITICIANS THAT SOLD US DOWN THE RIVER...
...THE CAR COMPANIES THAT OUTSOURCED JOBS AND LEFT US WITH NOTHING BUT DRUGS AND *AMERICAN IDOL.*
...THEY TOOK US FROM BEING AN INDUSTRIAL POWERHOUSE TO HALF THE CITY UPPING AND LEAVING US WITH OVER EIGHTY THOUSAND EMPTY BUILDINGS.
...IT'S ONLY RIGHT WE GOT A LITTLE PAYBACK FOR THOSE THREE GENERATIONS OF *CORRUPTION* AND *NEGLECT.*

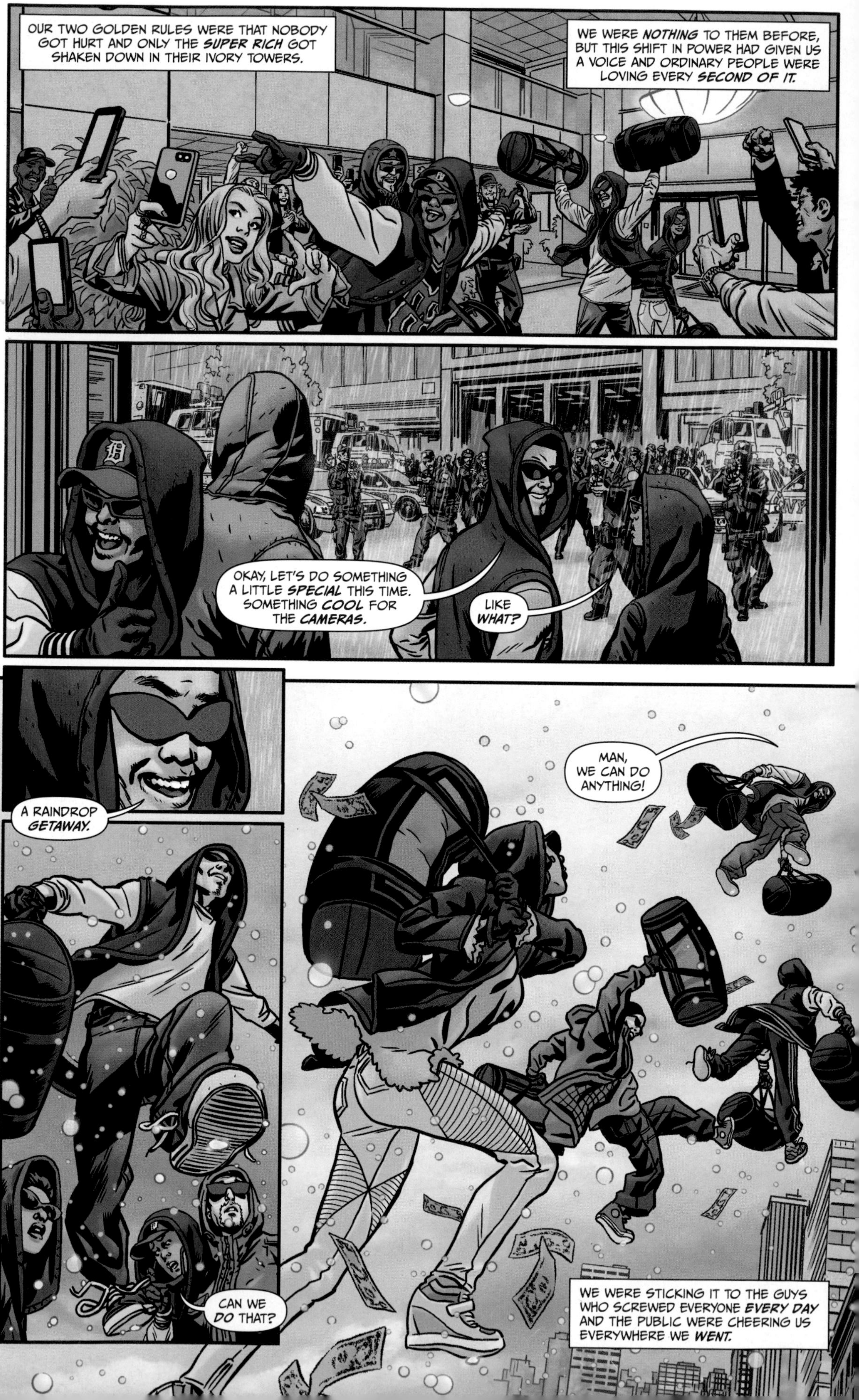
OUR TWO GOLDEN RULES WERE THAT NOBODY GOT HURT AND ONLY THE SUPER RICH GOT SHAKEN DOWN IN THEIR IVORY TOWERS.
WE WERE NOTHING TO THEM BEFORE, BUT THIS SHIFT IN POWER HAD GIVEN US A VOICE AND ORDINARY PEOPLE WERE LOVING EVERY SECOND OF IT.
OKAY, LET'S DO SOMETHING A LITTLE SPECIAL THIS TIME. SOMETHING COOL FOR THE CAMERAS.
LIKE WHAT?
A RAINDROP GETAWAY.
CAN WE DO THAT?
MAN, WE CAN DO ANYTHING!
WE WERE STICKING IT TO THE GUYS WHO SCREWED EVERYONE EVERY DAY AND THE PUBLIC WERE CHEERING US EVERYWHERE WE WENT.

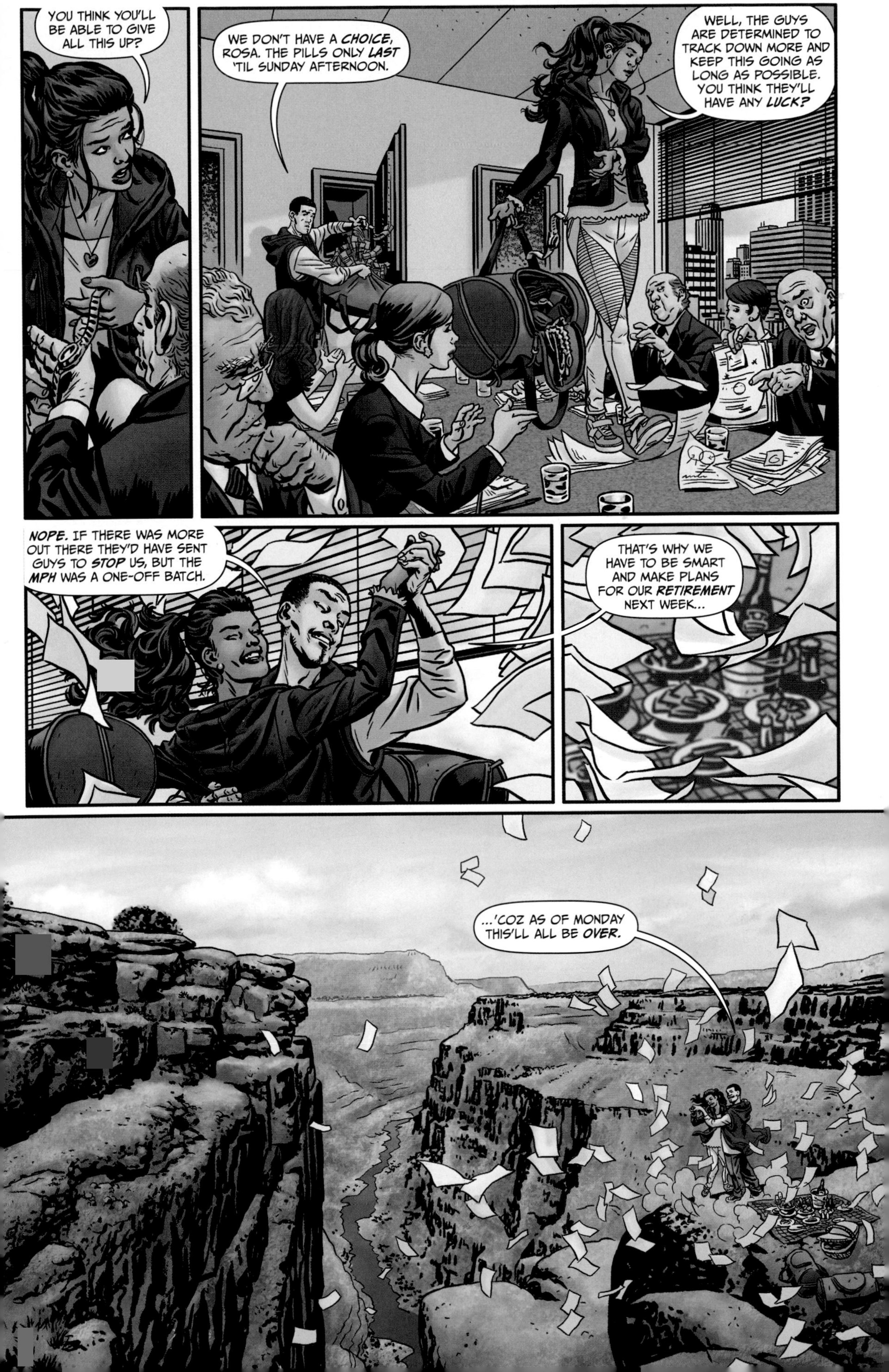
YOU THINK YOU'LL BE ABLE TO GIVE ALL THIS UP?
WE DON'T HAVE A CHOICE, ROSA. THE PILLS ONLY LAST 'TIL SUNDAY AFTERNOON.
WELL, THE GUYS ARE DETERMINED TO TRACK DOWN MORE AND KEEP THIS GOING AS LONG AS POSSIBLE. YOU THINK THEY'LL HAVE ANY LUCK?
NOPE. IF THERE WAS MORE OUT THERE THEY'D HAVE SENT GUYS TO STOP US, BUT THE MPH WAS A ONE-OFF BATCH.
THAT'S WHY WE HAVE TO BE SMART AND MAKE PLANS FOR OUR RETIREMENT NEXT WEEK...
...'COZ AS OF MONDAY THIS'LL ALL BE OVER.

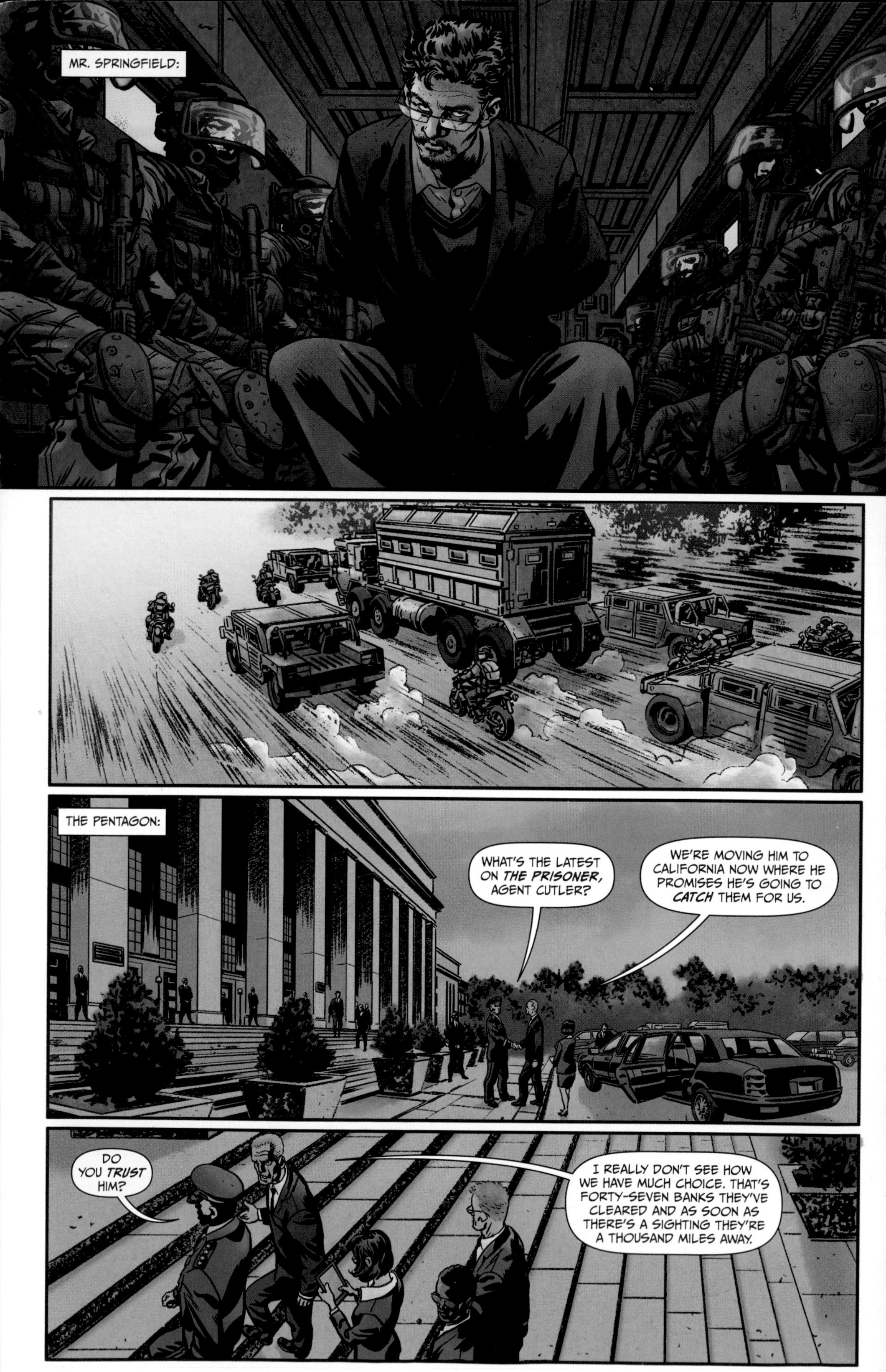
MR. SPRINGFIELD:
THE PENTAGON:
WHAT'S THE LATEST ON THE PRISONER, AGENT CUTLER?
WE'RE MOVING HIM TO CALIFORNIA NOW WHERE HE PROMISES HE'S GOING TO CATCH THEM FOR US.
DO YOU TRUST HIM?
I REALLY DON'T SEE HOW WE HAVE MUCH CHOICE. THAT'S FORTY-SEVEN BANKS THEY'VE CLEARED AND AS SOON AS THERE'S A SIGHTING THEY'RE A THOUSAND MILES AWAY.

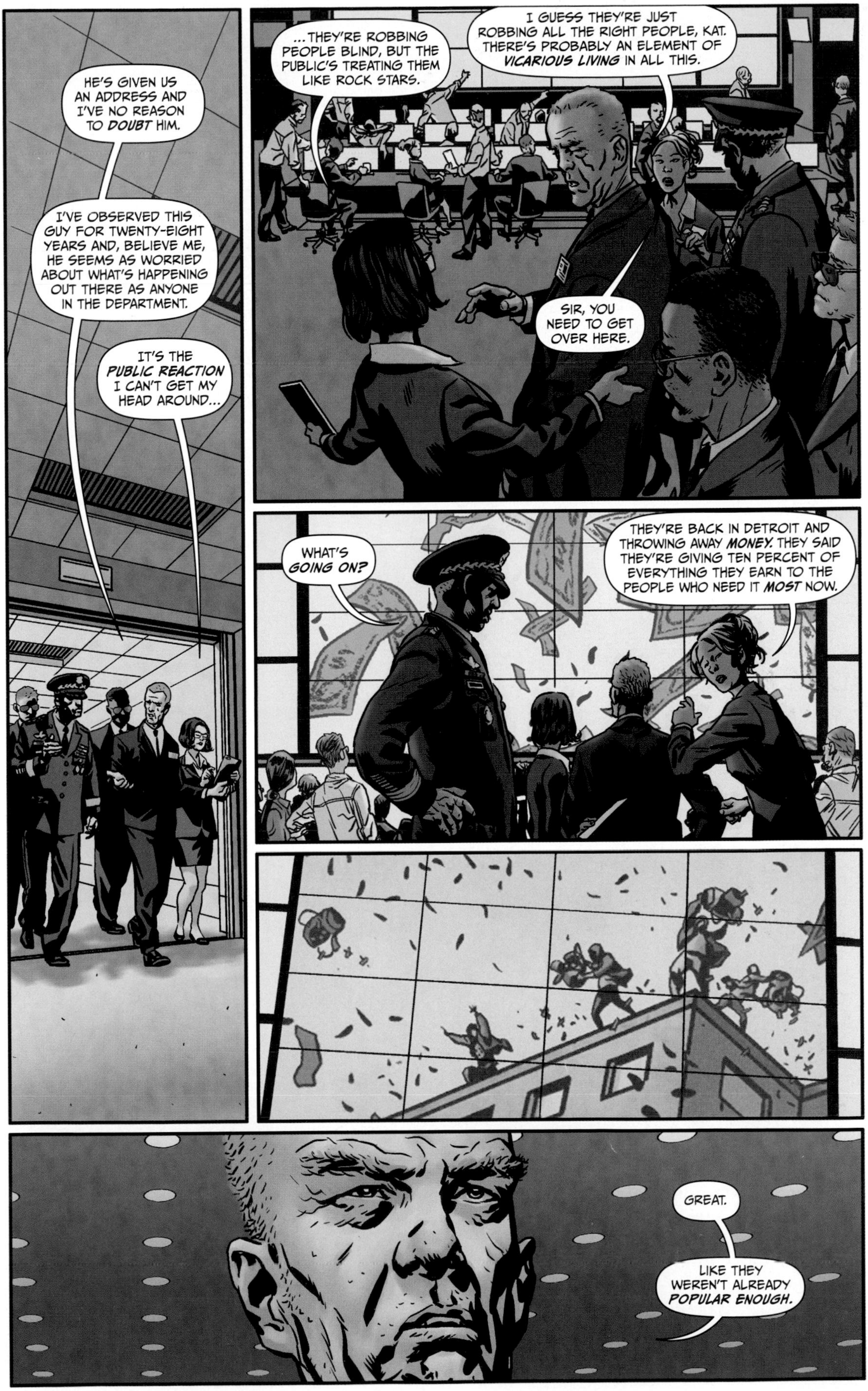
HE'S GIVEN US AN ADDRESS AND I'VE NO REASON TO DOUBT HIM.
I'VE OBSERVED THIS GUY FOR TWENTY-EIGHT YEARS AND, BELIEVE ME, HE SEEMS AS WORRIED ABOUT WHAT'S HAPPENING OUT THERE AS ANYONE IN THE DEPARTMENT.
IT'S THE PUBLIC REACTION I CAN'T GET MY HEAD AROUND...
...THEY'RE ROBBING PEOPLE BLIND, BUT THE PUBLIC'S TREATING THEM LIKE ROCK STARS.
I GUESS THEY'RE JUST ROBBING ALL THE RIGHT PEOPLE, KAT. THERE'S PROBABLY AN ELEMENT OF VICARIOUS LIVING IN ALL THIS.
SIR, YOU NEED TO GET OVER HERE.
WHAT'S GOING ON?
THEY'RE BACK IN DETROIT AND THROWING AWAY MONEY. THEY SAID THEY'RE GIVING TEN PERCENT OF EVERYTHING THEY EARN TO THE PEOPLE WHO NEED IT MOST NOW.
GREAT.
LIKE THEY WEREN'T ALREADY POPULAR ENOUGH.

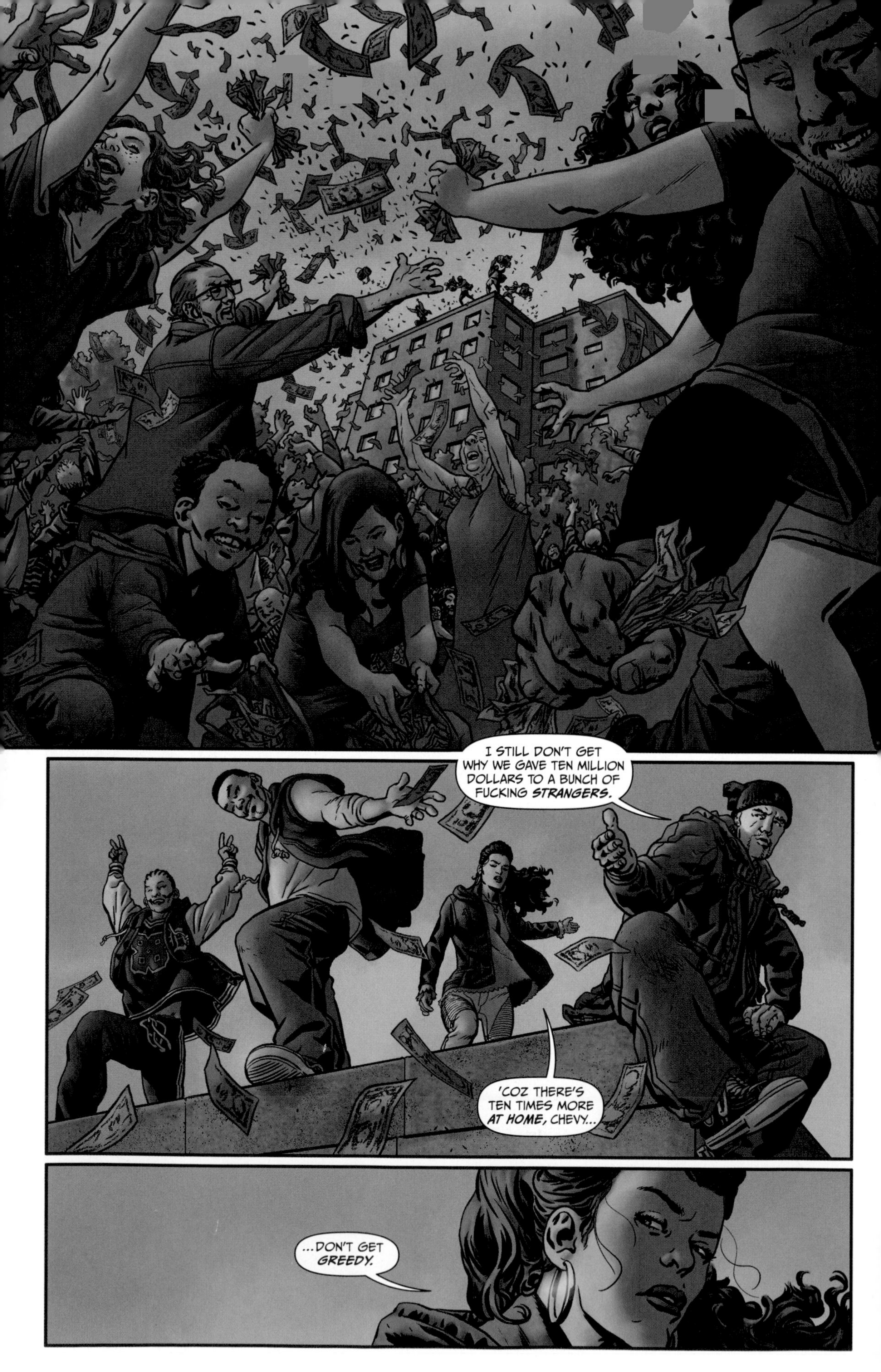
I STILL DON'T GET WHY WE GAVE TEN MILLION DOLLARS TO A BUNCH OF FUCKING STRANGERS.
'COZ THERE'S TEN TIMES MORE AT HOME, CHEVY...
...DON'T GET GREEDY.

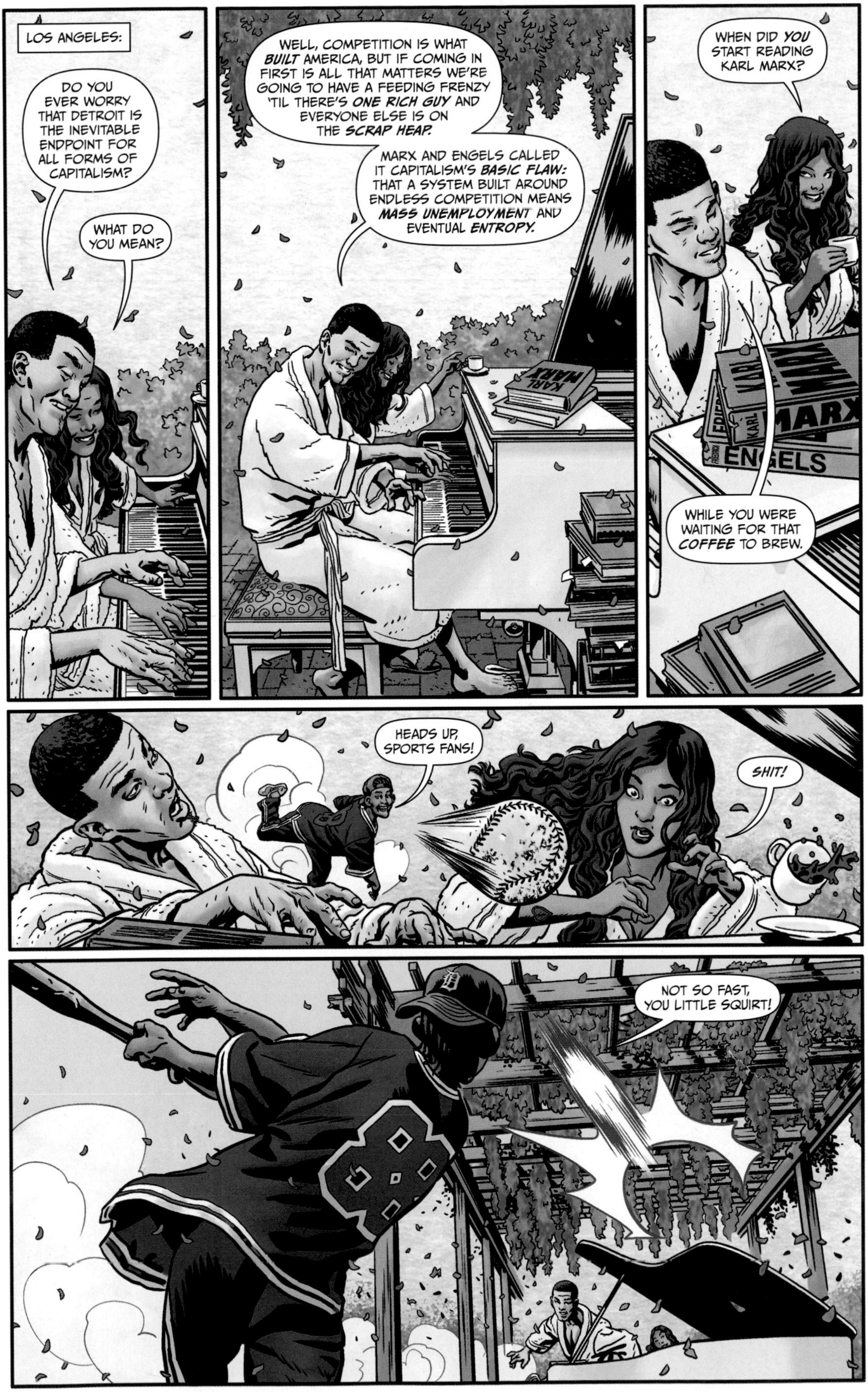
LOS ANGELES:
DO YOU EVER WORRY THAT DETROIT IS THE INEVITABLE ENDPOINT FOR ALL FORMS OF CAPITALISM?
WHAT DO YOU MEAN?
WELL, COMPETITION IS WHAT BUILT AMERICA, BUT IF COMING IN FIRST IS ALL THAT MATTERS WE'RE GOING TO HAVE A FEEDING FRENZY 'TIL THERE'S ONE RICH GUY AND EVERYONE ELSE IS ON THE SCRAP HEAP.
MARX AND ENGELS CALLED IT CAPITALISM'S BASIC FLAW: THAT A SYSTEM BUILT AROUND ENDLESS COMPETITION MEANS MASS UNEMPLOYMENT AND EVENTUAL ENTROPY.
KARL MARX
WHEN DID YOU START READING KARL MARX?
KARL MARX
ENGELS
WHILE YOU WERE WAITING FOR THAT COFFEE TO BREW.
HEADS UP, SPORTS FANS!
SHIT!
NOT SO FAST, YOU LITTLE SQUIRT!

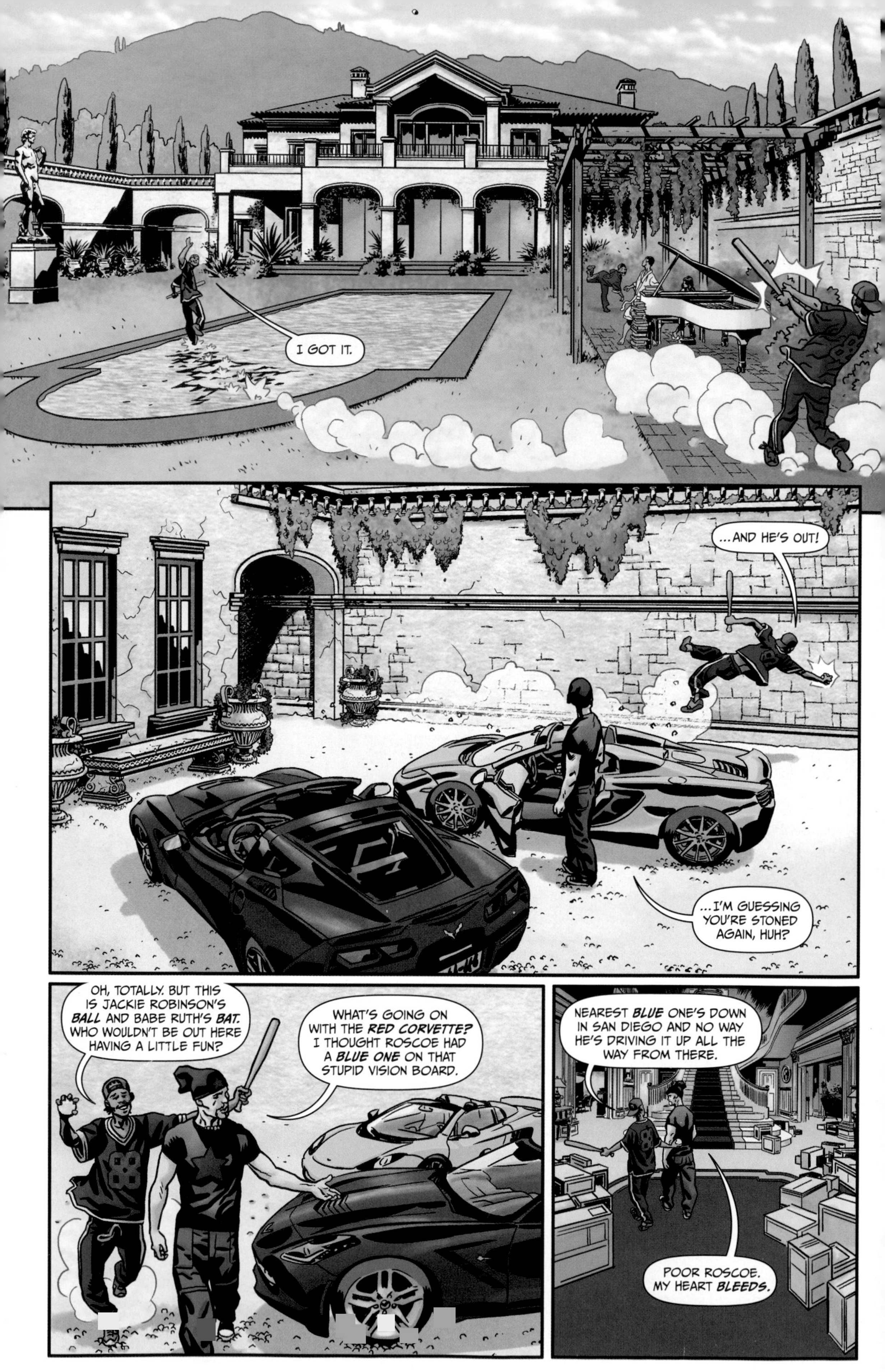
I GOT IT.
...AND HE'S OUT!
...I'M GUESSING YOU'RE STONED AGAIN, HUH?
OH, TOTALLY. BUT THIS IS JACKIE ROBINSON'S BALL AND BABE RUTH'S BAT. WHO WOULDN'T BE OUT HERE HAVING A LITTLE FUN?
WHAT'S GOING ON WITH THE RED CORVETTE? I THOUGHT ROSCOE HAD A BLUE ONE ON THAT STUPID VISION BOARD.
NEAREST BLUE ONE'S DOWN IN SAN DIEGO AND NO WAY HE'S DRIVING IT UP ALL THE WAY FROM THERE.
POOR ROSCOE. MY HEART BLEEDS.

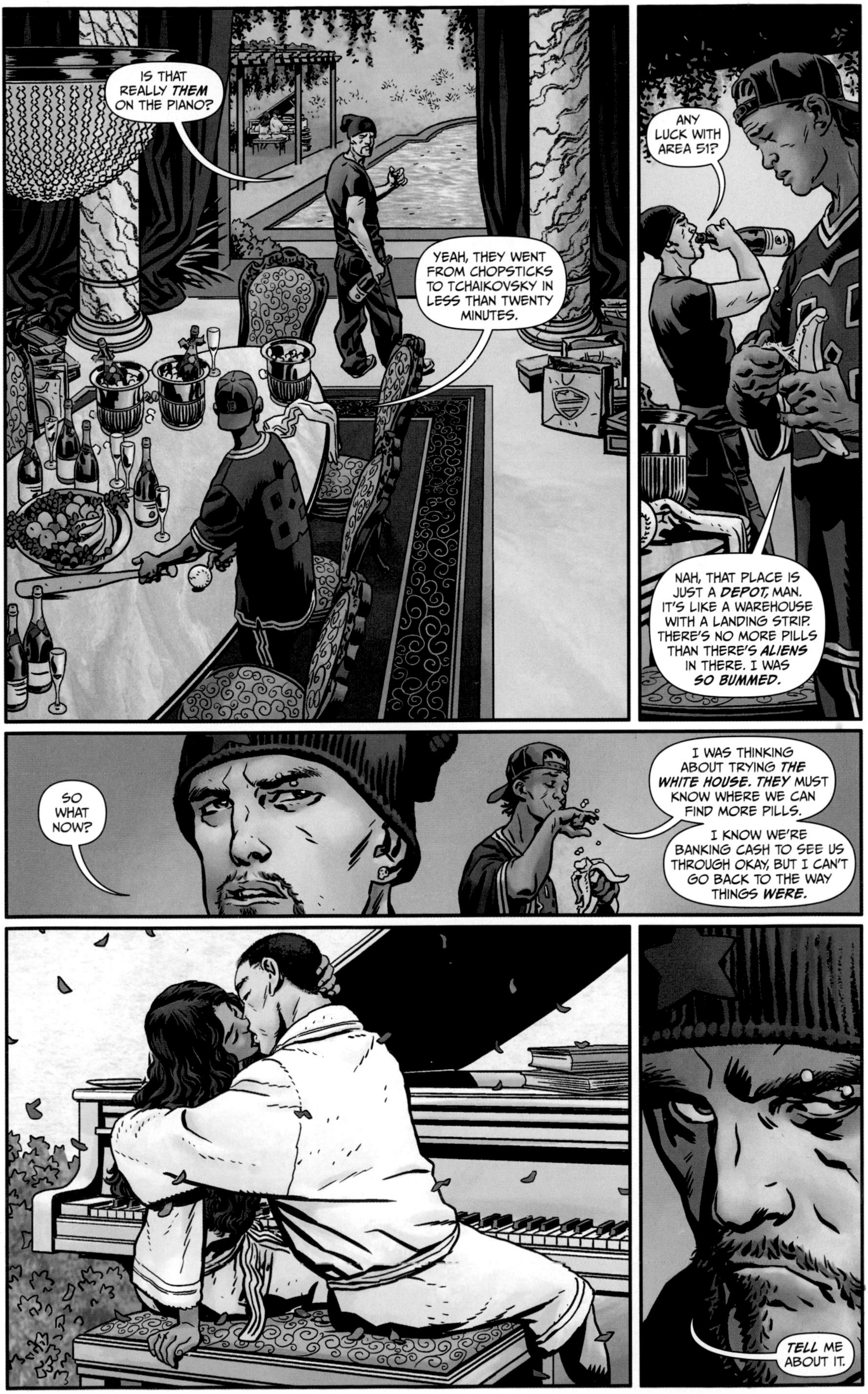
IS THAT REALLY THEM ON THE PIANO?
YEAH, THEY WENT FROM CHOPSTICKS TO TCHAIKOVSKY IN LESS THAN TWENTY MINUTES.
ANY LUCK WITH AREA 51?
NAH, THAT PLACE IS JUST A DEPOT, MAN. IT'S LIKE A WAREHOUSE WITH A LANDING STRIP. THERE'S NO MORE PILLS THAN THERE'S ALIENS IN THERE. I WAS SO BUMMED.
SO WHAT NOW?
I WAS THINKING ABOUT TRYING THE WHITE HOUSE. THEY MUST KNOW WHERE WE CAN FIND MORE PILLS.
I KNOW WE'RE BANKING CASH TO SEE US THROUGH OKAY, BUT I CAN'T GO BACK TO THE WAY THINGS WERE.
TELL ME ABOUT IT.

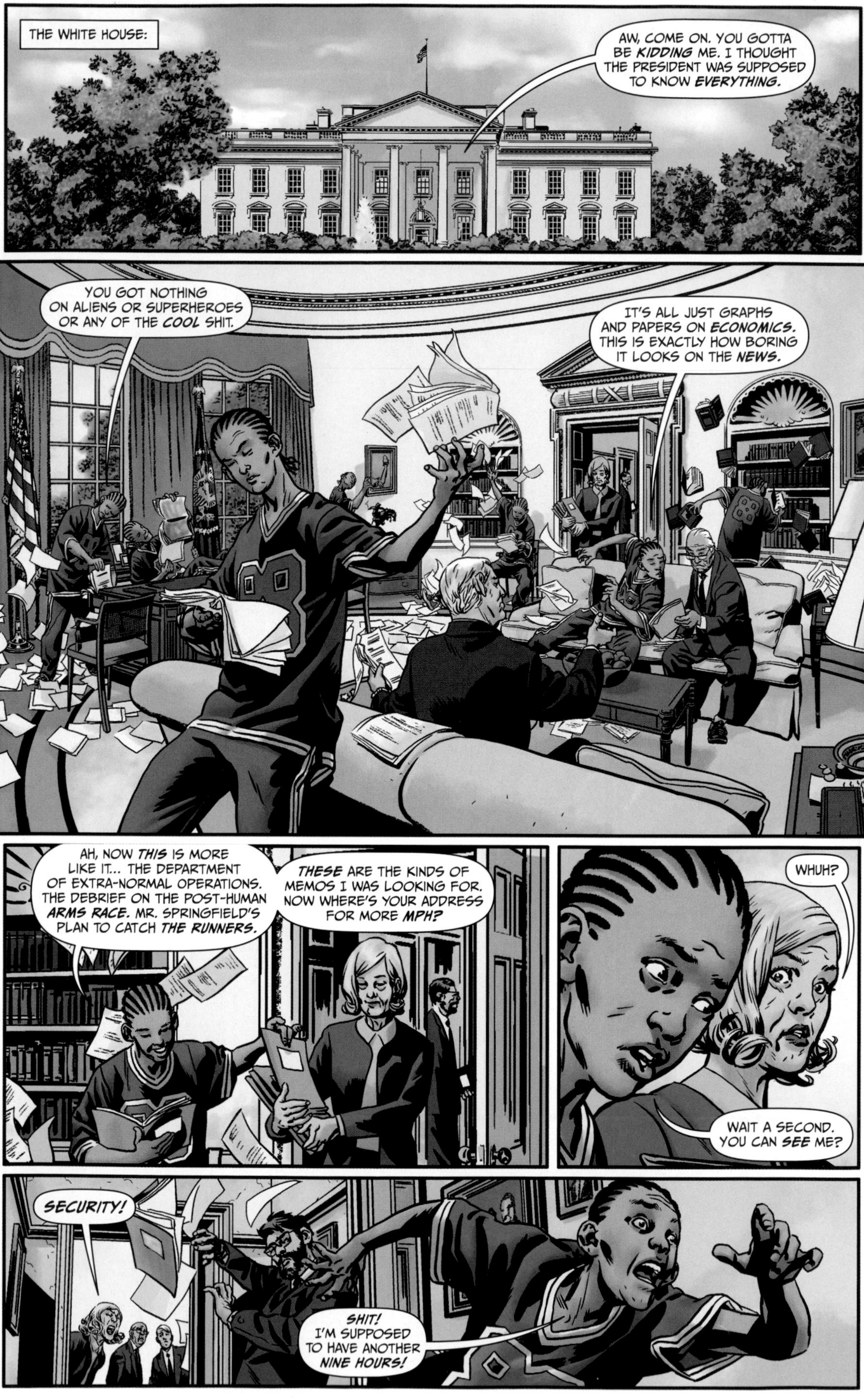
THE WHITE HOUSE:
AW, COME ON. YOU GOTTA BE KIDDING ME. I THOUGHT THE PRESIDENT WAS SUPPOSED TO KNOW EVERYTHING.
YOU GOT NOTHING ON ALIENS OR SUPERHEROES OR ANY OF THE COOL SHIT.
IT'S ALL JUST GRAPHS AND PAPERS ON ECONOMICS. THIS IS EXACTLY HOW BORING IT LOOKS ON THE NEWS.
AH, NOW THIS IS MORE LIKE IT... THE DEPARTMENT OF EXTRA-NORMAL OPERATIONS. THE DEBRIEF ON THE POST-HUMAN ARMS RACE. MR. SPRINGFIELD'S PLAN TO CATCH THE RUNNERS.
THESE ARE THE KINDS OF MEMOS I WAS LOOKING FOR. NOW WHERE'S YOUR ADDRESS FOR MORE MPH?
WHUH?
WAIT A SECOND. YOU CAN SEE ME?
SECURITY!
SHIT! I'M SUPPOSED TO HAVE ANOTHER NINE HOURS!

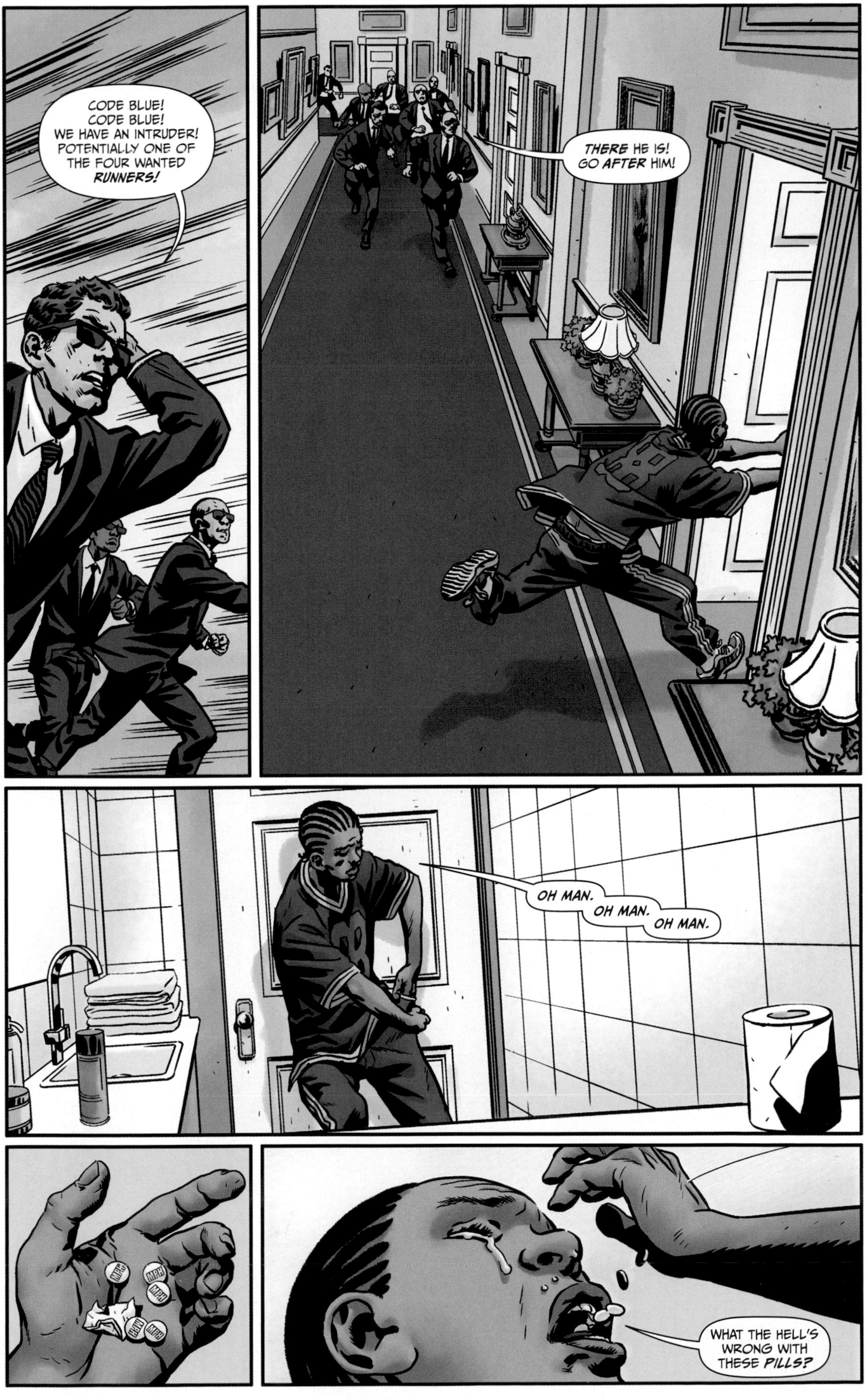
CODE BLUE! CODE BLUE! WE HAVE AN INTRUDER! POTENTIALLY ONE OF THE FOUR WANTED RUNNERS!
THERE HE IS! GO AFTER HIM!
OH MAN.
OH MAN.
OH MAN.
WHAT THE HELL'S WRONG WITH THESE PILLS?

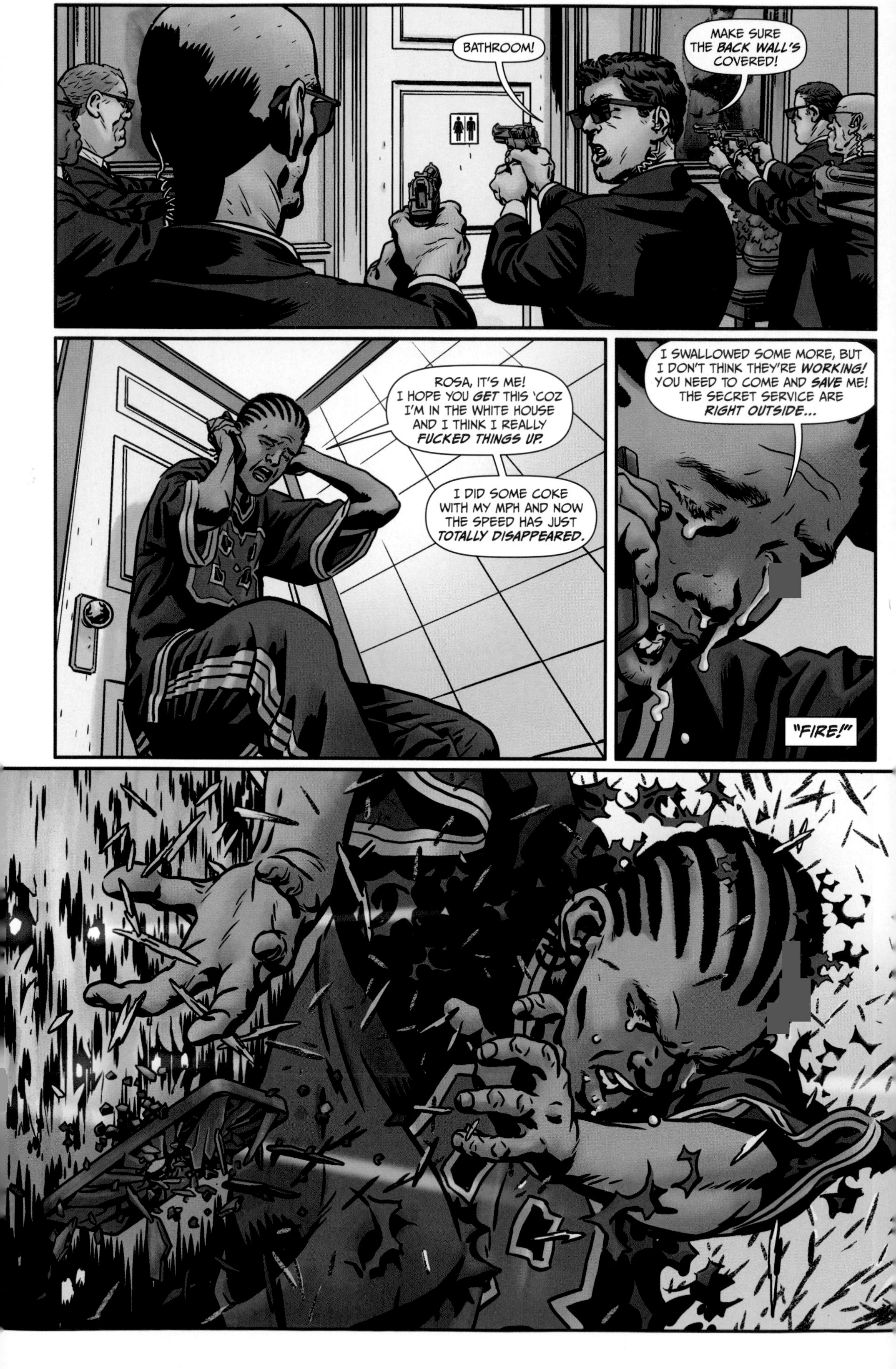
BATHROOM!
MAKE SURE THE BACK WALL'S COVERED!
ROSA, IT'S ME! I HOPE YOU GET THIS 'COZ I'M IN THE WHITE HOUSE AND I THINK I REALLY FUCKED THINGS UP.
I DID SOME COKE WITH MY MPH AND NOW THE SPEED HAS JUST TOTALLY DISAPPEARED.
I SWALLOWED SOME MORE, BUT I DON'T THINK THEY'RE WORKING! YOU NEED TO COME AND SAVE ME! THE SECRET SERVICE ARE RIGHT OUTSIDE...
"FIRE!"

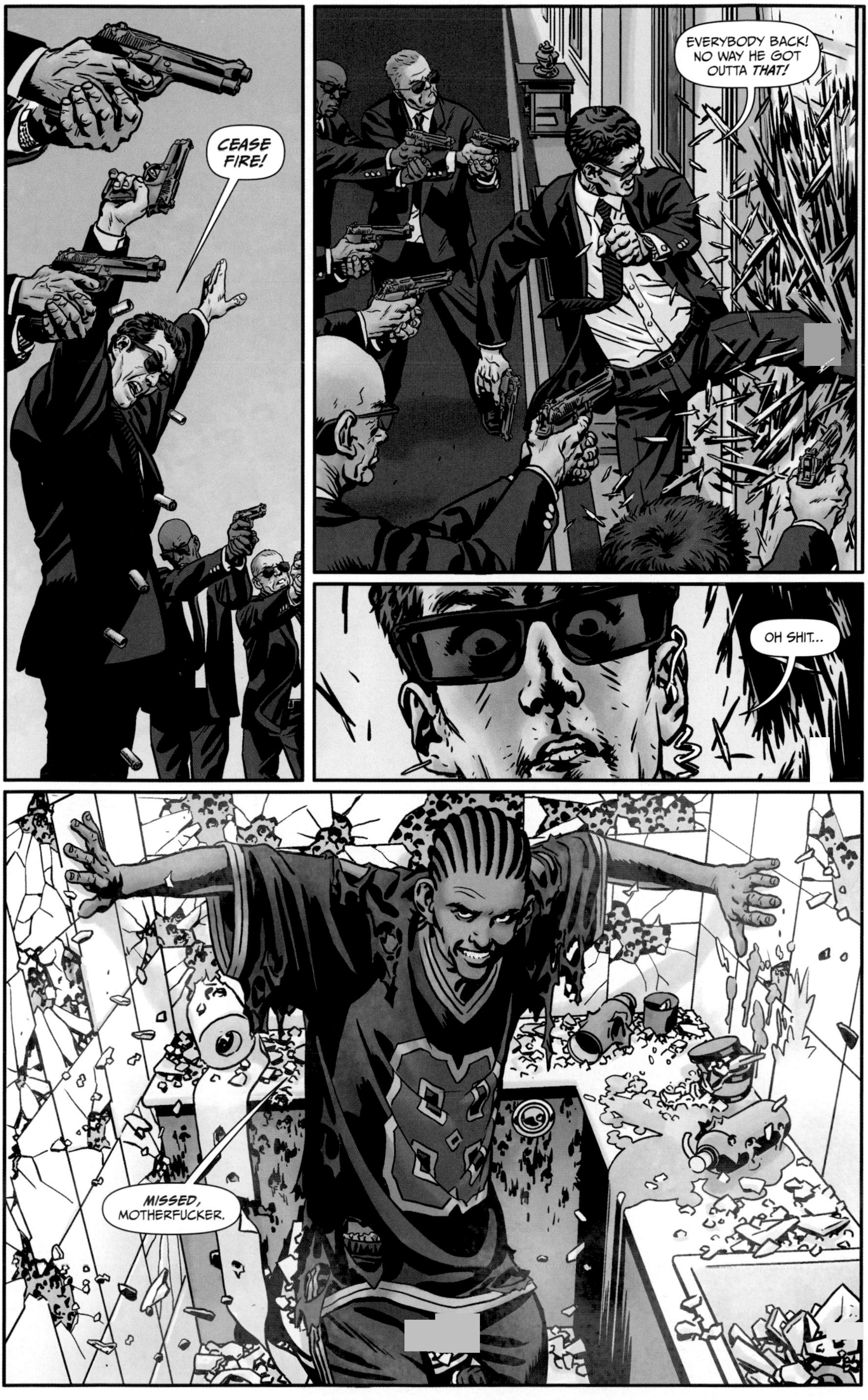
CEASE FIRE!
EVERYBODY BACK! NO WAY HE GOT OUTTA THAT!
OH SHIT...
MISSED, MOTHERFUCKER.

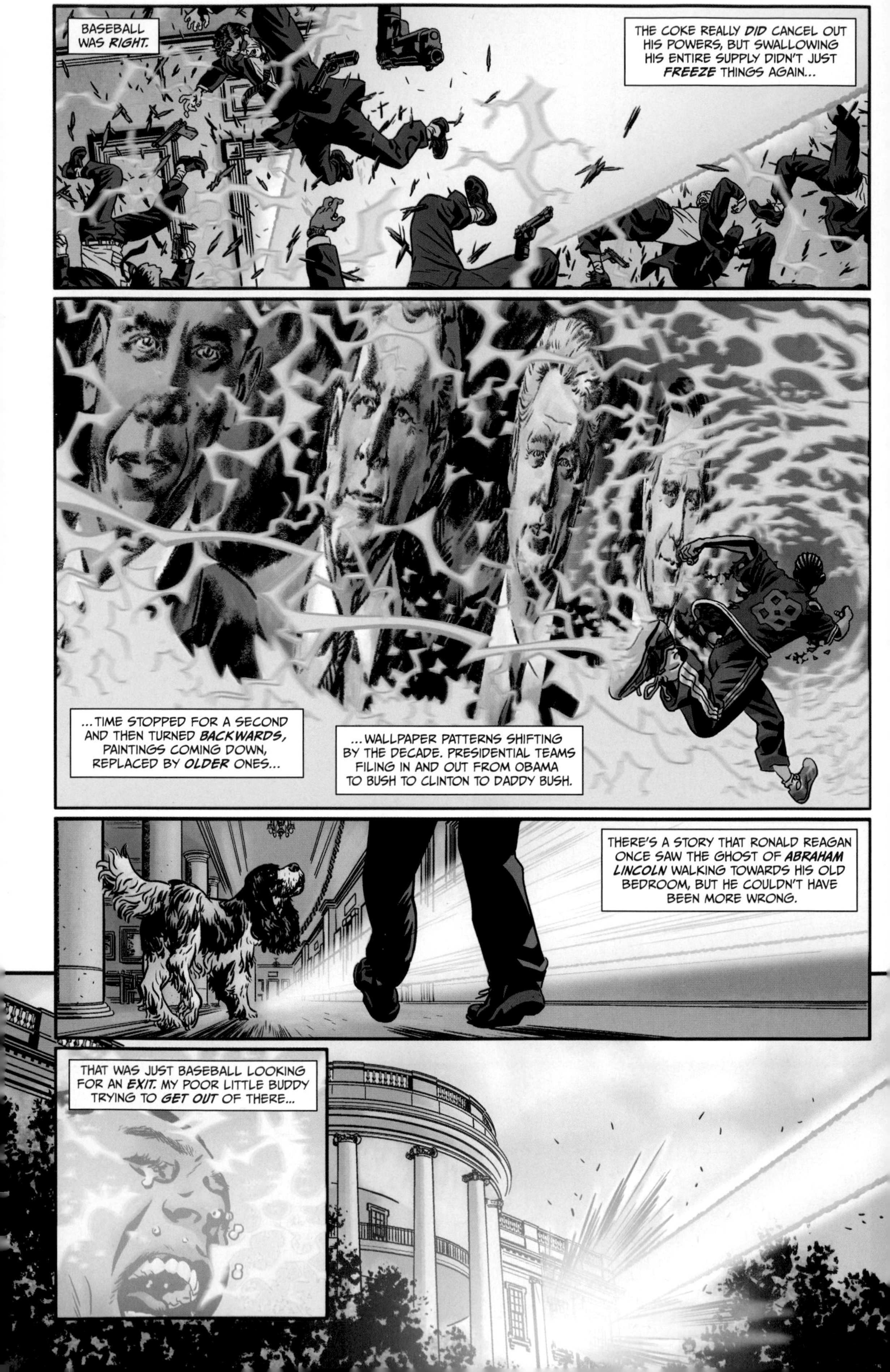
BASEBALL WAS RIGHT.
THE COKE REALLY DID CANCEL OUT HIS POWERS, BUT SWALLOWING HIS ENTIRE SUPPLY DIDN'T JUST FREEZE THINGS AGAIN...
...TIME STOPPED FOR A SECOND AND THEN TURNED BACKWARDS, PAINTINGS COMING DOWN, REPLACED BY OLDER ONES...
...WALLPAPER PATTERNS SHIFTING BY THE DECADE. PRESIDENTIAL TEAMS FILING IN AND OUT FROM OBAMA TO BUSH TO CLINTON TO DADDY BUSH.
THERE'S A STORY THAT RONALD REAGAN ONCE SAW THE GHOST OF ABRAHAM LINCOLN WALKING TOWARDS HIS OLD BEDROOM, BUT HE COULDN'T HAVE BEEN MORE WRONG.
THAT WAS JUST BASEBALL LOOKING FOR AN EXIT. MY POOR LITTLE BUDDY TRYING TO GET OUT OF THERE...

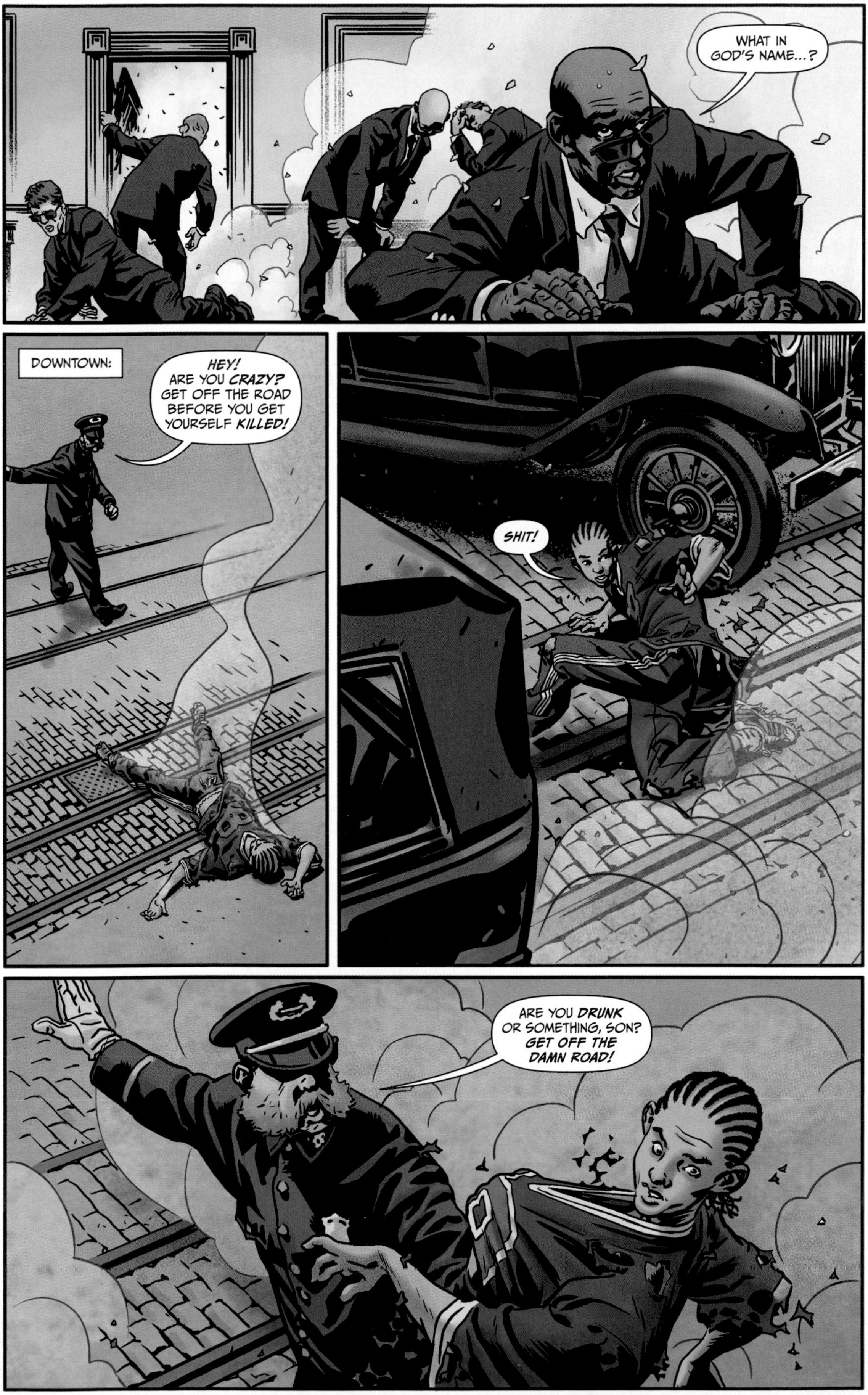
WHAT IN GOD'S NAME...?
DOWNTOWN:
HEY! ARE YOU CRAZY? GET OFF THE ROAD BEFORE YOU GET YOURSELF KILLED!
SHIT!
ARE YOU DRUNK OR SOMETHING, SON? GET OFF THE DAMN ROAD!

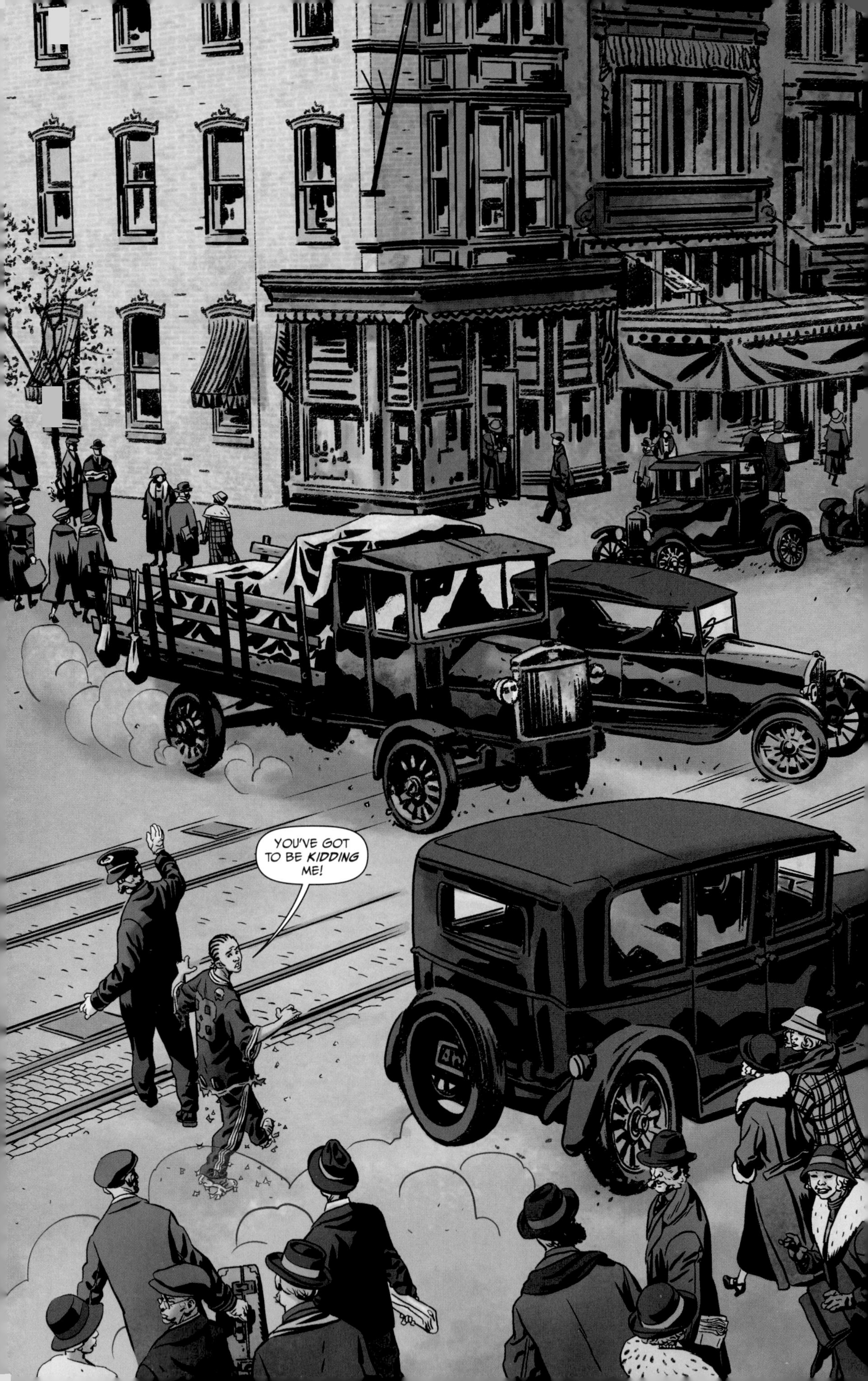
YOU'VE GOT TO BE *KIDDING* ME!

CHAPTER

FOUR

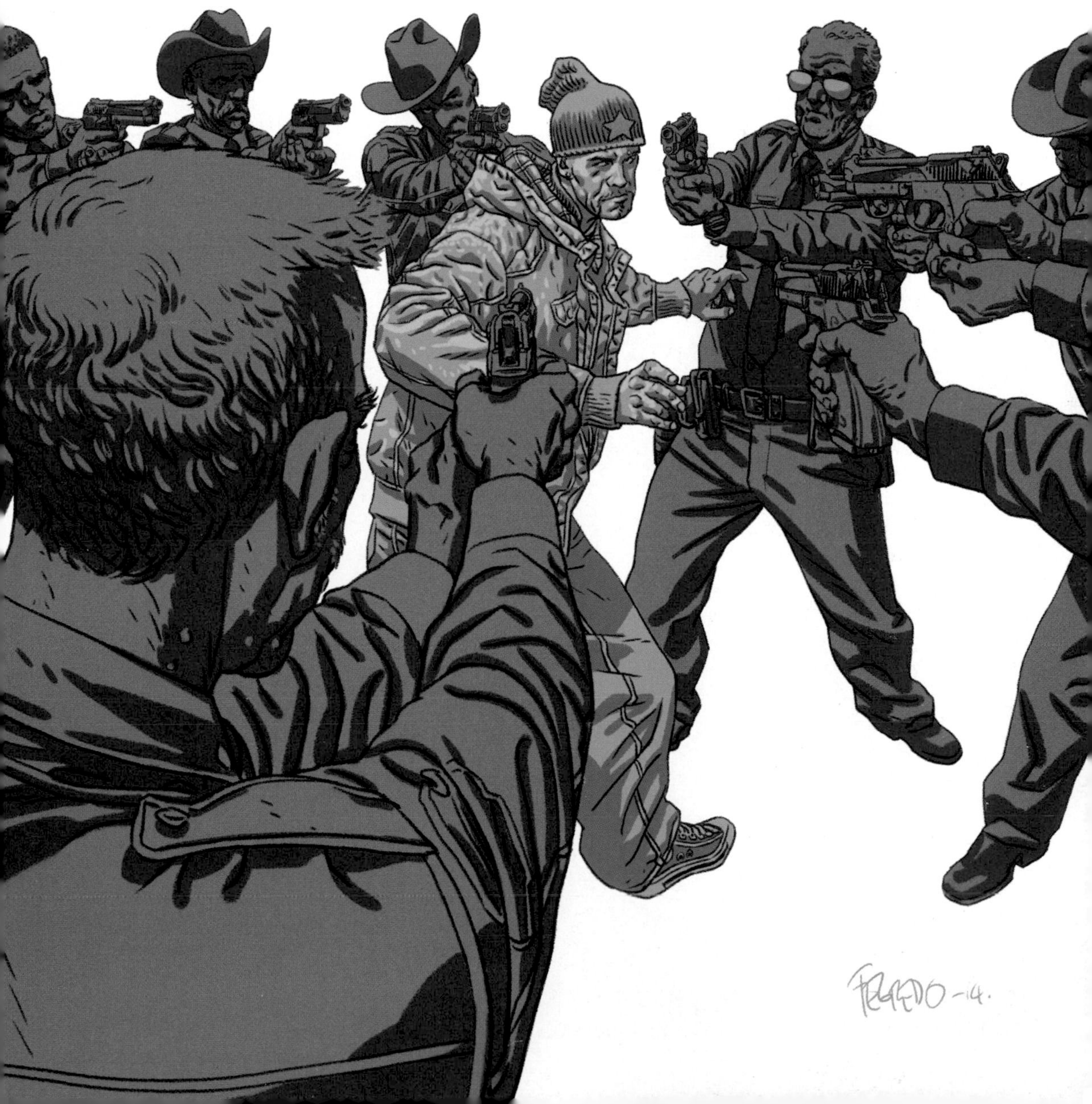

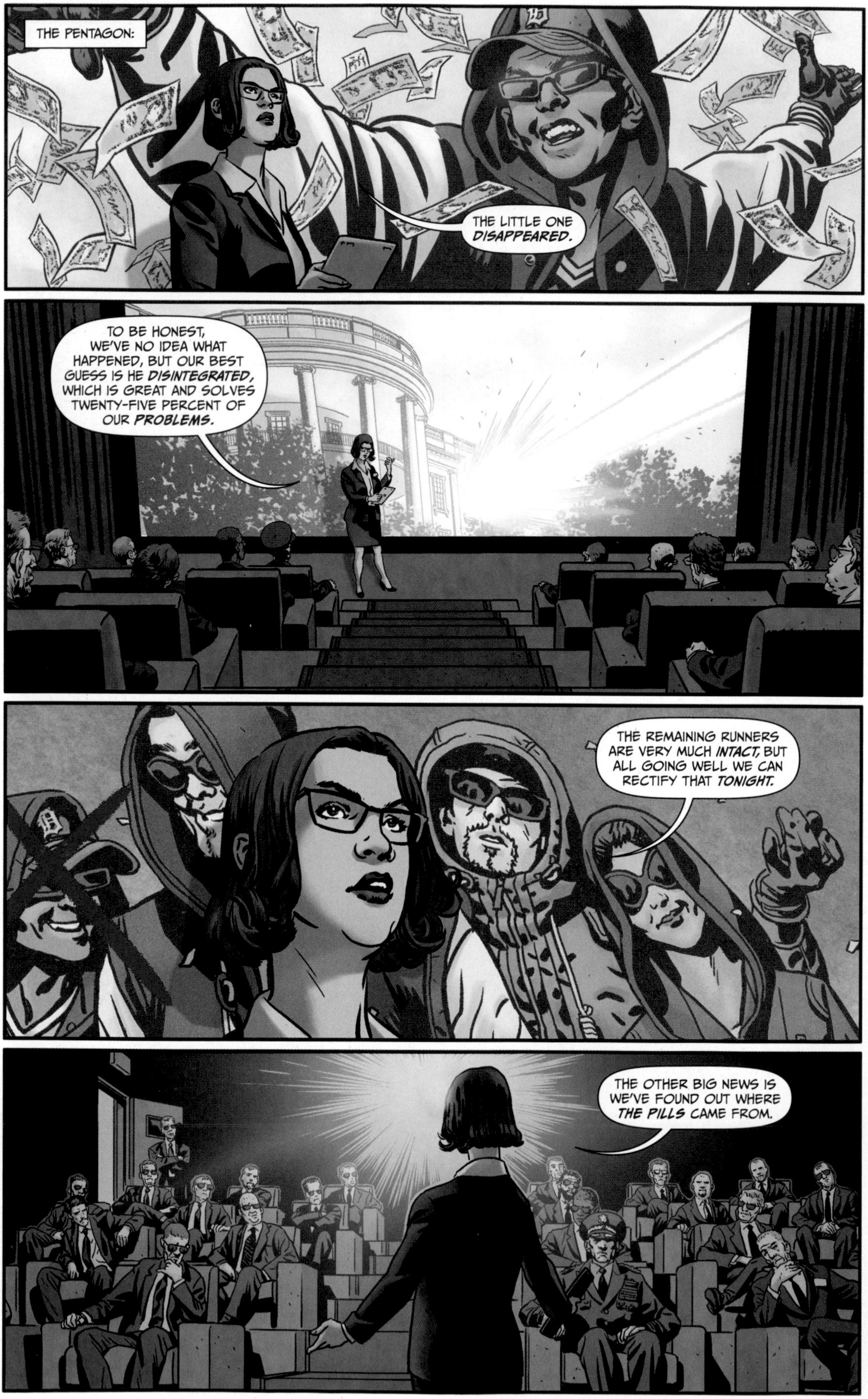
THE PENTAGON:
THE LITTLE ONE DISAPPEARED.
TO BE HONEST, WE'VE NO IDEA WHAT HAPPENED, BUT OUR BEST GUESS IS HE DISINTEGRATED, WHICH IS GREAT AND SOLVES TWENTY-FIVE PERCENT OF OUR PROBLEMS.
THE REMAINING RUNNERS ARE VERY MUCH INTACT, BUT ALL GOING WELL WE CAN RECTIFY THAT TONIGHT.
THE OTHER BIG NEWS IS WE'VE FOUND OUT WHERE THE PILLS CAME FROM.

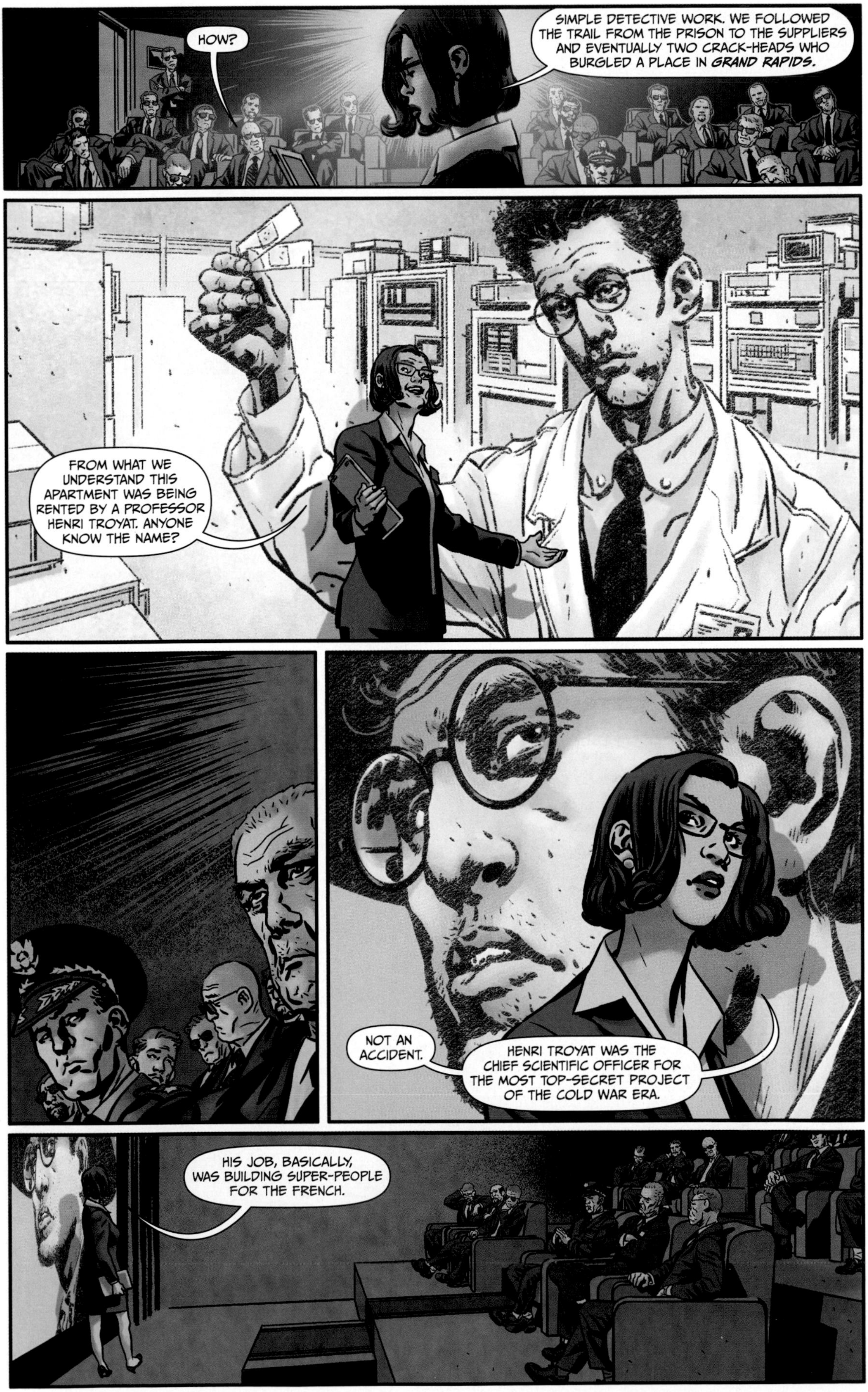
HOW?
SIMPLE DETECTIVE WORK. WE FOLLOWED THE TRAIL FROM THE PRISON TO THE SUPPLIERS AND EVENTUALLY TWO CRACK-HEADS WHO BURGLED A PLACE IN GRAND RAPIDS.
FROM WHAT WE UNDERSTAND THIS APARTMENT WAS BEING RENTED BY A PROFESSOR HENRI TROYAT. ANYONE KNOW THE NAME?
NOT AN ACCIDENT.
HENRI TROYAT WAS THE CHIEF SCIENTIFIC OFFICER FOR THE MOST TOP-SECRET PROJECT OF THE COLD WAR ERA.
HIS JOB, BASICALLY, WAS BUILDING SUPER-PEOPLE FOR THE FRENCH.

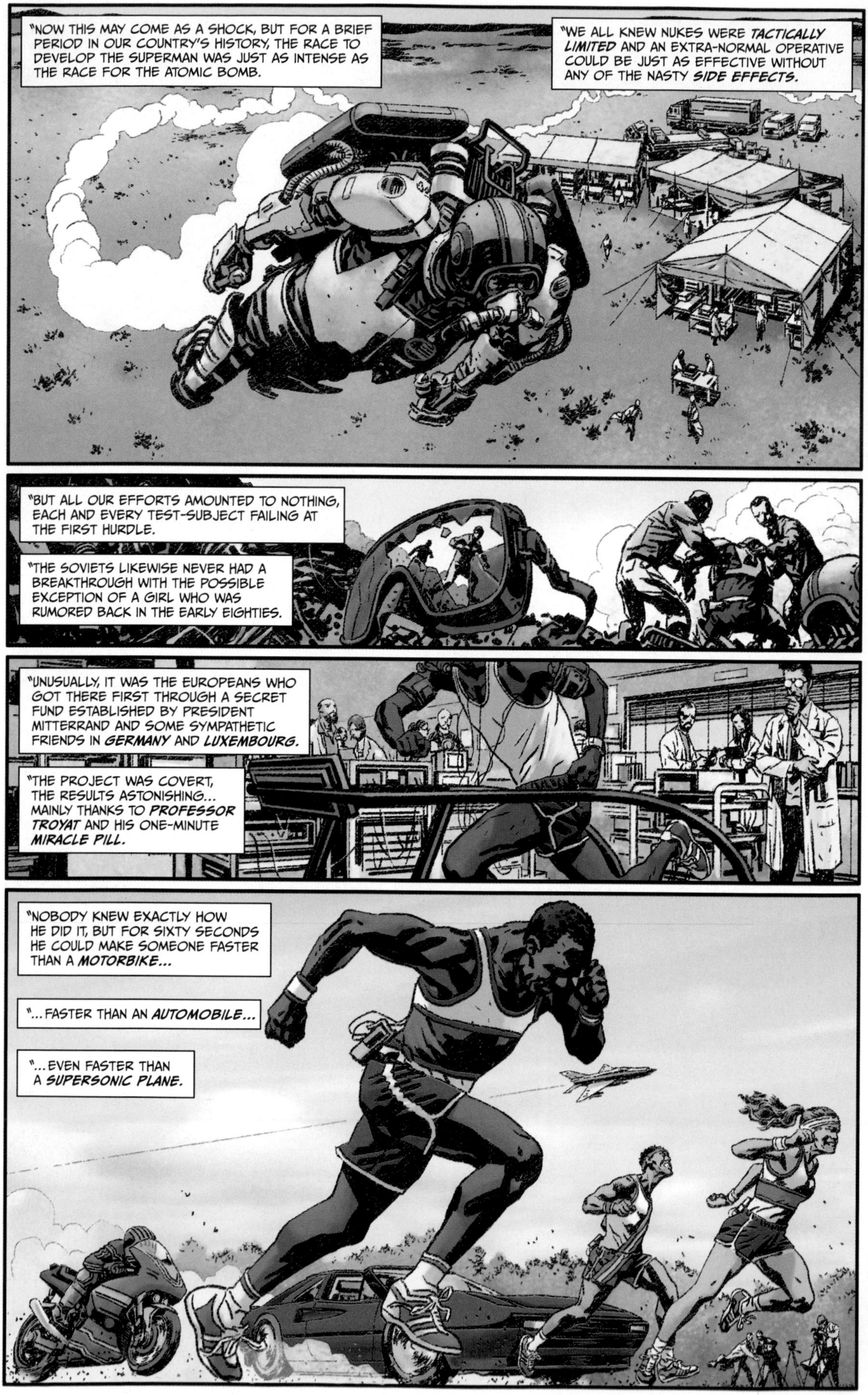
"NOW THIS MAY COME AS A SHOCK, BUT FOR A BRIEF PERIOD IN OUR COUNTRY'S HISTORY, THE RACE TO DEVELOP THE SUPERMAN WAS JUST AS INTENSE AS THE RACE FOR THE ATOMIC BOMB.
"WE ALL KNEW NUKES WERE *TACTICALLY LIMITED* AND AN EXTRA-NORMAL OPERATIVE COULD BE JUST AS EFFECTIVE WITHOUT ANY OF THE NASTY *SIDE EFFECTS.*
"BUT ALL OUR EFFORTS AMOUNTED TO NOTHING, EACH AND EVERY TEST-SUBJECT FAILING AT THE FIRST HURDLE.
"THE SOVIETS LIKEWISE NEVER HAD A BREAKTHROUGH WITH THE POSSIBLE EXCEPTION OF A GIRL WHO WAS RUMORED BACK IN THE EARLY EIGHTIES.
"UNUSUALLY, IT WAS THE EUROPEANS WHO GOT THERE FIRST THROUGH A SECRET FUND ESTABLISHED BY PRESIDENT MITTERRAND AND SOME SYMPATHETIC FRIENDS IN *GERMANY* AND *LUXEMBOURG.*
"THE PROJECT WAS COVERT, THE RESULTS ASTONISHING... MAINLY THANKS TO *PROFESSOR TROYAT* AND HIS ONE-MINUTE *MIRACLE PILL.*
"NOBODY KNEW EXACTLY HOW HE DID IT, BUT FOR SIXTY SECONDS HE COULD MAKE SOMEONE FASTER THAN A *MOTORBIKE...*
"...FASTER THAN AN *AUTOMOBILE...*
"...EVEN FASTER THAN A *SUPERSONIC PLANE.*

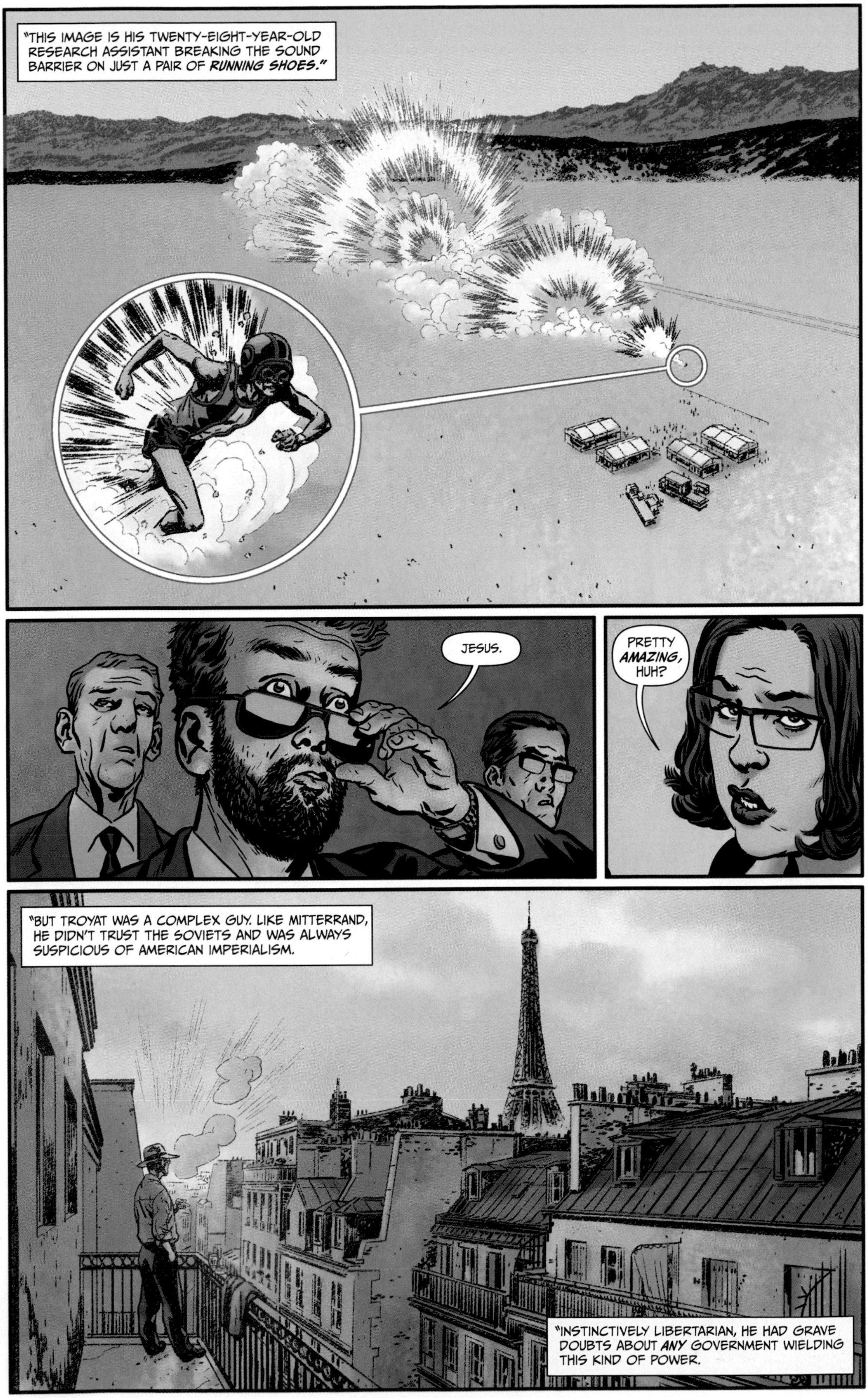
"THIS IMAGE IS HIS TWENTY-EIGHT-YEAR-OLD RESEARCH ASSISTANT BREAKING THE SOUND BARRIER ON JUST A PAIR OF *RUNNING SHOES.*"
JESUS.
PRETTY *AMAZING,* HUH?
"BUT TROYAT WAS A COMPLEX GUY. LIKE MITTERRAND, HE DIDN'T TRUST THE SOVIETS AND WAS ALWAYS SUSPICIOUS OF AMERICAN IMPERIALISM.
"INSTINCTIVELY LIBERTARIAN, HE HAD GRAVE DOUBTS ABOUT *ANY* GOVERNMENT WIELDING THIS KIND OF POWER.

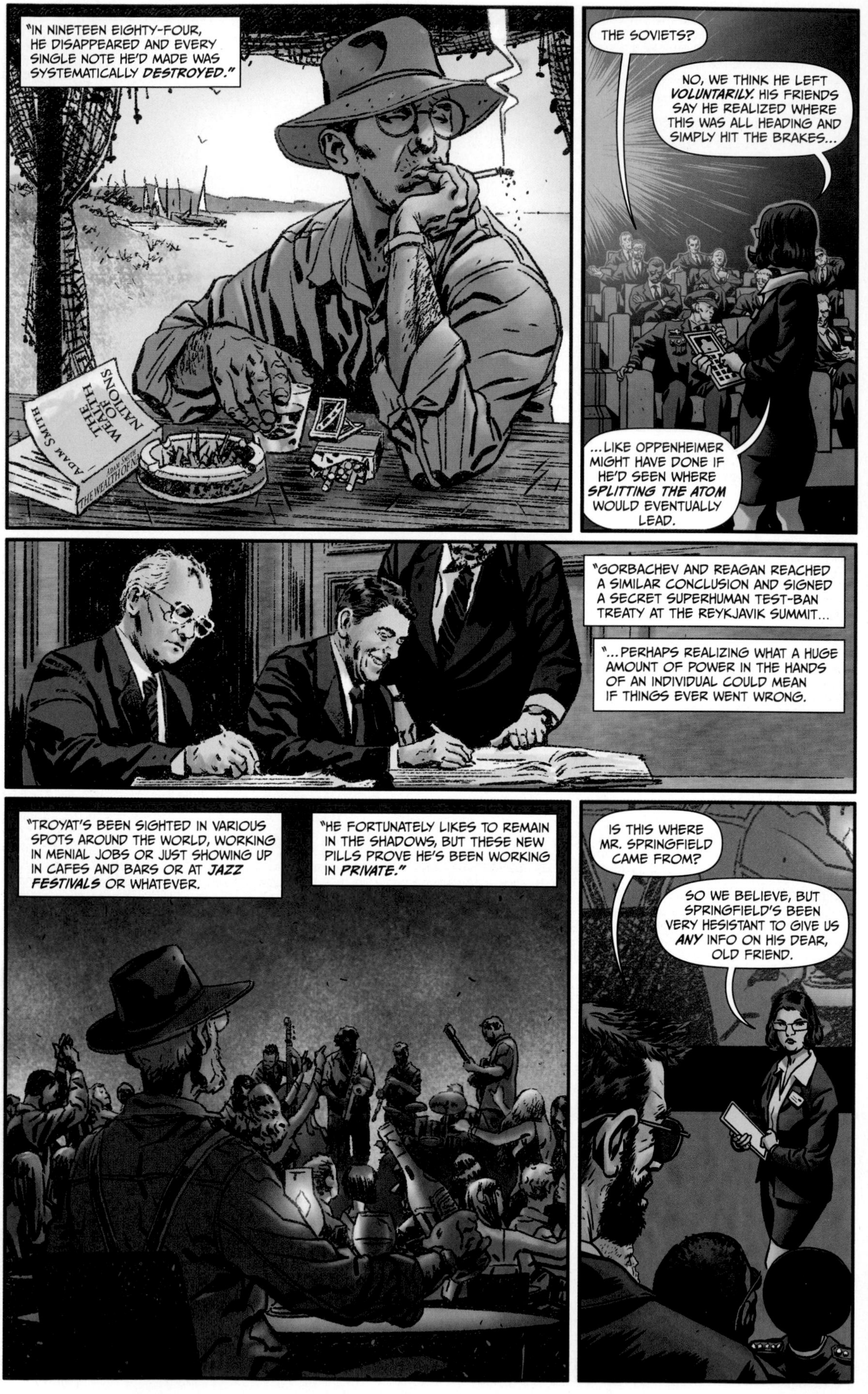
"IN NINETEEN EIGHTY-FOUR, HE DISAPPEARED AND EVERY SINGLE NOTE HE'D MADE WAS SYSTEMATICALLY DESTROYED."
THE WEALTH OF NATIONS
ADAM SMITH
THE SOVIETS?
NO, WE THINK HE LEFT VOLUNTARILY. HIS FRIENDS SAY HE REALIZED WHERE THIS WAS ALL HEADING AND SIMPLY HIT THE BRAKES...
...LIKE OPPENHEIMER MIGHT HAVE DONE IF HE'D SEEN WHERE SPLITTING THE ATOM WOULD EVENTUALLY LEAD.
"GORBACHEV AND REAGAN REACHED A SIMILAR CONCLUSION AND SIGNED A SECRET SUPERHUMAN TEST-BAN TREATY AT THE REYKJAVIK SUMMIT...
"...PERHAPS REALIZING WHAT A HUGE AMOUNT OF POWER IN THE HANDS OF AN INDIVIDUAL COULD MEAN IF THINGS EVER WENT WRONG.
"TROYAT'S BEEN SIGHTED IN VARIOUS SPOTS AROUND THE WORLD, WORKING IN MENIAL JOBS OR JUST SHOWING UP IN CAFES AND BARS OR AT JAZZ FESTIVALS OR WHATEVER.
"HE FORTUNATELY LIKES TO REMAIN IN THE SHADOWS, BUT THESE NEW PILLS PROVE HE'S BEEN WORKING IN PRIVATE."
IS THIS WHERE MR. SPRINGFIELD CAME FROM?
SO WE BELIEVE, BUT SPRINGFIELD'S BEEN VERY HESISTANT TO GIVE US ANY INFO ON HIS DEAR, OLD FRIEND.

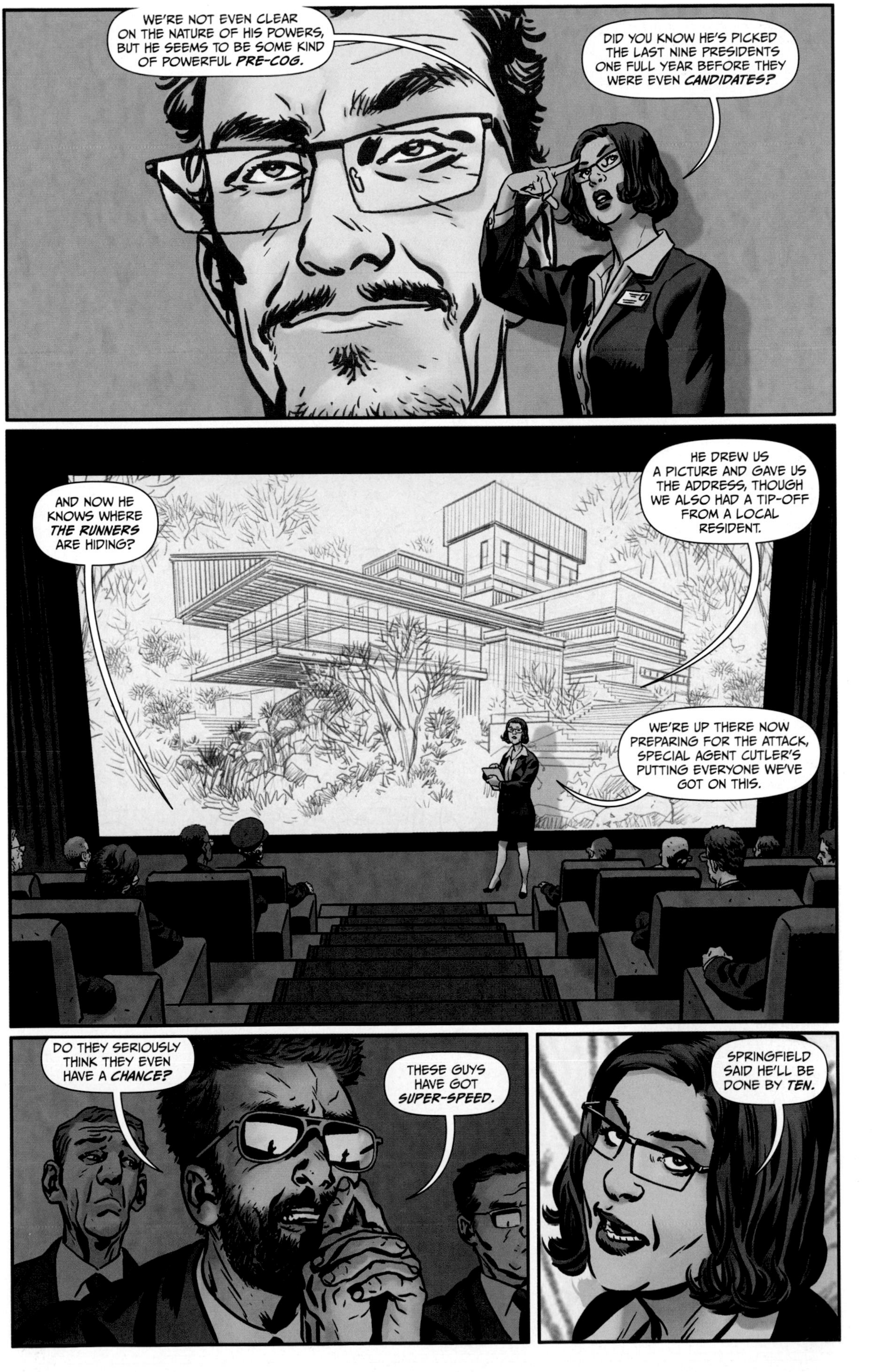
WE'RE NOT EVEN CLEAR ON THE NATURE OF HIS POWERS, BUT HE SEEMS TO BE SOME KIND OF POWERFUL PRE-COG.
DID YOU KNOW HE'S PICKED THE LAST NINE PRESIDENTS ONE FULL YEAR BEFORE THEY WERE EVEN CANDIDATES?
AND NOW HE KNOWS WHERE THE RUNNERS ARE HIDING?
HE DREW US A PICTURE AND GAVE US THE ADDRESS, THOUGH WE ALSO HAD A TIP-OFF FROM A LOCAL RESIDENT.
WE'RE UP THERE NOW PREPARING FOR THE ATTACK, SPECIAL AGENT CUTLER'S PUTTING EVERYONE WE'VE GOT ON THIS.
DO THEY SERIOUSLY THINK THEY EVEN HAVE A CHANCE?
THESE GUYS HAVE GOT SUPER-SPEED.
SPRINGFIELD SAID HE'LL BE DONE BY TEN.

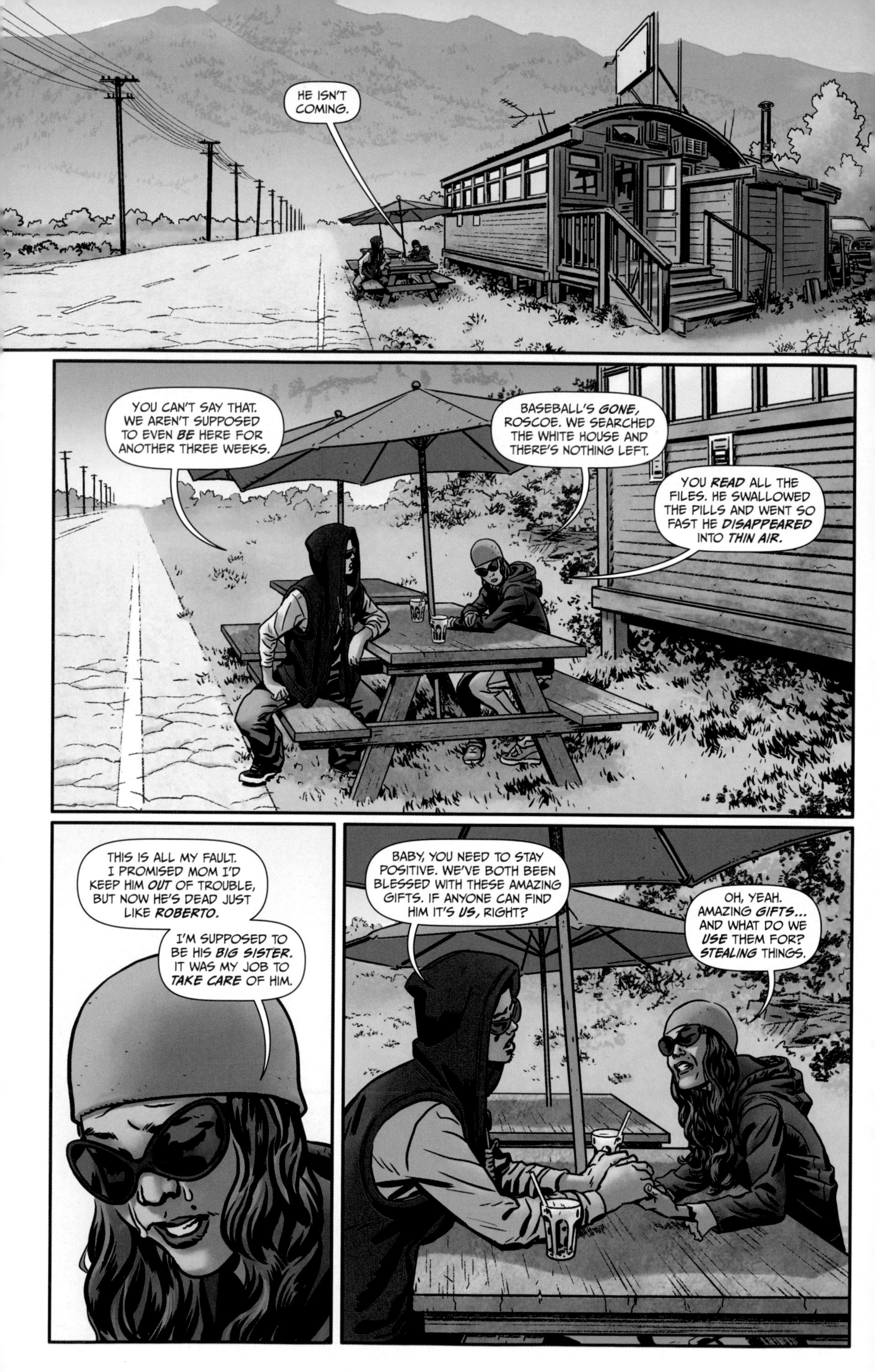
HE ISN'T COMING.
YOU CAN'T SAY THAT. WE AREN'T SUPPOSED TO EVEN BE HERE FOR ANOTHER THREE WEEKS.
BASEBALL'S GONE, ROSCOE. WE SEARCHED THE WHITE HOUSE AND THERE'S NOTHING LEFT.
YOU READ ALL THE FILES. HE SWALLOWED THE PILLS AND WENT SO FAST HE DISAPPEARED INTO THIN AIR.
THIS IS ALL MY FAULT. I PROMISED MOM I'D KEEP HIM OUT OF TROUBLE, BUT NOW HE'S DEAD JUST LIKE ROBERTO.
I'M SUPPOSED TO BE HIS BIG SISTER. IT WAS MY JOB TO TAKE CARE OF HIM.
BABY, YOU NEED TO STAY POSITIVE. WE'VE BOTH BEEN BLESSED WITH THESE AMAZING GIFTS. IF ANYONE CAN FIND HIM IT'S US, RIGHT?
OH, YEAH. AMAZING GIFTS... AND WHAT DO WE USE THEM FOR? STEALING THINGS.

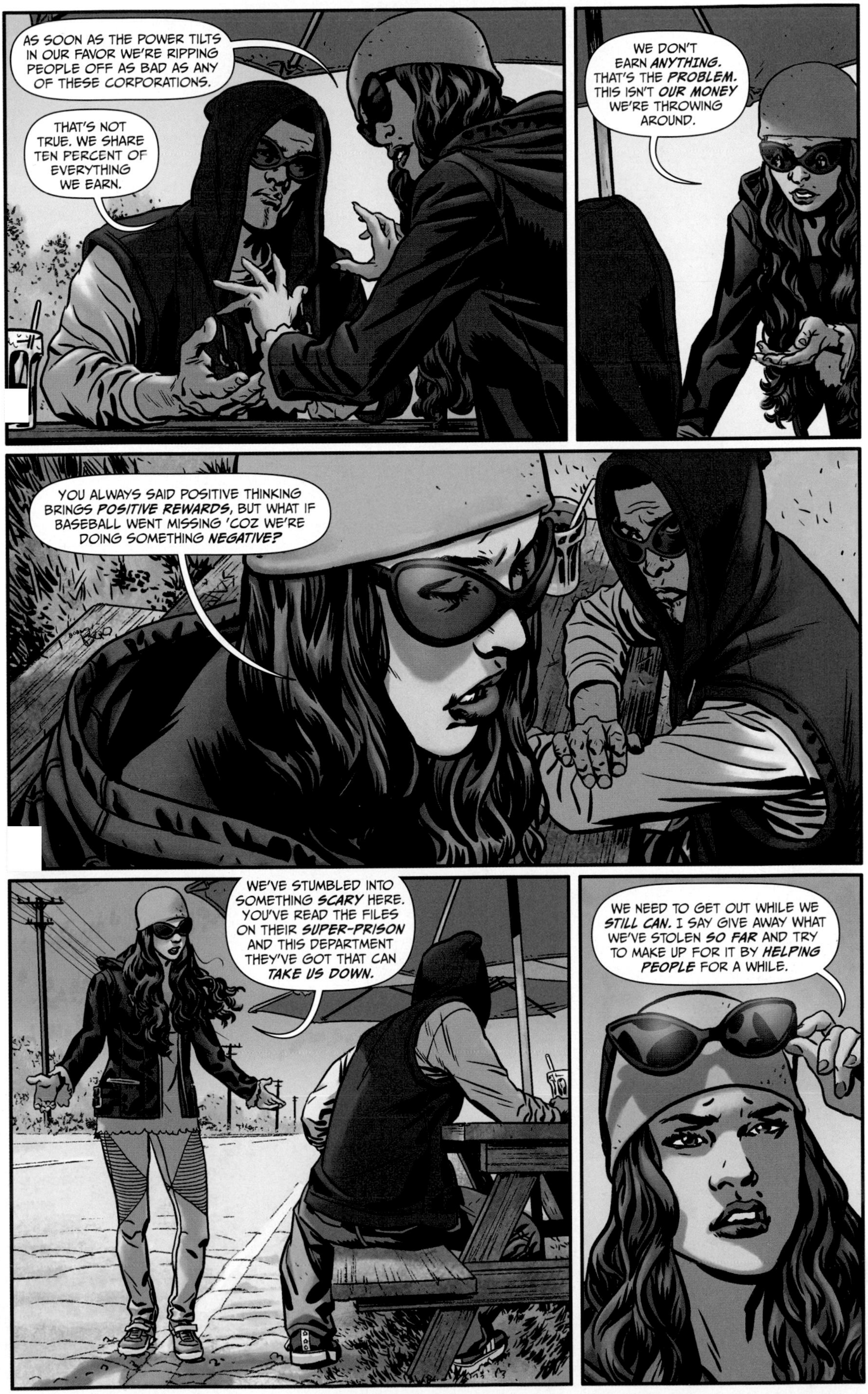
AS SOON AS THE POWER TILTS IN OUR FAVOR WE'RE RIPPING PEOPLE OFF AS BAD AS ANY OF THESE CORPORATIONS.
THAT'S NOT TRUE. WE SHARE TEN PERCENT OF EVERYTHING WE EARN.
WE DON'T EARN ANYTHING. THAT'S THE PROBLEM. THIS ISN'T OUR MONEY WE'RE THROWING AROUND.
YOU ALWAYS SAID POSITIVE THINKING BRINGS POSITIVE REWARDS, BUT WHAT IF BASEBALL WENT MISSING 'COZ WE'RE DOING SOMETHING NEGATIVE?
WE'VE STUMBLED INTO SOMETHING SCARY HERE. YOU'VE READ THE FILES ON THEIR SUPER-PRISON AND THIS DEPARTMENT THEY'VE GOT THAT CAN TAKE US DOWN.
WE NEED TO GET OUT WHILE WE STILL CAN. I SAY GIVE AWAY WHAT WE'VE STOLEN SO FAR AND TRY TO MAKE UP FOR IT BY HELPING PEOPLE FOR A WHILE.

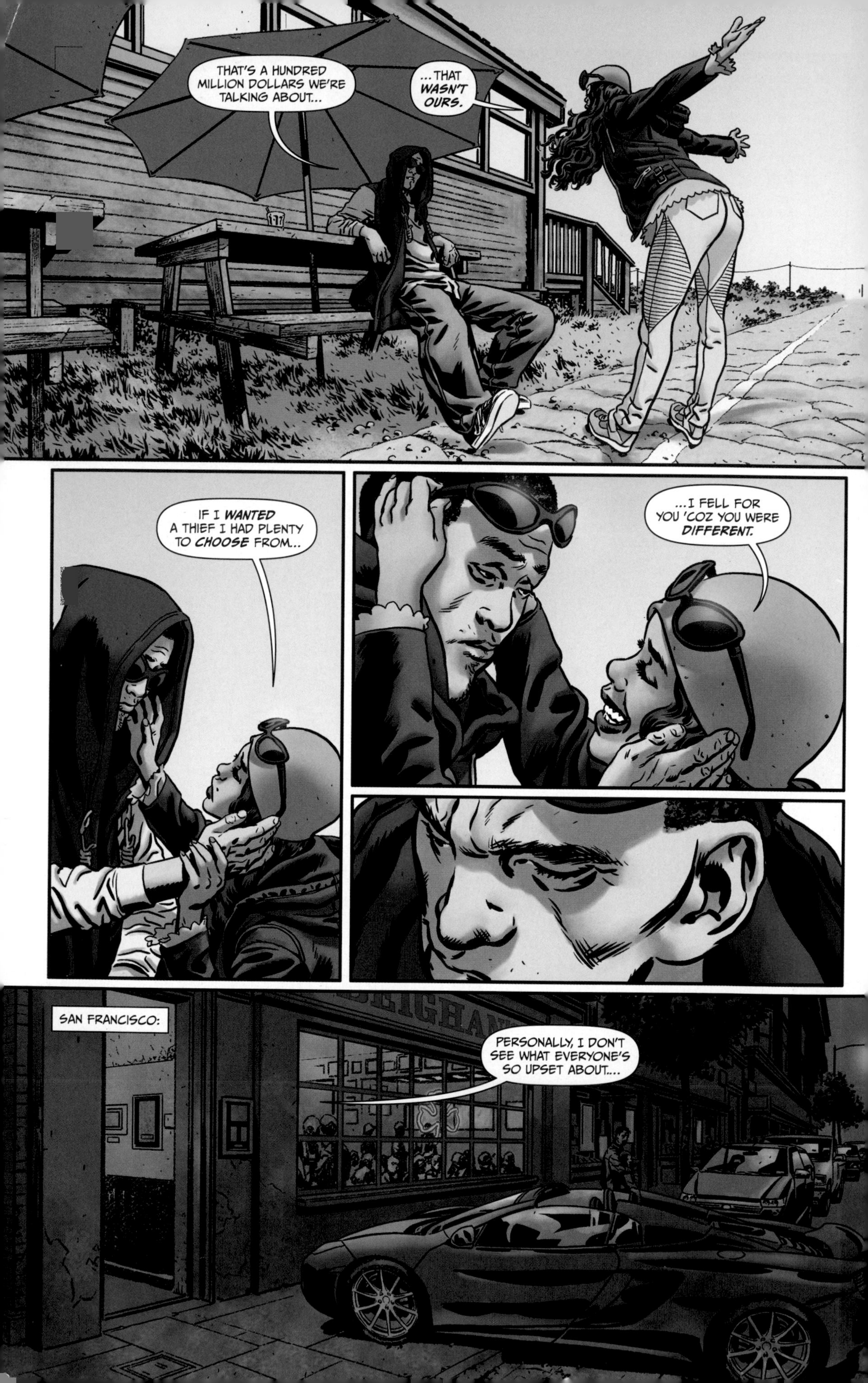
THAT'S A HUNDRED MILLION DOLLARS WE'RE TALKING ABOUT...
...THAT *WASN'T OURS.*
IF I *WANTED* A THIEF I HAD PLENTY TO *CHOOSE* FROM...
...I FELL FOR YOU 'COZ YOU WERE *DIFFERENT.*
SAN FRANCISCO:
PERSONALLY, I DON'T SEE WHAT EVERYONE'S SO UPSET ABOUT....

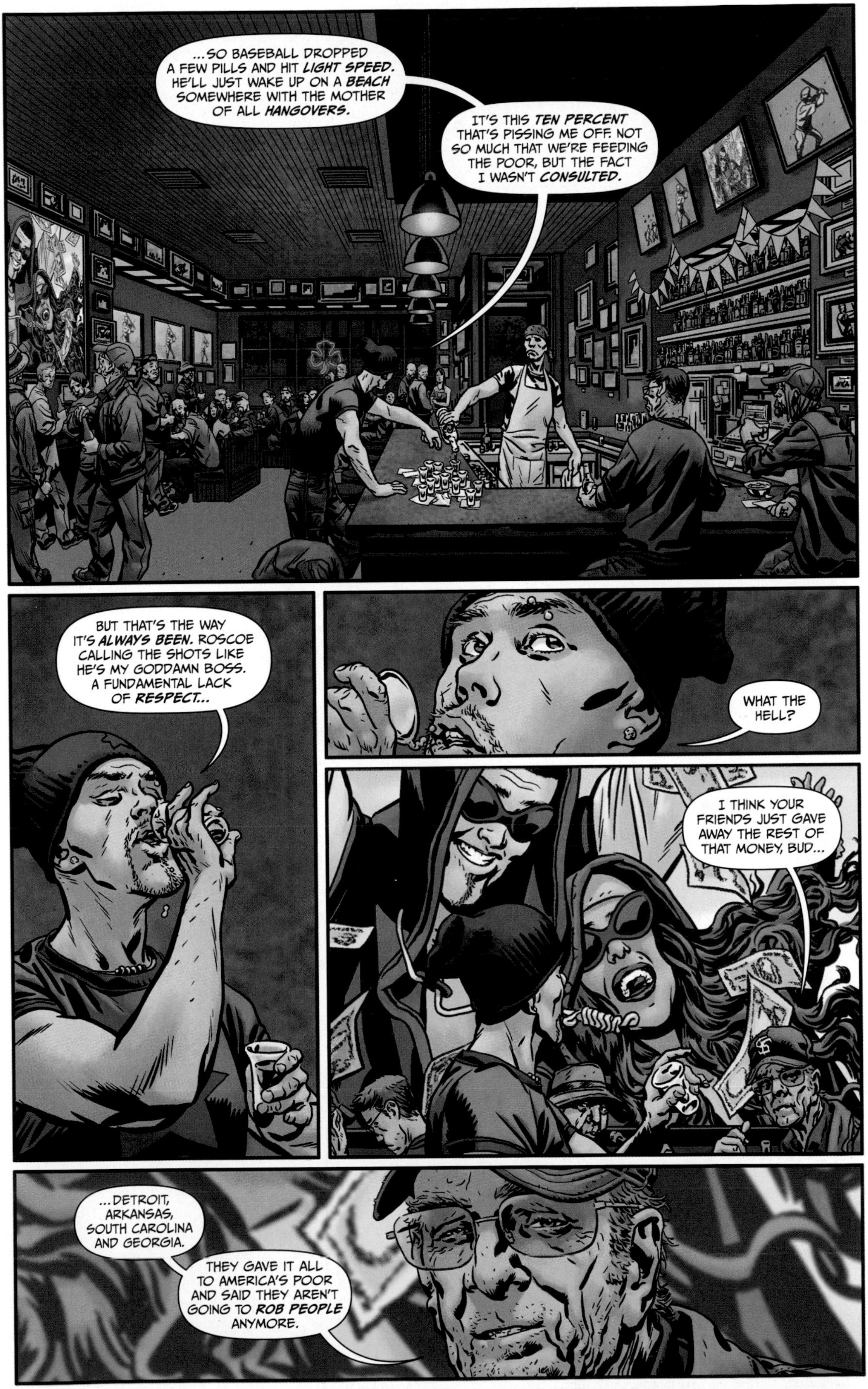
...SO BASEBALL DROPPED A FEW PILLS AND HIT LIGHT SPEED. HE'LL JUST WAKE UP ON A BEACH SOMEWHERE WITH THE MOTHER OF ALL HANGOVERS.
IT'S THIS TEN PERCENT THAT'S PISSING ME OFF. NOT SO MUCH THAT WE'RE FEEDING THE POOR, BUT THE FACT I WASN'T CONSULTED.
BUT THAT'S THE WAY IT'S ALWAYS BEEN. ROSCOE CALLING THE SHOTS LIKE HE'S MY GODDAMN BOSS. A FUNDAMENTAL LACK OF RESPECT...
WHAT THE HELL?
I THINK YOUR FRIENDS JUST GAVE AWAY THE REST OF THAT MONEY, BUD...
...DETROIT, ARKANSAS, SOUTH CAROLINA AND GEORGIA.
THEY GAVE IT ALL TO AMERICA'S POOR AND SAID THEY AREN'T GOING TO ROB PEOPLE ANYMORE.

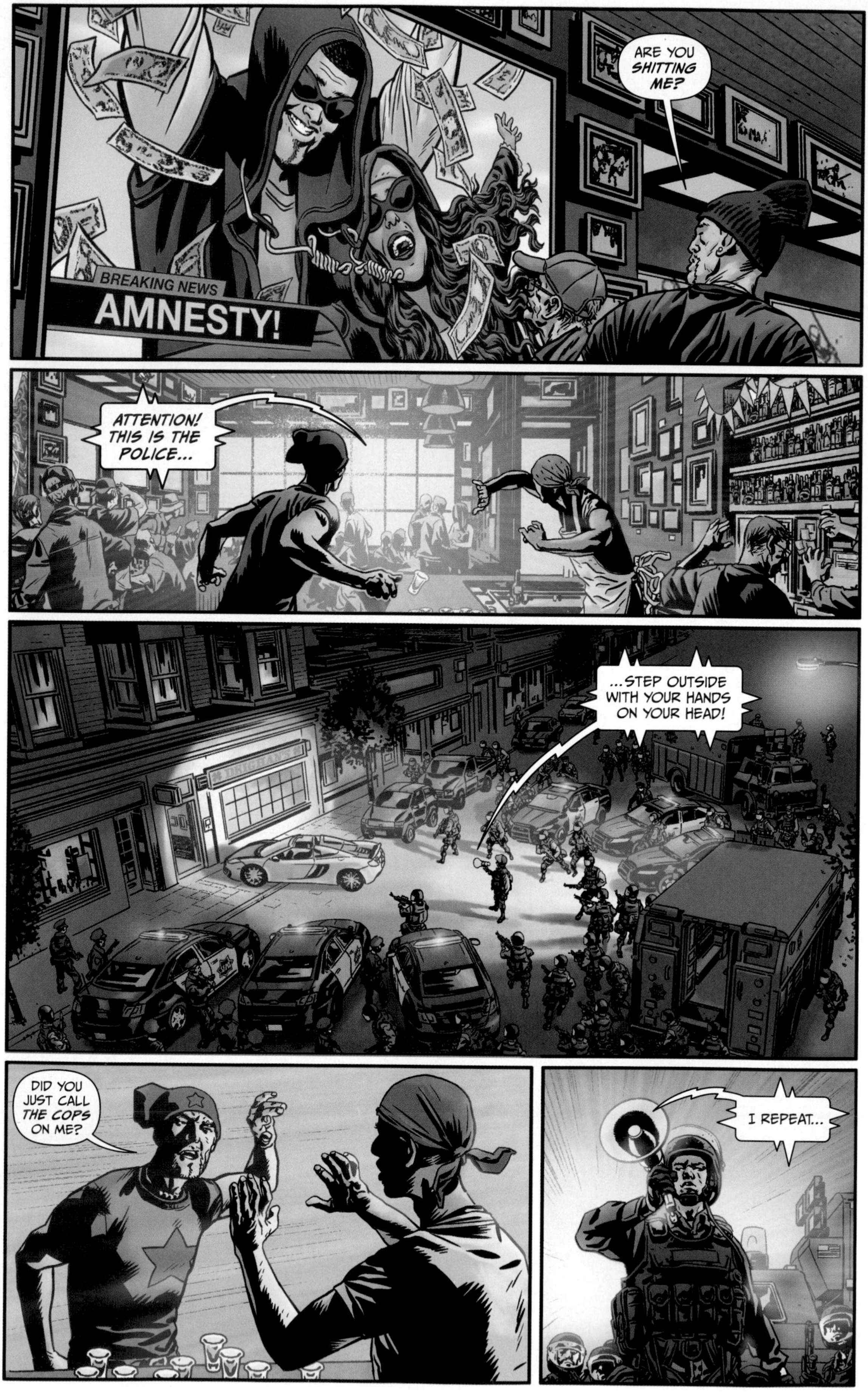
BREAKING NEWS
AMNESTY!
ARE YOU SHITTING ME?
ATTENTION! THIS IS THE POLICE...
...STEP OUTSIDE WITH YOUR HANDS ON YOUR HEAD!
DID YOU JUST CALL THE COPS ON ME?
I REPEAT...

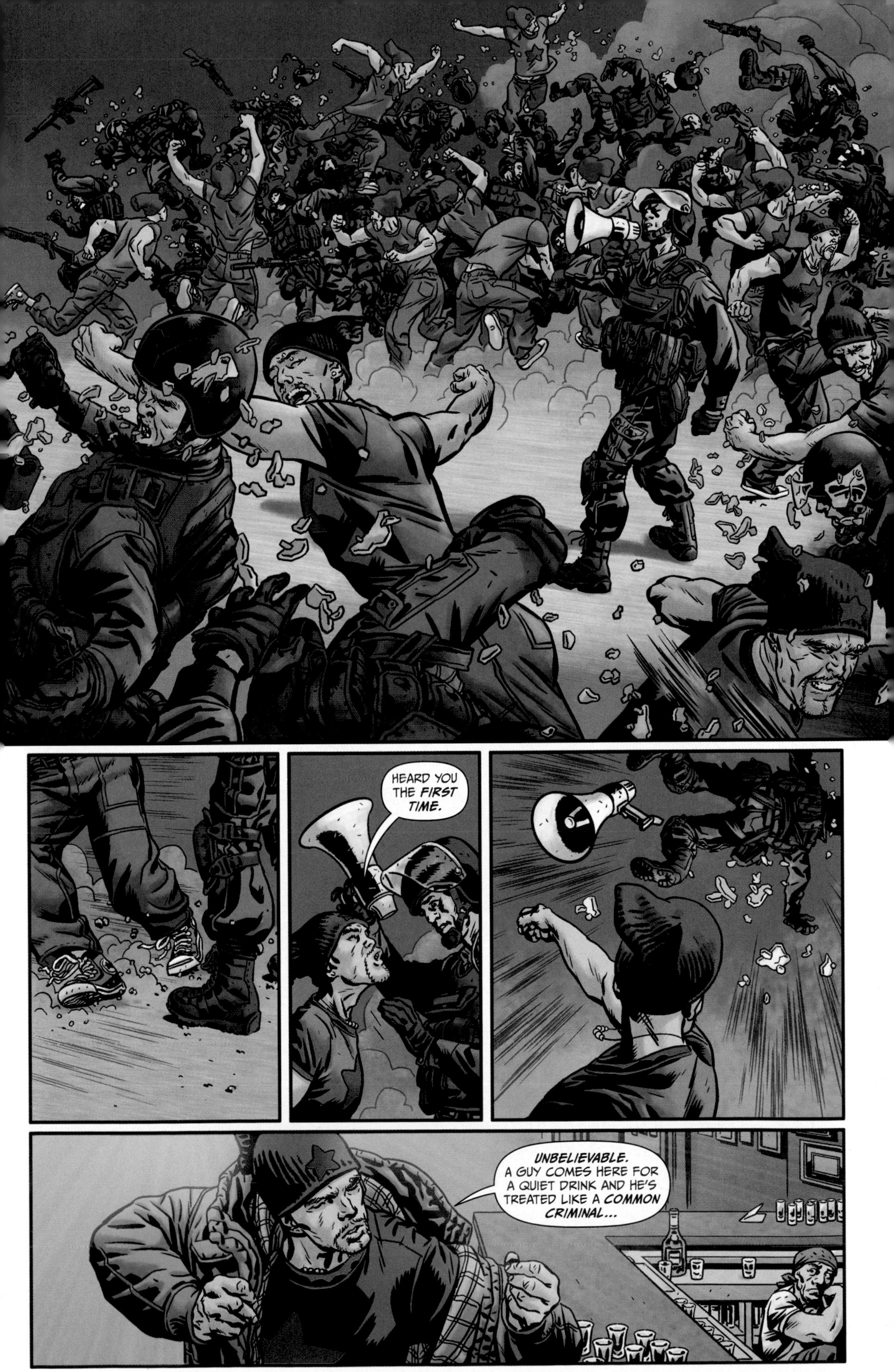
HEARD YOU THE *FIRST TIME.*
UNBELIEVABLE. A GUY COMES HERE FOR A QUIET DRINK AND HE'S TREATED LIKE A *COMMON CRIMINAL...*

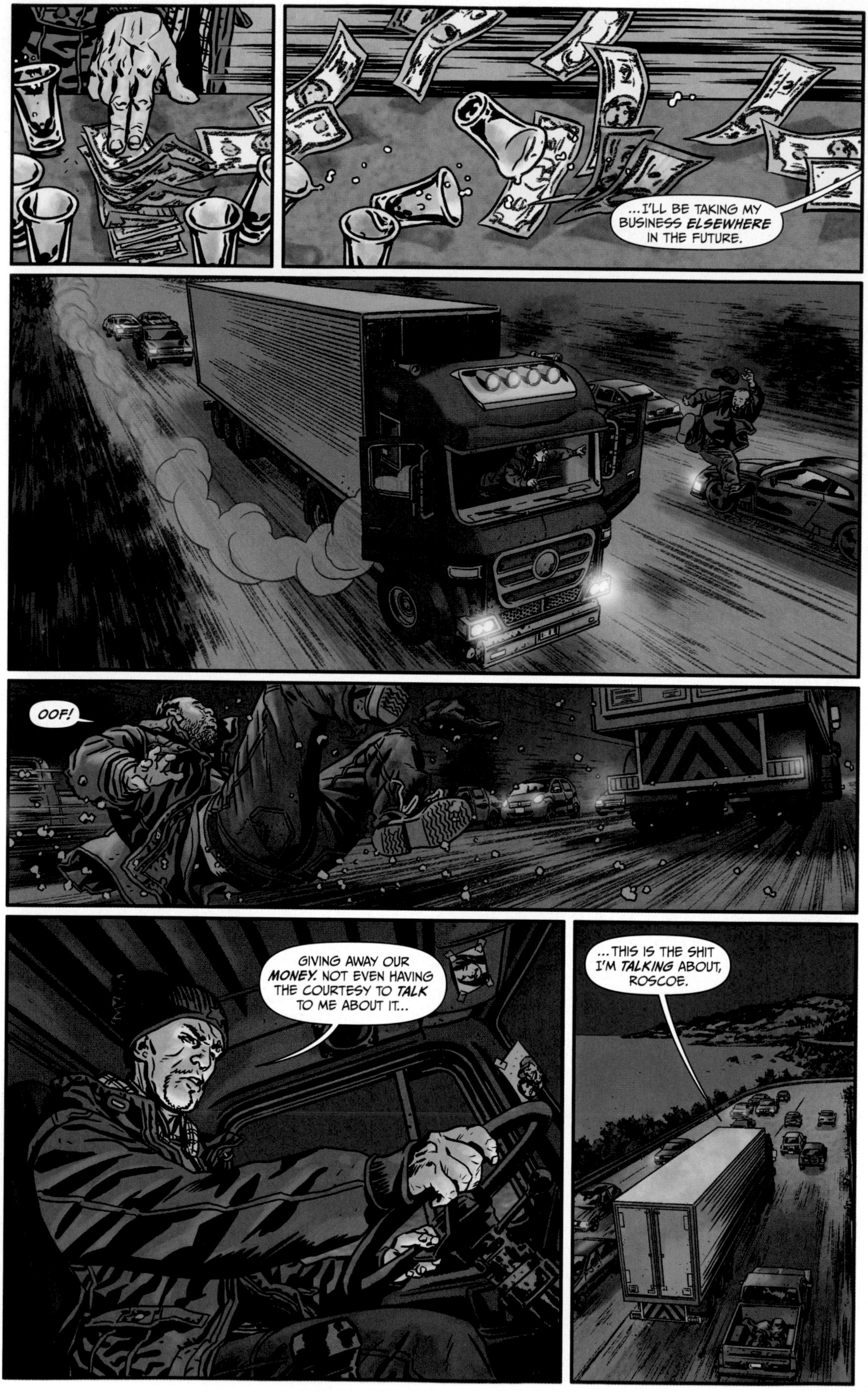
...I'LL BE TAKING MY BUSINESS ELSEWHERE IN THE FUTURE.
OOF!
GIVING AWAY OUR MONEY. NOT EVEN HAVING THE COURTESY TO TALK TO ME ABOUT IT...
...THIS IS THE SHIT I'M TALKING ABOUT, ROSCOE.

THE WOODS:

SMELL *NICE?*

AFTER TWENTY-EIGHT YEARS OF RECYCLED AIR YOU HAVE NO IDEA.

WE'VE EVACUATED THE AREA JUST LIKE YOU ASKED, MR. SPRINGFIELD. SATELLITE'S PICKING UP *CHEVY* IN THE HOUSE, BUT STILL NO SIGN OF *ROSCOE* AND *ROSA.*

THEY'LL *BE* HERE.

I'M ACTUALLY REALLY *EXCITED* ABOUT ALL THIS. THIS IS EVERYTHING I'VE WANTED SINCE I JOINED THE *DEPARTMENT.*

I GREW UP READING *DC* COMICS AND WATCHING GEORGE REEVES ON *TV* SO YOU CAN GUESS WHAT I SAID WHEN I HEARD THEY WERE STARTING A *SUPER-CRIME* DIVISION.

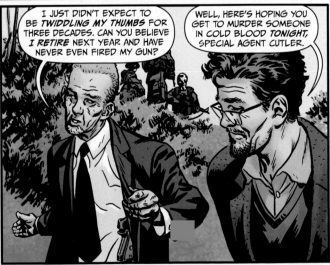

I JUST DIDN'T EXPECT TO BE *TWIDDLING MY THUMBS* FOR THREE DECADES. CAN YOU BELIEVE *I RETIRE* NEXT YEAR AND HAVE NEVER EVEN FIRED MY GUN?

WELL, HERE'S HOPING YOU GET TO MURDER SOMEONE IN COLD BLOOD *TONIGHT,* SPECIAL AGENT CUTLER.

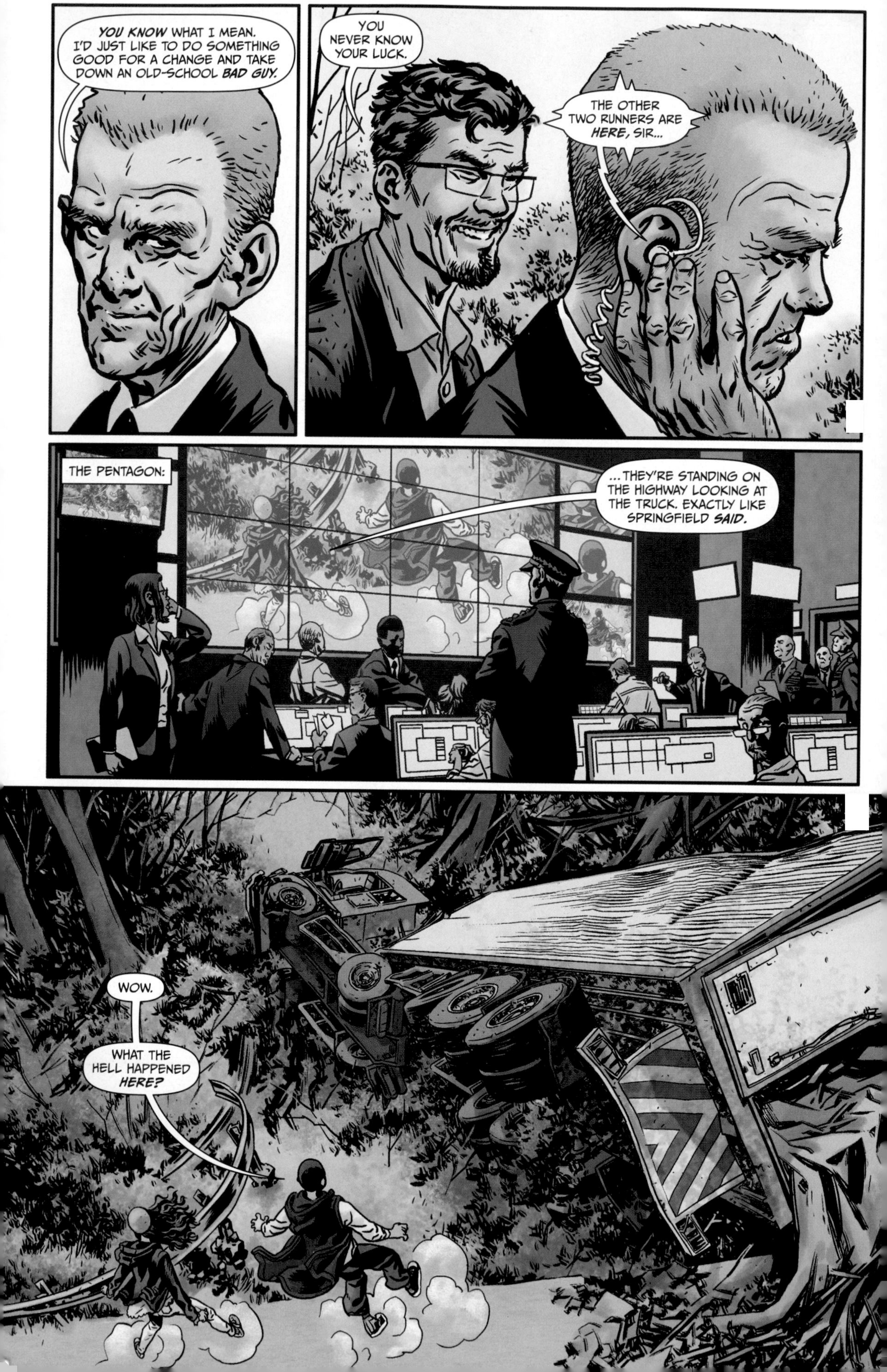
YOU KNOW WHAT I MEAN. I'D JUST LIKE TO DO SOMETHING GOOD FOR A CHANGE AND TAKE DOWN AN OLD-SCHOOL BAD GUY.
YOU NEVER KNOW YOUR LUCK.
THE OTHER TWO RUNNERS ARE HERE, SIR...
THE PENTAGON:
...THEY'RE STANDING ON THE HIGHWAY LOOKING AT THE TRUCK. EXACTLY LIKE SPRINGFIELD SAID.
WOW.
WHAT THE HELL HAPPENED HERE?

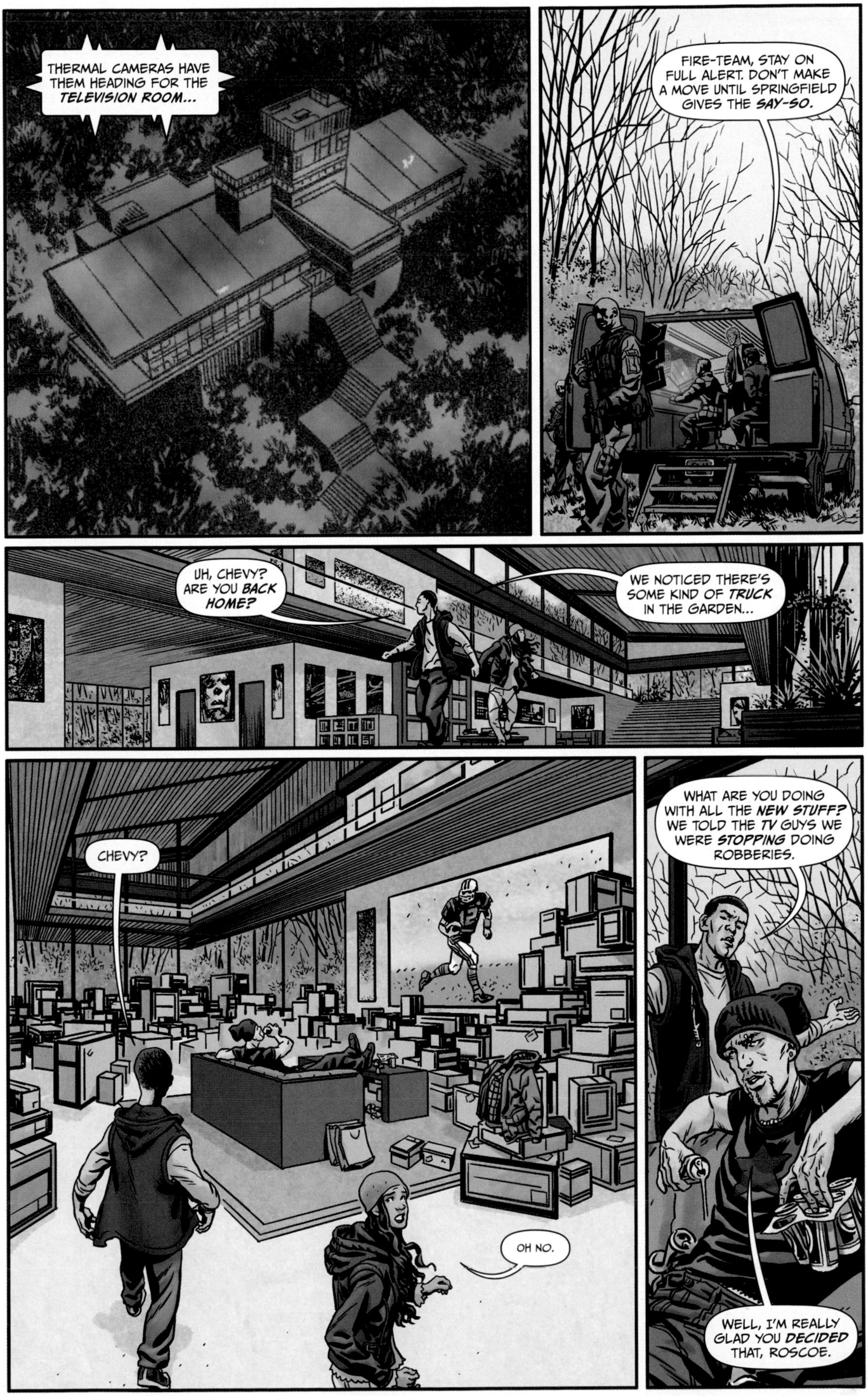
THERMAL CAMERAS HAVE THEM HEADING FOR THE *TELEVISION ROOM...*
FIRE-TEAM, STAY ON FULL ALERT. DON'T MAKE A MOVE UNTIL SPRINGFIELD GIVES THE *SAY-SO.*
UH, CHEVY? ARE YOU *BACK HOME?*
WE NOTICED THERE'S SOME KIND OF *TRUCK* IN THE GARDEN...
CHEVY?
OH NO.
WHAT ARE YOU DOING WITH ALL THE *NEW STUFF?* WE TOLD THE *TV* GUYS WE WERE *STOPPING* DOING ROBBERIES.
WELL, I'M REALLY GLAD YOU *DECIDED* THAT, ROSCOE.

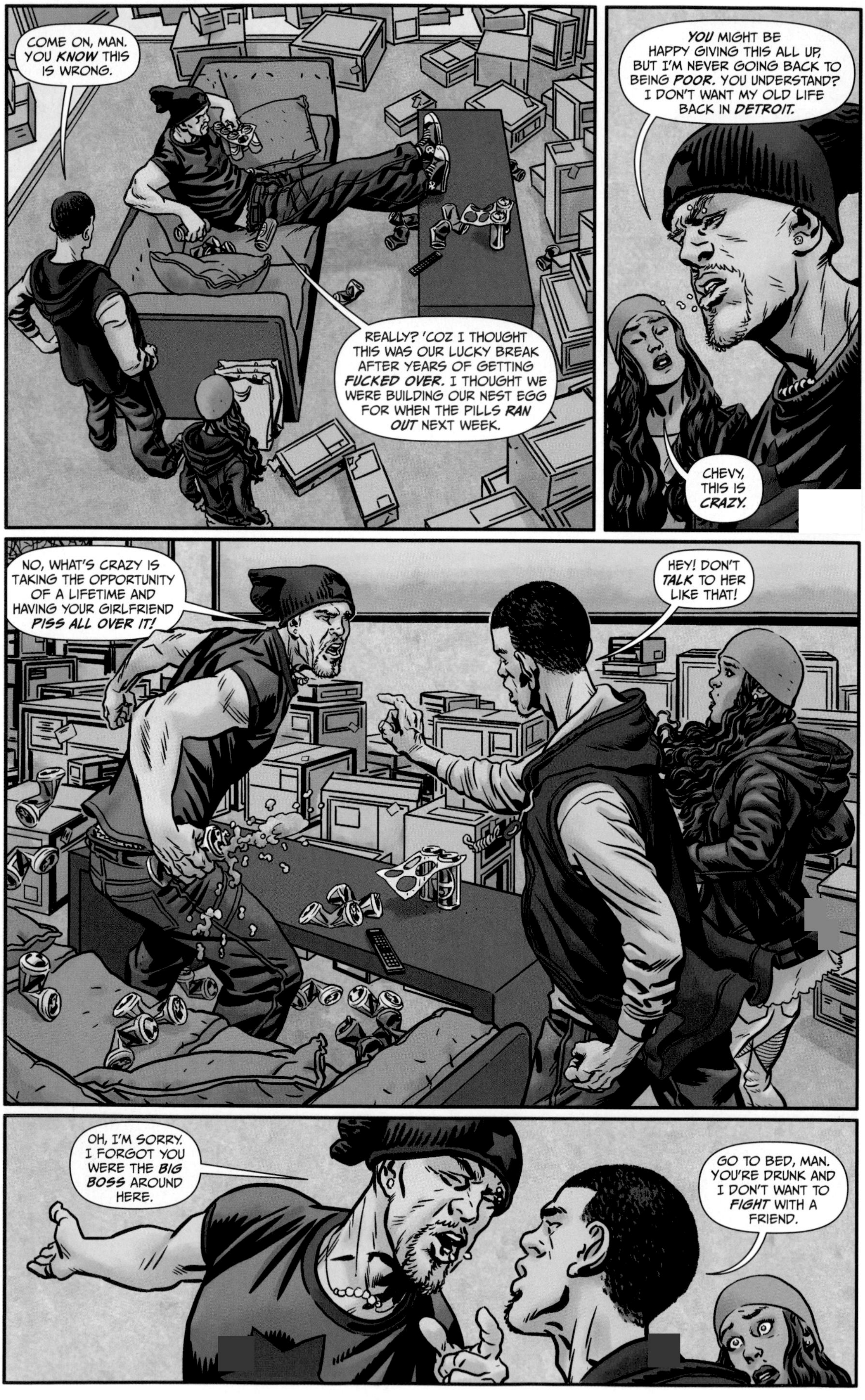
COME ON, MAN. YOU *KNOW* THIS IS WRONG.
REALLY? 'COZ I THOUGHT THIS WAS OUR LUCKY BREAK AFTER YEARS OF GETTING *FUCKED OVER.* I THOUGHT WE WERE BUILDING OUR NEST EGG FOR WHEN THE PILLS *RAN OUT* NEXT WEEK.
YOU MIGHT BE HAPPY GIVING THIS ALL UP, BUT I'M NEVER GOING BACK TO BEING *POOR.* YOU UNDERSTAND? I DON'T WANT MY OLD LIFE BACK IN *DETROIT.*
CHEVY, THIS IS *CRAZY.*
NO, WHAT'S CRAZY IS TAKING THE OPPORTUNITY OF A LIFETIME AND HAVING YOUR GIRLFRIEND *PISS ALL OVER IT!*
HEY! DON'T *TALK* TO HER LIKE THAT!
OH, I'M SORRY. I FORGOT YOU WERE THE *BIG BOSS* AROUND HERE.
GO TO BED, MAN. YOU'RE DRUNK AND I DON'T WANT TO *FIGHT* WITH A FRIEND.

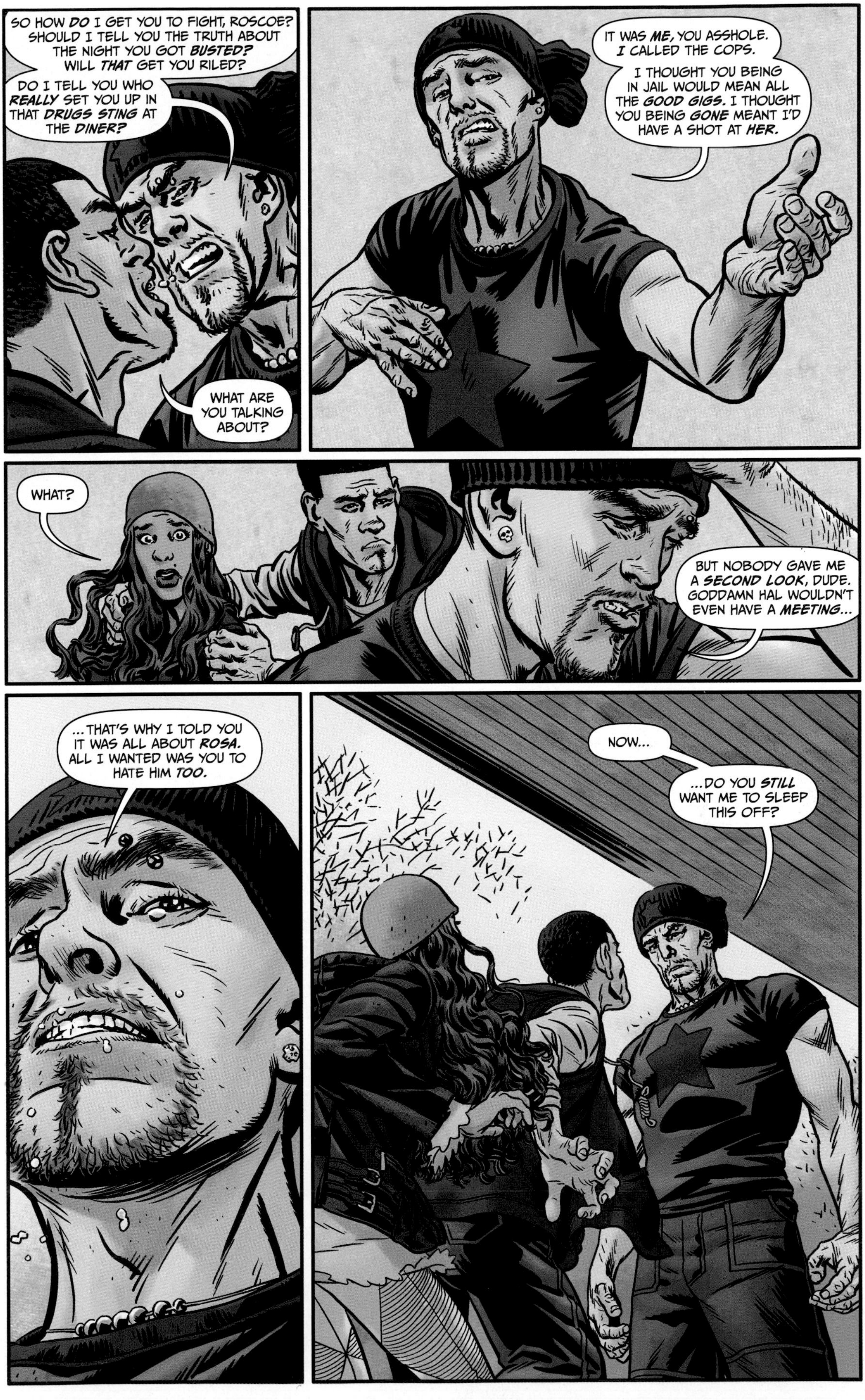
SO HOW DO I GET YOU TO FIGHT, ROSCOE? SHOULD I TELL YOU THE TRUTH ABOUT THE NIGHT YOU GOT BUSTED? WILL THAT GET YOU RILED?
DO I TELL YOU WHO REALLY SET YOU UP IN THAT DRUGS STING AT THE DINER?
WHAT ARE YOU TALKING ABOUT?
IT WAS ME, YOU ASSHOLE. I CALLED THE COPS.
I THOUGHT YOU BEING IN JAIL WOULD MEAN ALL THE GOOD GIGS. I THOUGHT YOU BEING GONE MEANT I'D HAVE A SHOT AT HER.
WHAT?
BUT NOBODY GAVE ME A SECOND LOOK, DUDE. GODDAMN HAL WOULDN'T EVEN HAVE A MEETING...
...THAT'S WHY I TOLD YOU IT WAS ALL ABOUT ROSA. ALL I WANTED WAS YOU TO HATE HIM TOO.
NOW...
...DO YOU STILL WANT ME TO SLEEP THIS OFF?

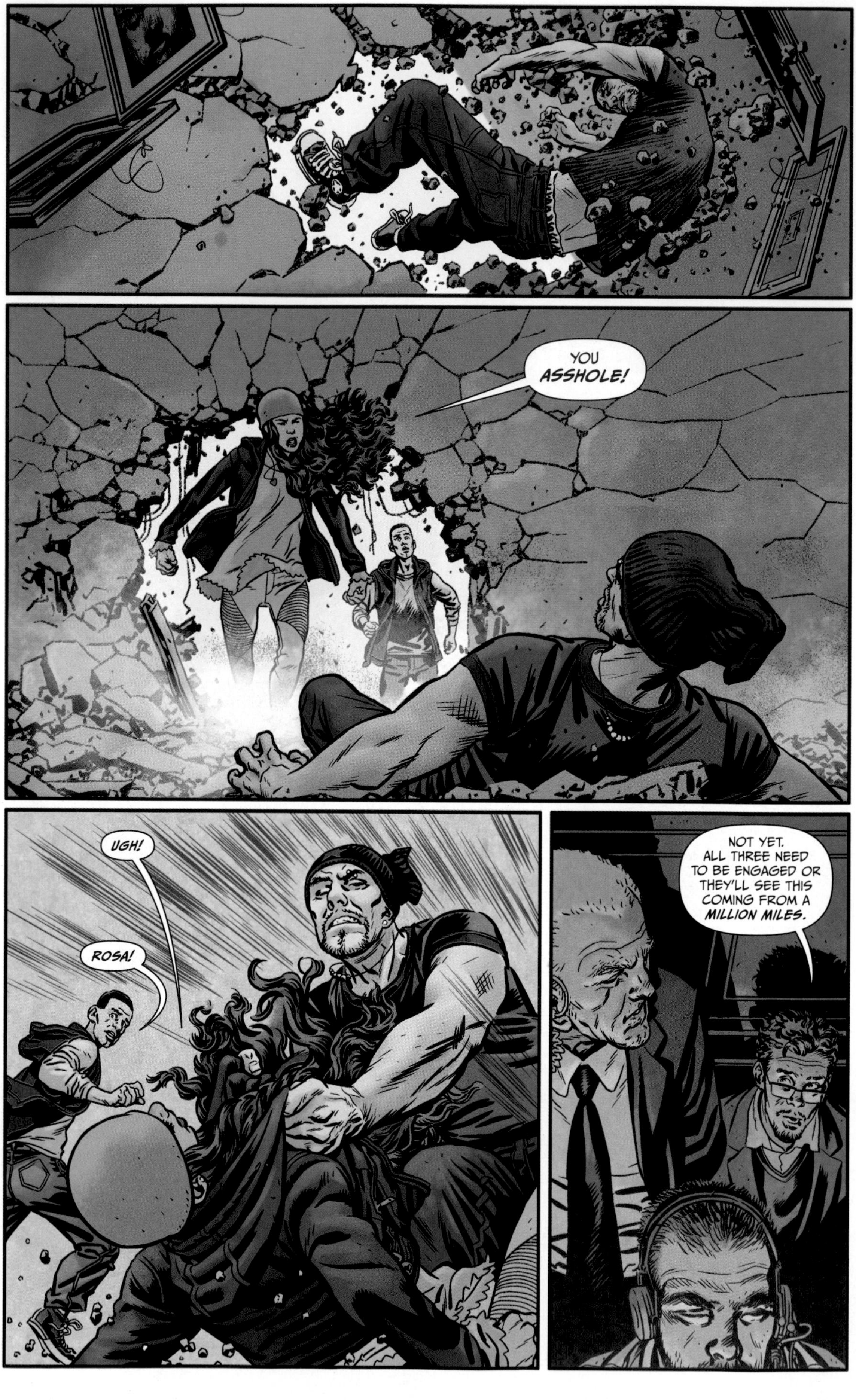
YOU ASSHOLE!
UGH!
ROSA!
NOT YET. ALL THREE NEED TO BE ENGAGED OR THEY'LL SEE THIS COMING FROM A MILLION MILES.

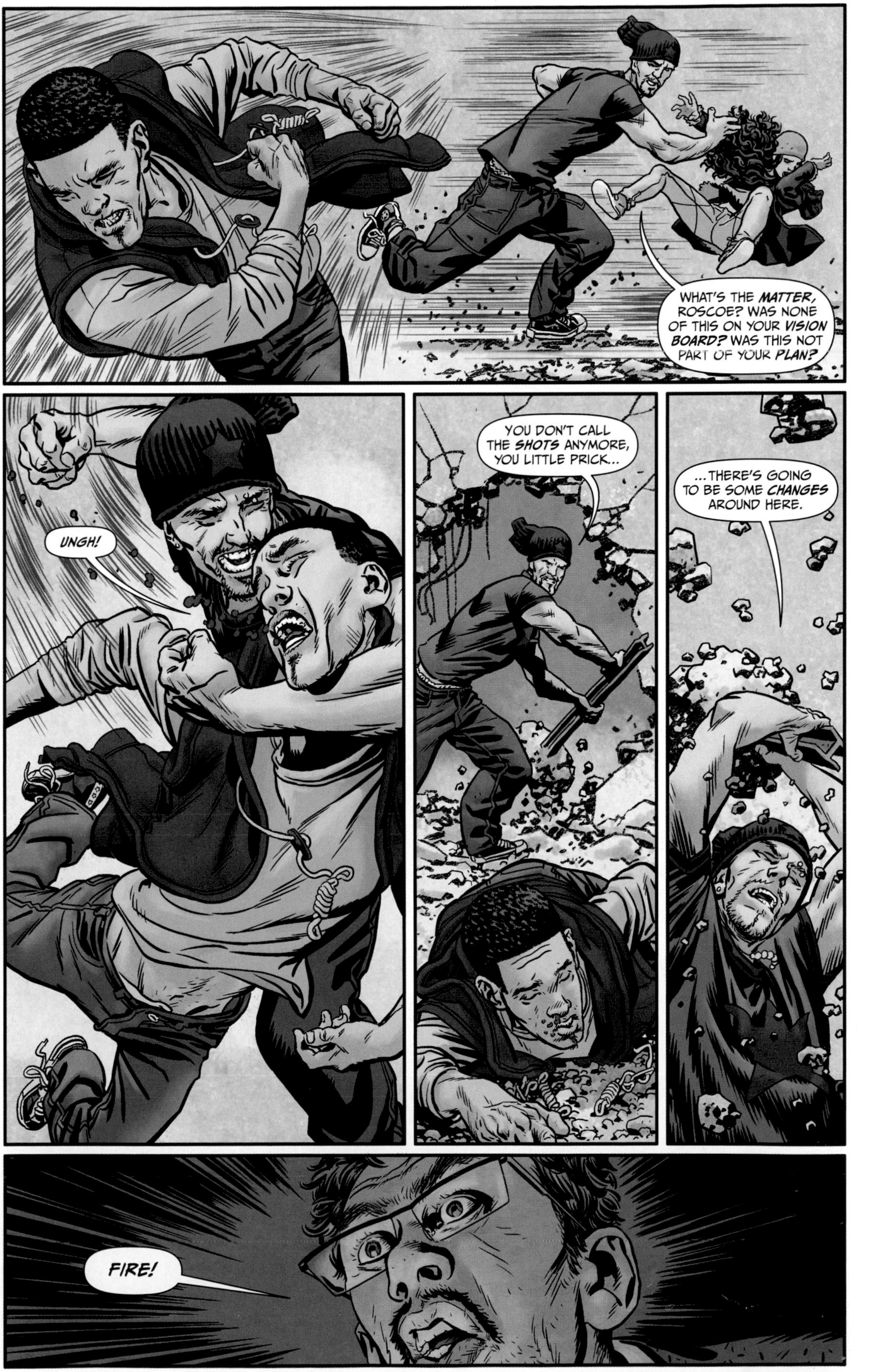
WHAT'S THE MATTER, ROSCOE? WAS NONE OF THIS ON YOUR VISION BOARD? WAS THIS NOT PART OF YOUR PLAN?
UNGH!
YOU DON'T CALL THE SHOTS ANYMORE, YOU LITTLE PRICK...
...THERE'S GOING TO BE SOME CHANGES AROUND HERE.
FIRE!

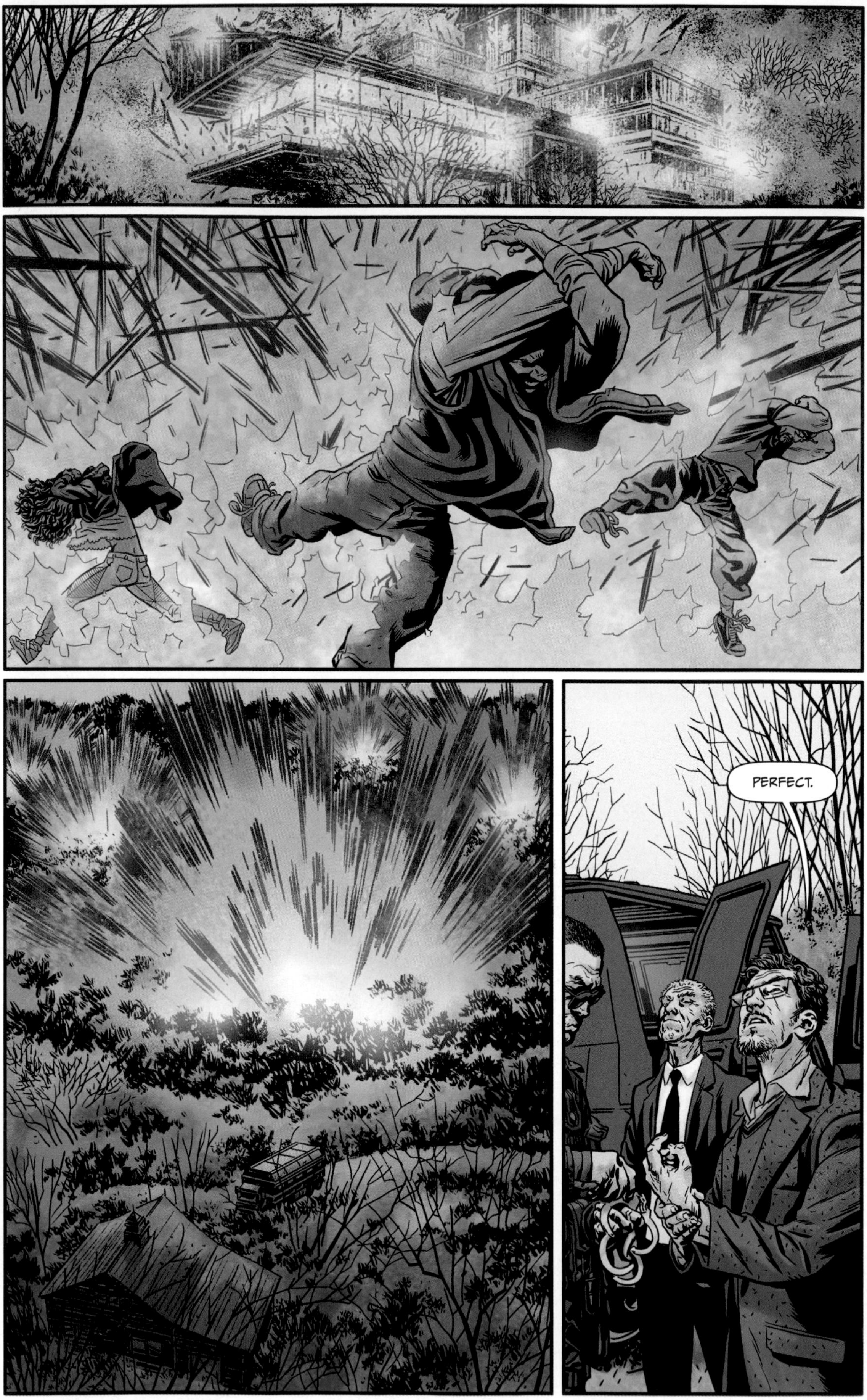
PERFECT.

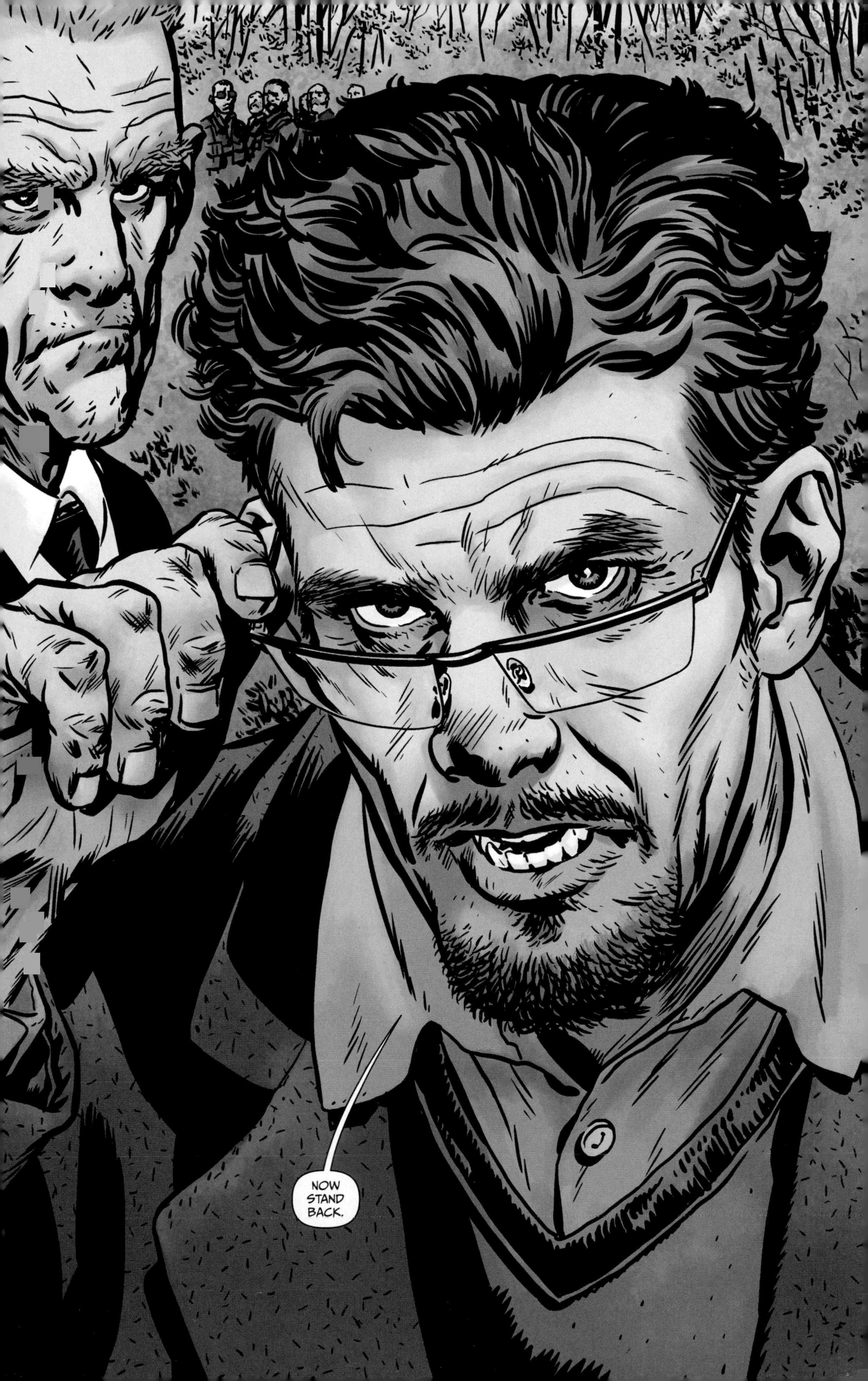
NOW STAND BACK.

CHAPTER FIVE

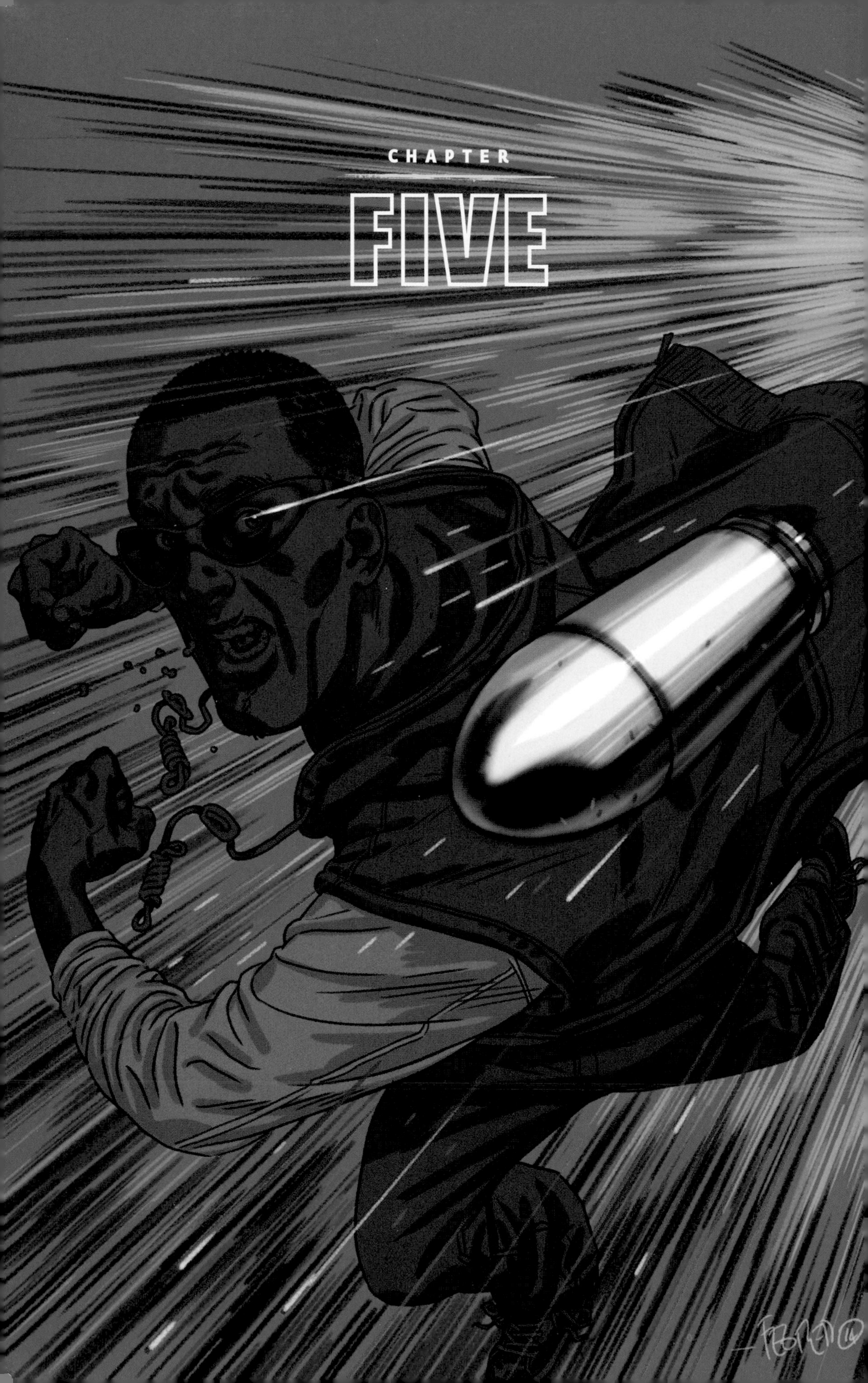

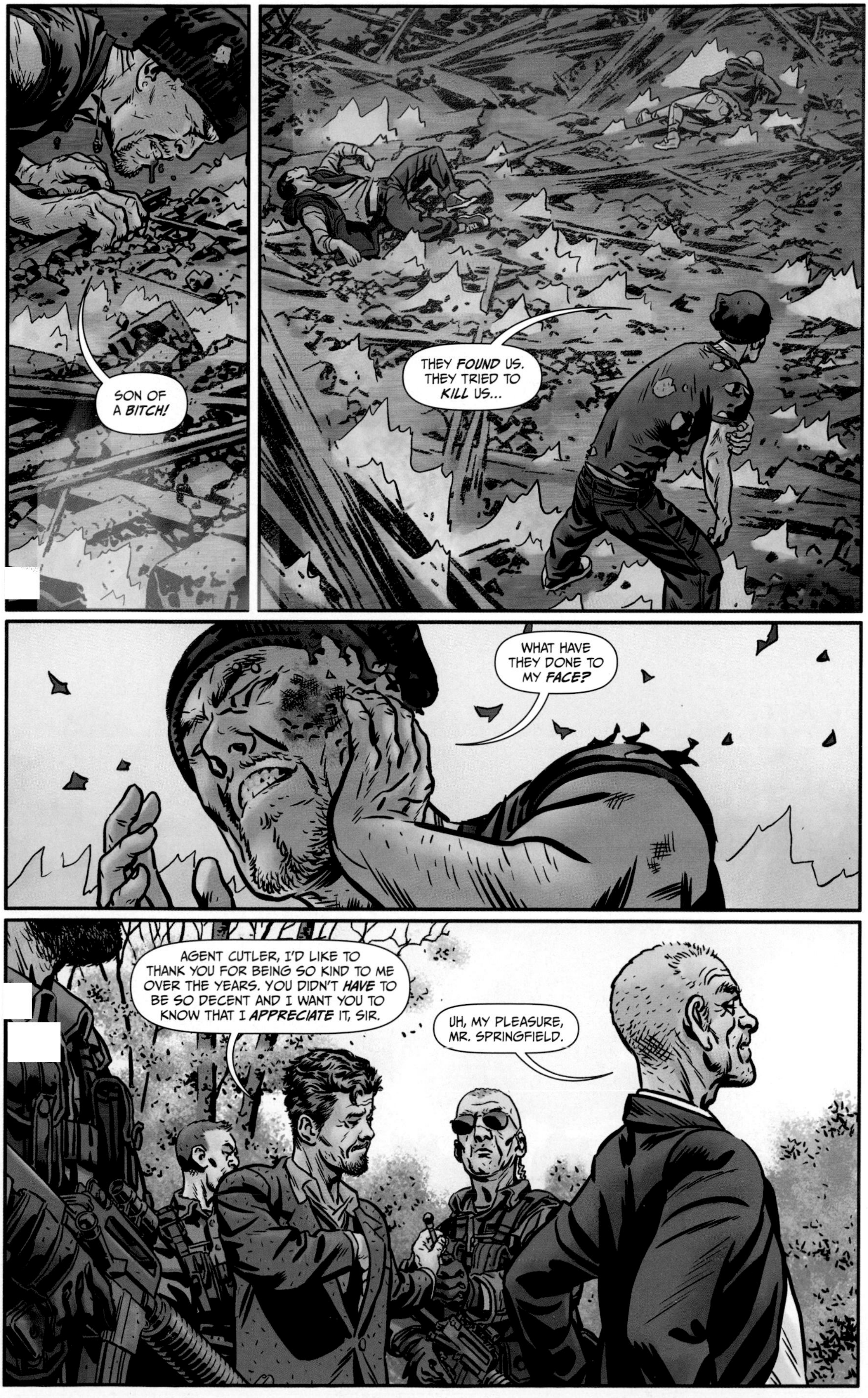
SON OF A *BITCH!*
THEY *FOUND* US. THEY TRIED TO *KILL* US...
WHAT HAVE THEY DONE TO MY *FACE?*
AGENT CUTLER, I'D LIKE TO THANK YOU FOR BEING SO KIND TO ME OVER THE YEARS. YOU DIDN'T *HAVE* TO BE SO DECENT AND I WANT YOU TO KNOW THAT I *APPRECIATE* IT, SIR.
UH, MY PLEASURE, MR. SPRINGFIELD.

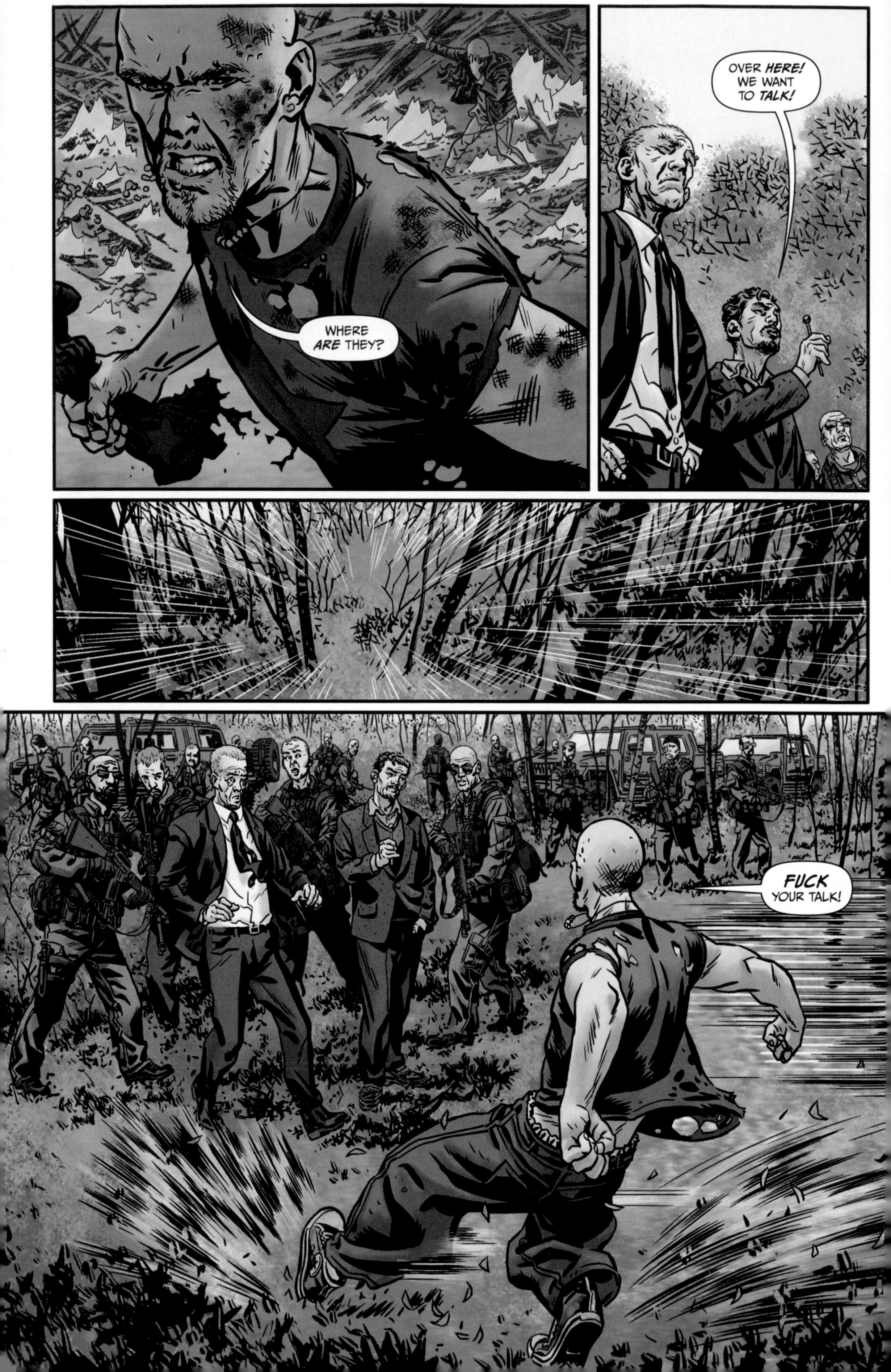
WHERE ARE THEY?
OVER HERE! WE WANT TO TALK!
FUCK YOUR TALK!

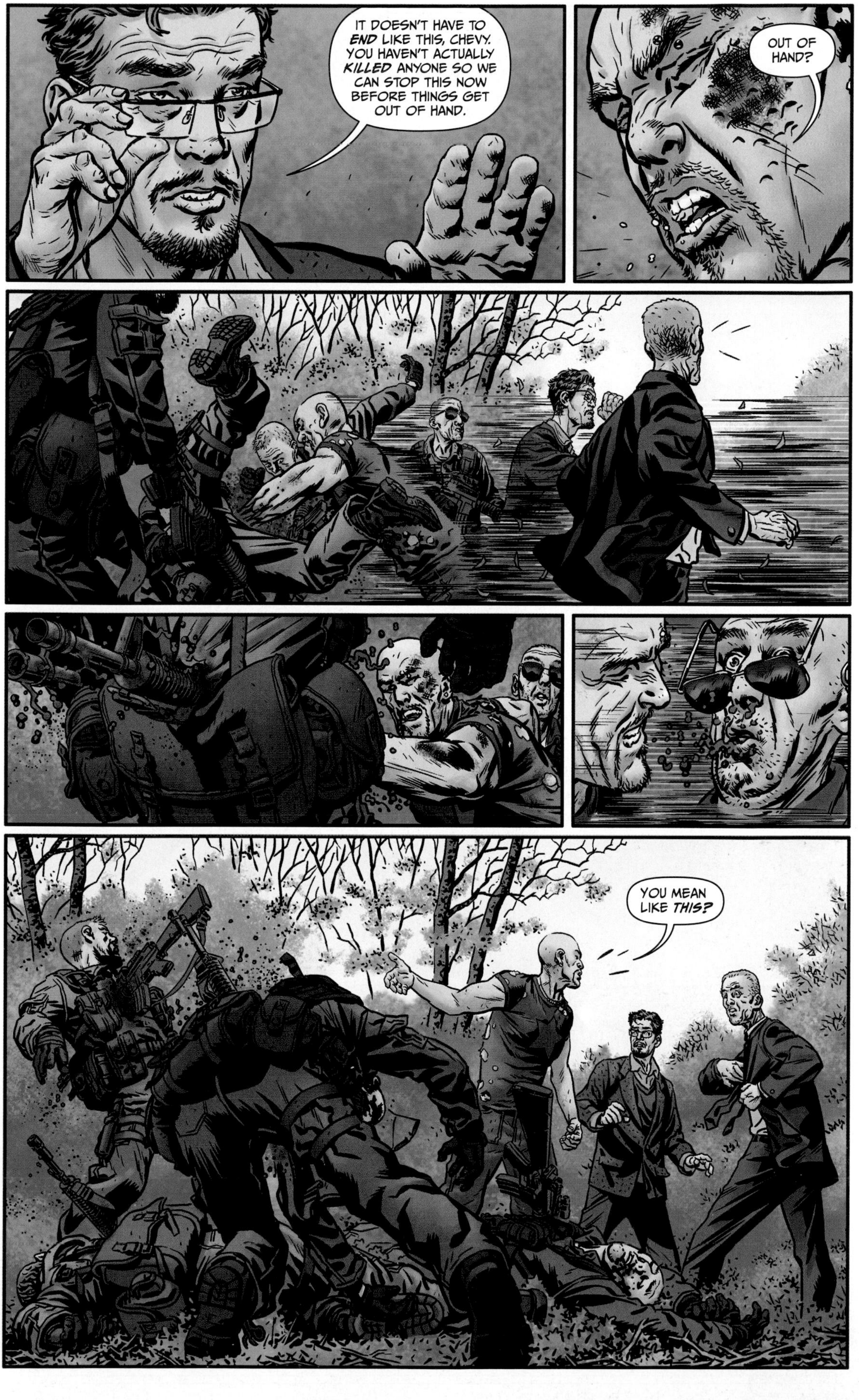
IT DOESN'T HAVE TO END LIKE THIS, CHEVY. YOU HAVEN'T ACTUALLY KILLED ANYONE SO WE CAN STOP THIS NOW BEFORE THINGS GET OUT OF HAND.
OUT OF HAND?
YOU MEAN LIKE THIS?

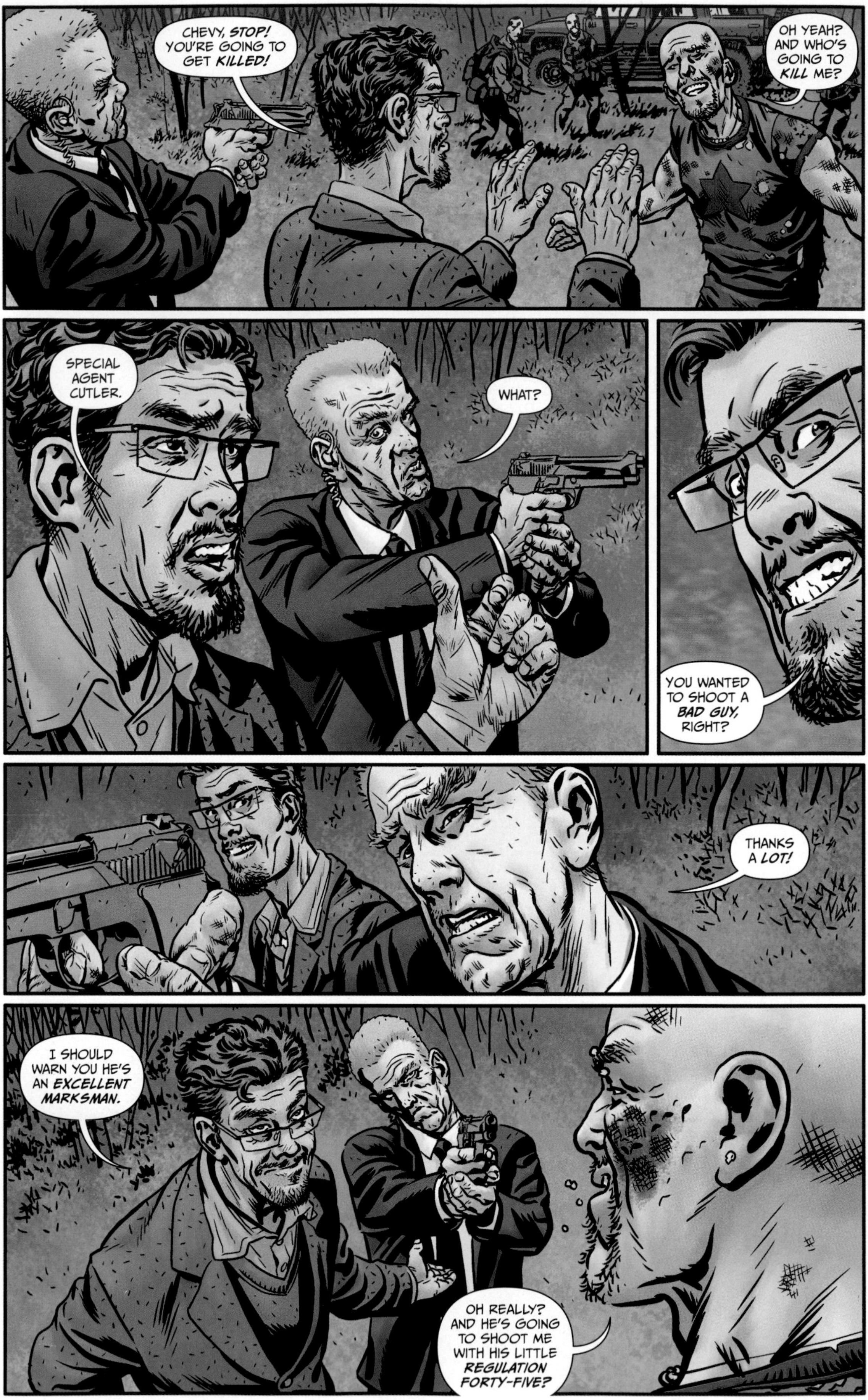
CHEVY, STOP! YOU'RE GOING TO GET KILLED!
OH YEAH? AND WHO'S GOING TO KILL ME?
SPECIAL AGENT CUTLER.
WHAT?
YOU WANTED TO SHOOT A BAD GUY, RIGHT?
THANKS A LOT!
I SHOULD WARN YOU HE'S AN EXCELLENT MARKSMAN.
OH REALLY? AND HE'S GOING TO SHOOT ME WITH HIS LITTLE REGULATION FORTY-FIVE?

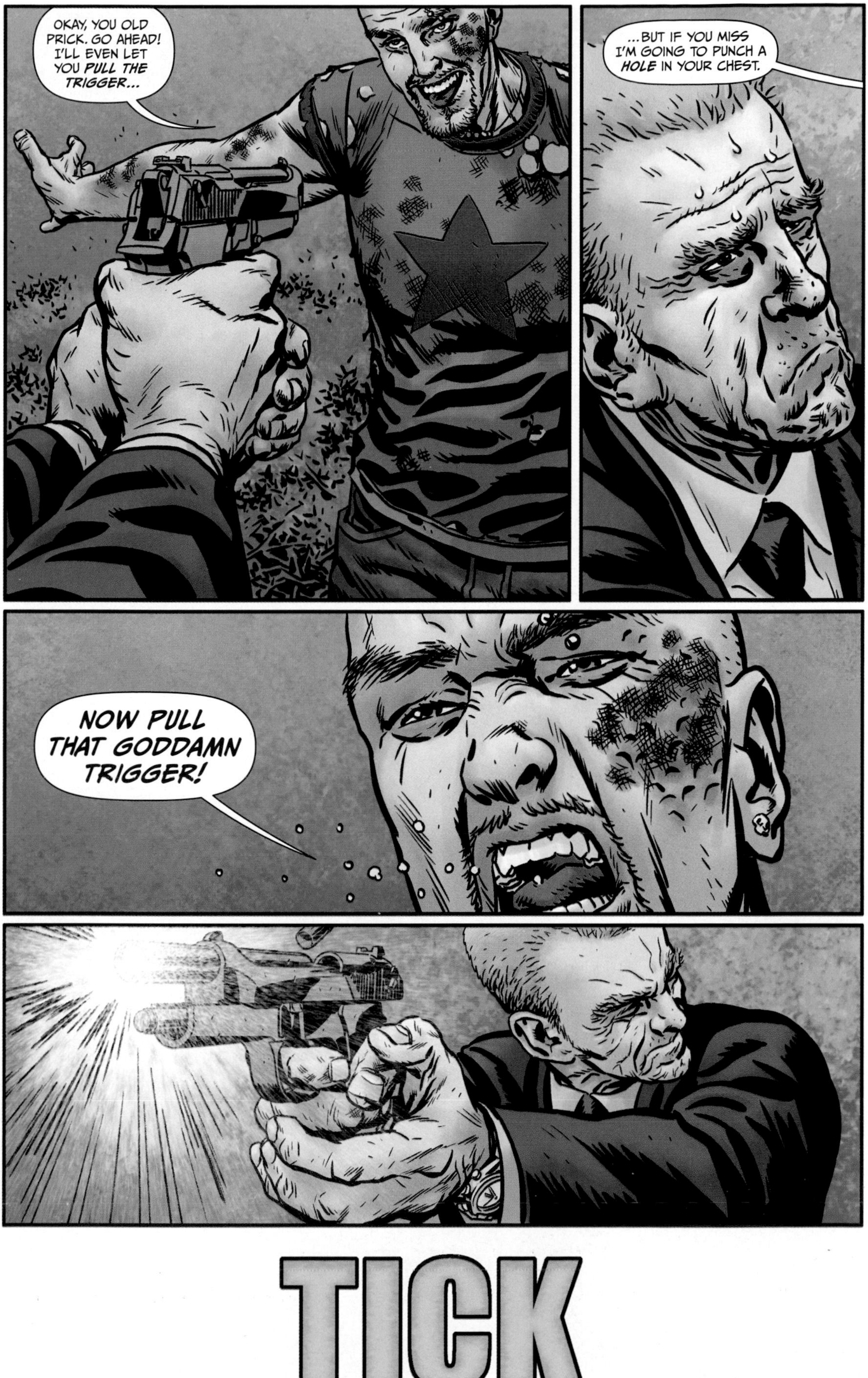
OKAY, YOU OLD PRICK. GO AHEAD! I'LL EVEN LET YOU PULL THE TRIGGER...
...BUT IF YOU MISS I'M GOING TO PUNCH A HOLE IN YOUR CHEST.
NOW PULL THAT GODDAMN TRIGGER!
TICK

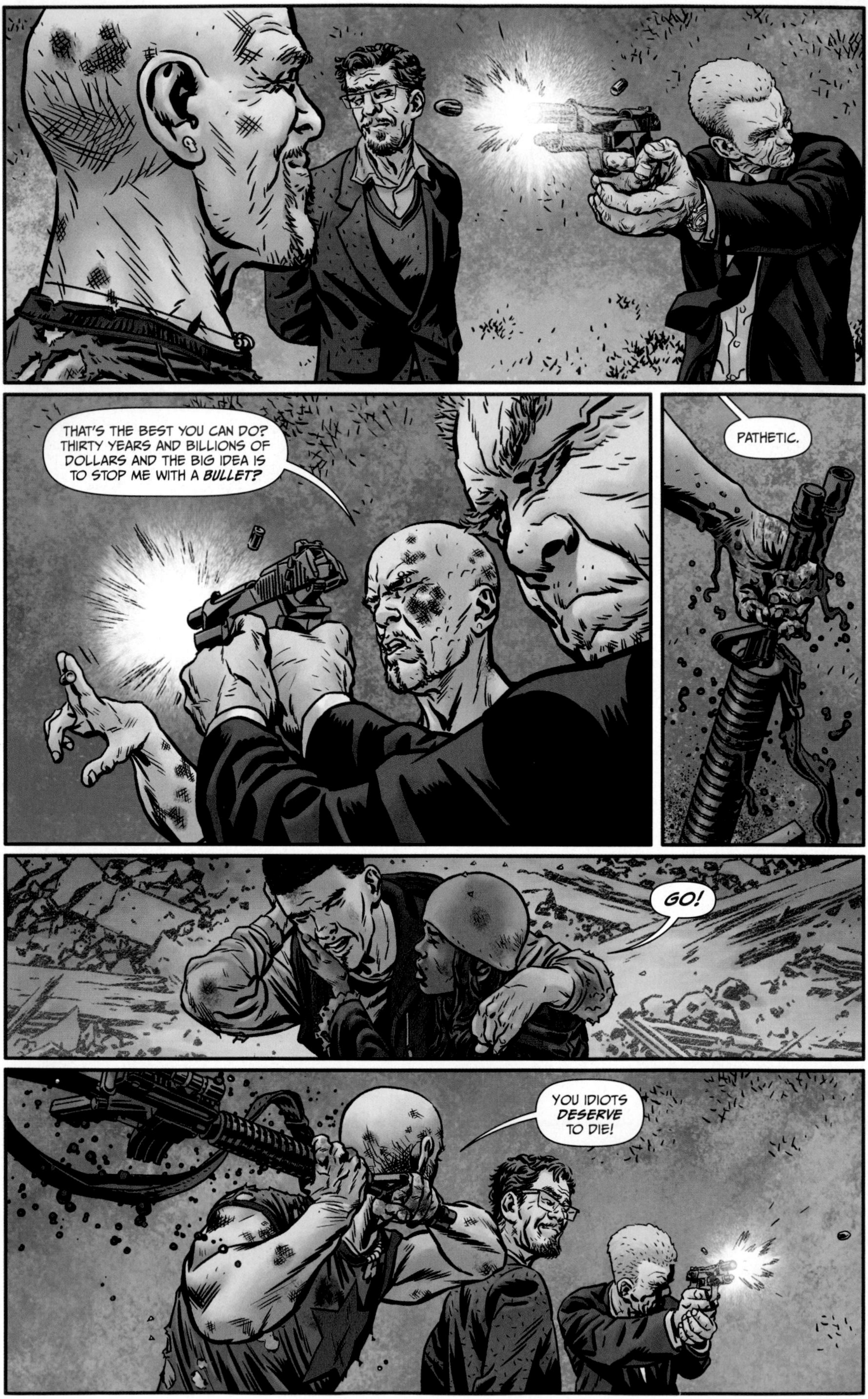
THAT'S THE BEST YOU CAN DO? THIRTY YEARS AND BILLIONS OF DOLLARS AND THE BIG IDEA IS TO STOP ME WITH A *BULLET?*
PATHETIC.
GO!
YOU IDIOTS *DESERVE* TO DIE!

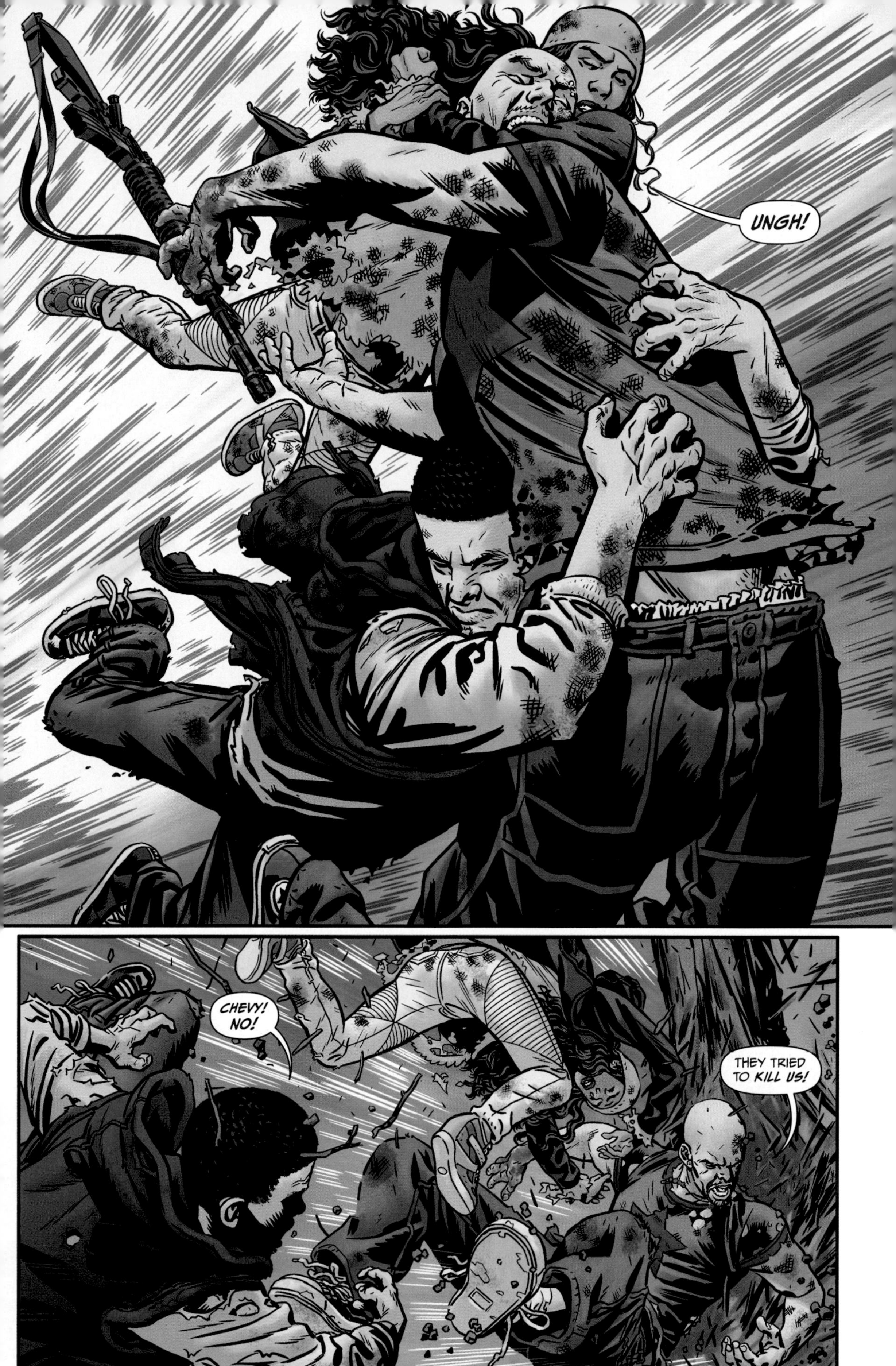
UNGH!
CHEVY! NO!
THEY TRIED TO KILL US!

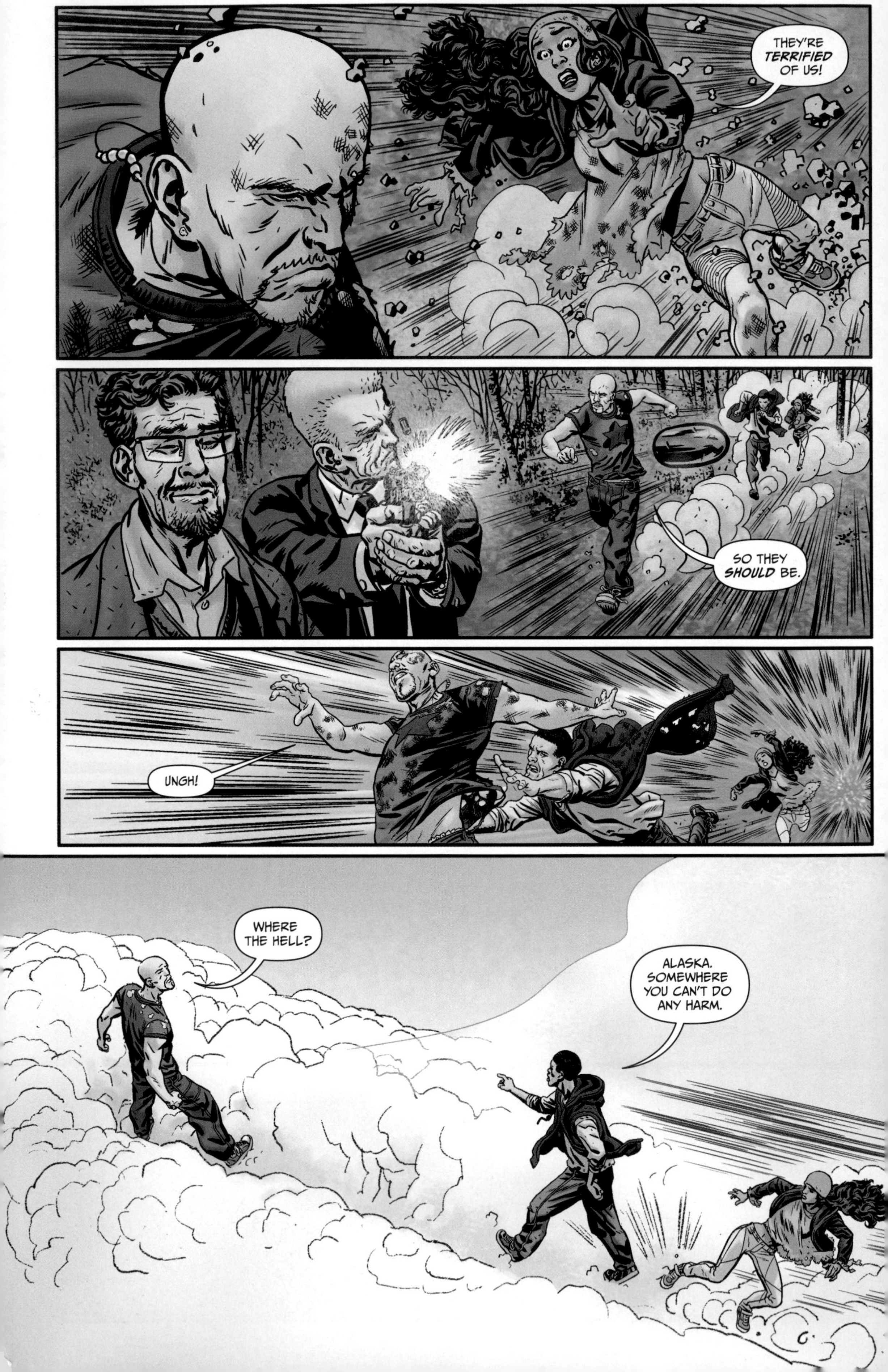
THEY'RE *TERRIFIED* OF US!
SO THEY ***SHOULD*** BE.
UNGH!
WHERE THE HELL?
ALASKA. SOMEWHERE YOU CAN'T DO ANY HARM.

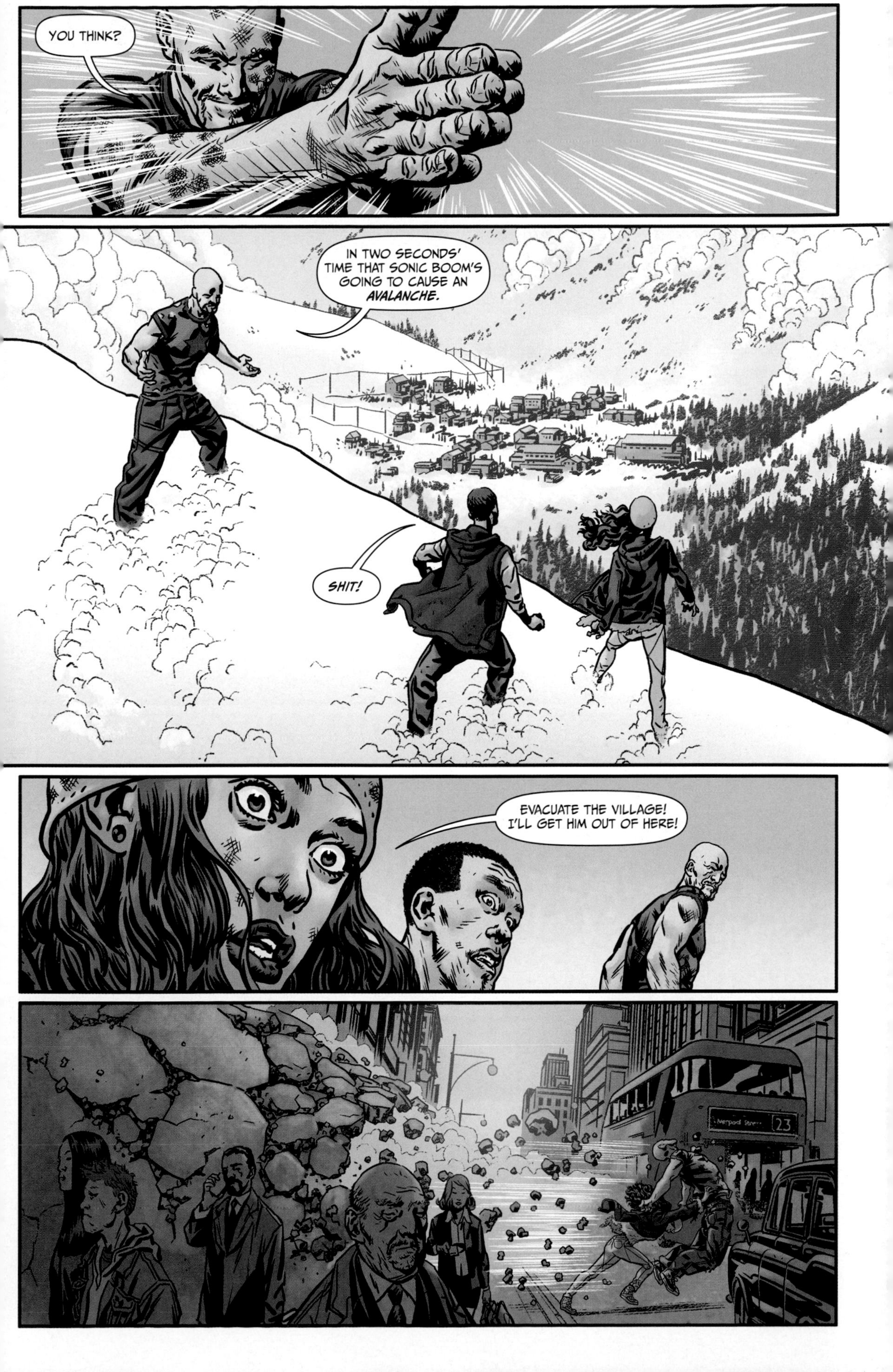
YOU THINK?
IN TWO SECONDS' TIME THAT SONIC BOOM'S GOING TO CAUSE AN *AVALANCHE.*
SHIT!
EVACUATE THE VILLAGE! I'LL GET HIM OUT OF HERE!
23

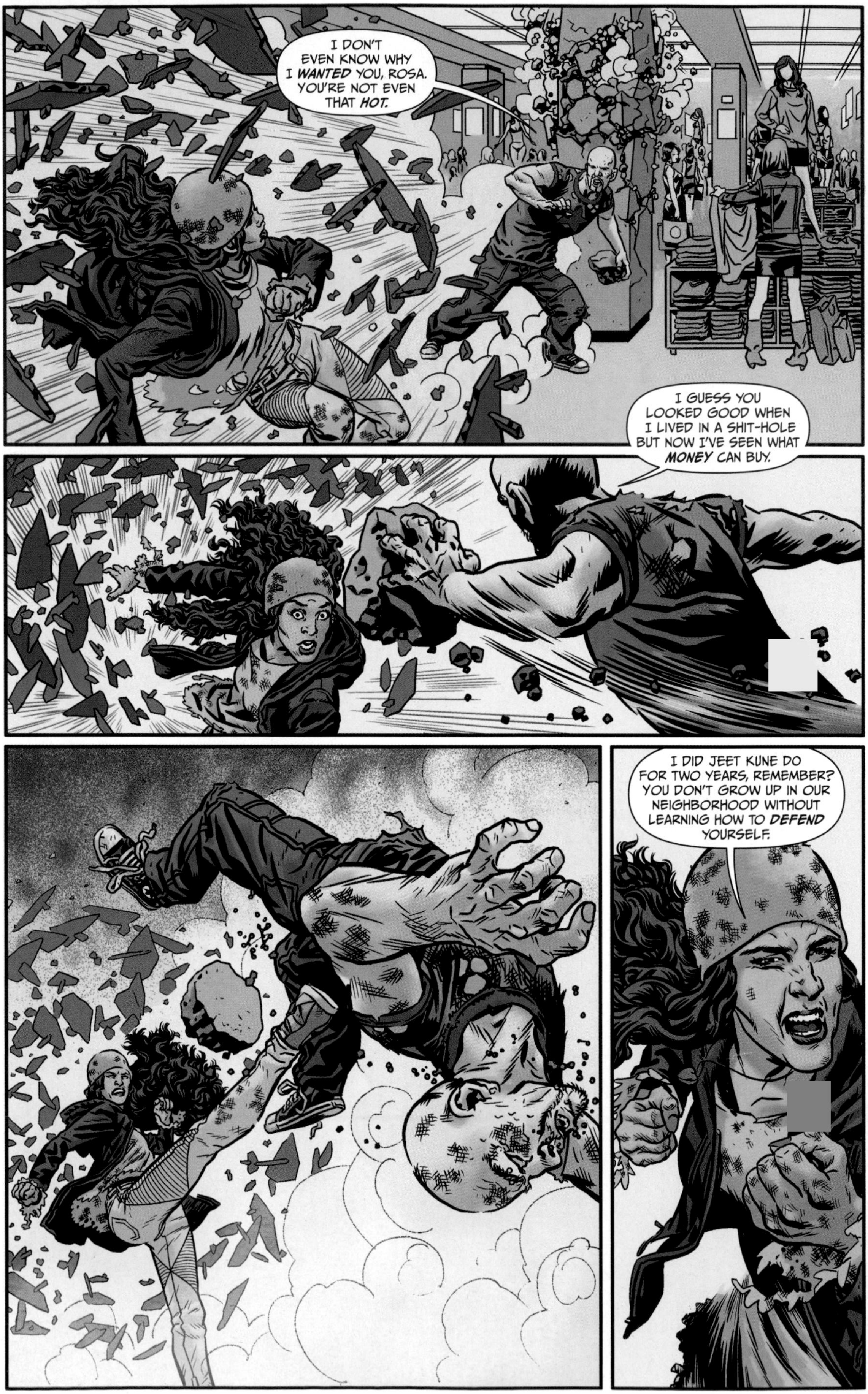
I DON'T EVEN KNOW WHY I WANTED YOU, ROSA. YOU'RE NOT EVEN THAT HOT.
I GUESS YOU LOOKED GOOD WHEN I LIVED IN A SHIT-HOLE BUT NOW I'VE SEEN WHAT MONEY CAN BUY.
I DID JEET KUNE DO FOR TWO YEARS, REMEMBER? YOU DON'T GROW UP IN OUR NEIGHBORHOOD WITHOUT LEARNING HOW TO DEFEND YOURSELF.

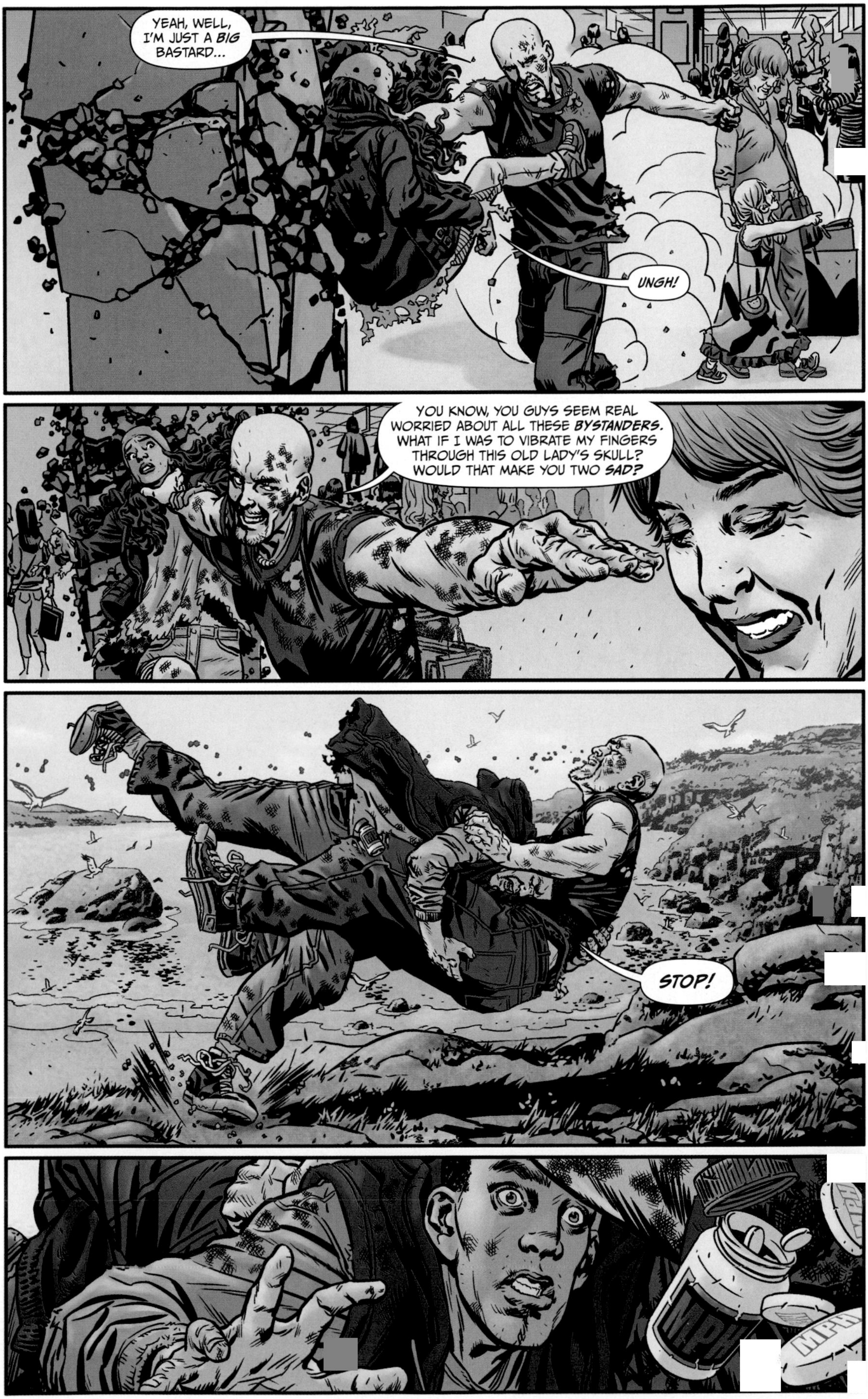
YEAH, WELL, I'M JUST A BIG BASTARD...
UNGH!
YOU KNOW, YOU GUYS SEEM REAL WORRIED ABOUT ALL THESE BYSTANDERS. WHAT IF I WAS TO VIBRATE MY FINGERS THROUGH THIS OLD LADY'S SKULL? WOULD THAT MAKE YOU TWO SAD?
STOP!

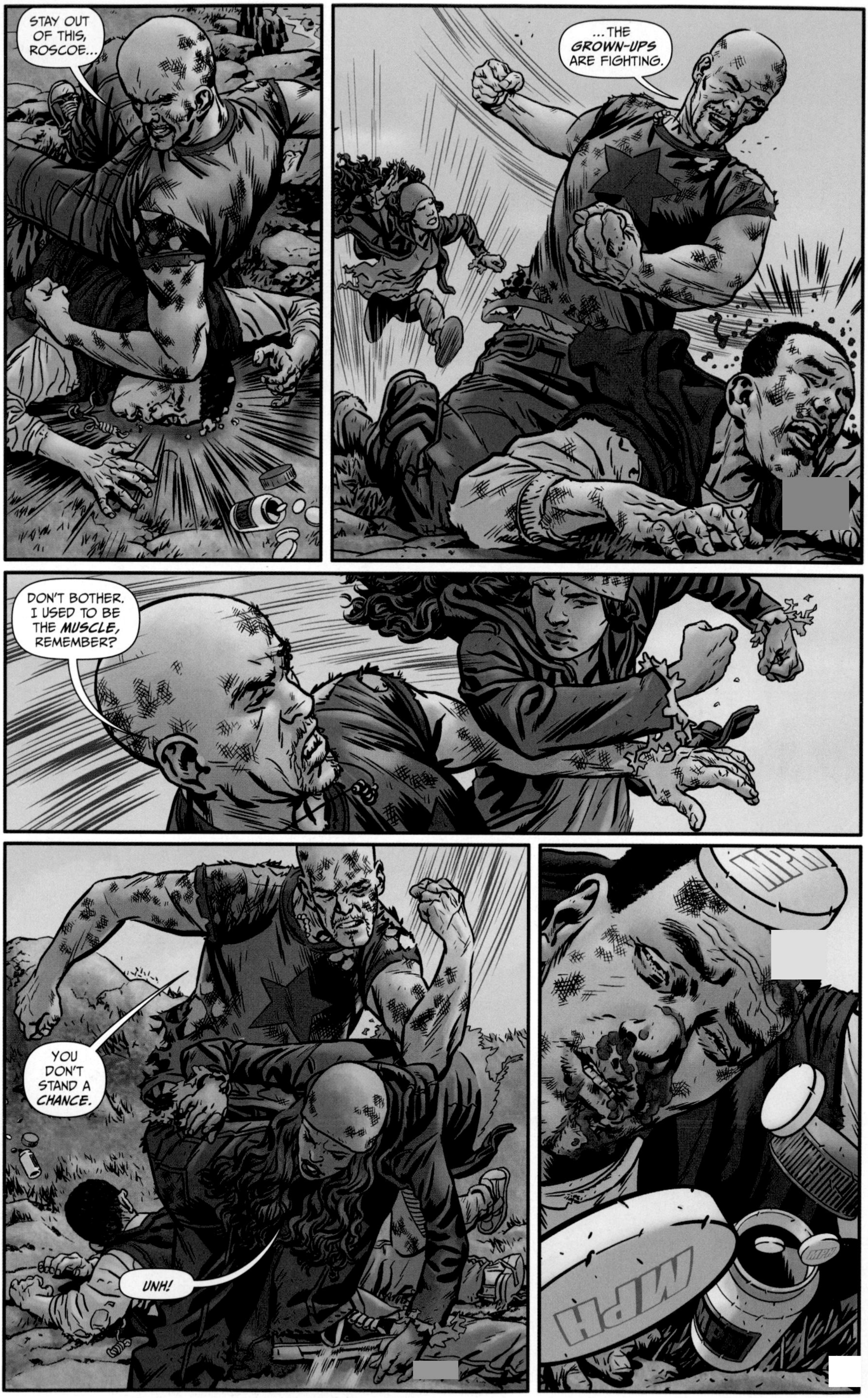
STAY OUT OF THIS, ROSCOE...
...THE GROWN-UPS ARE FIGHTING.
DON'T BOTHER. I USED TO BE THE MUSCLE, REMEMBER?
YOU DON'T STAND A CHANCE.
UNH!
MPH
MPH

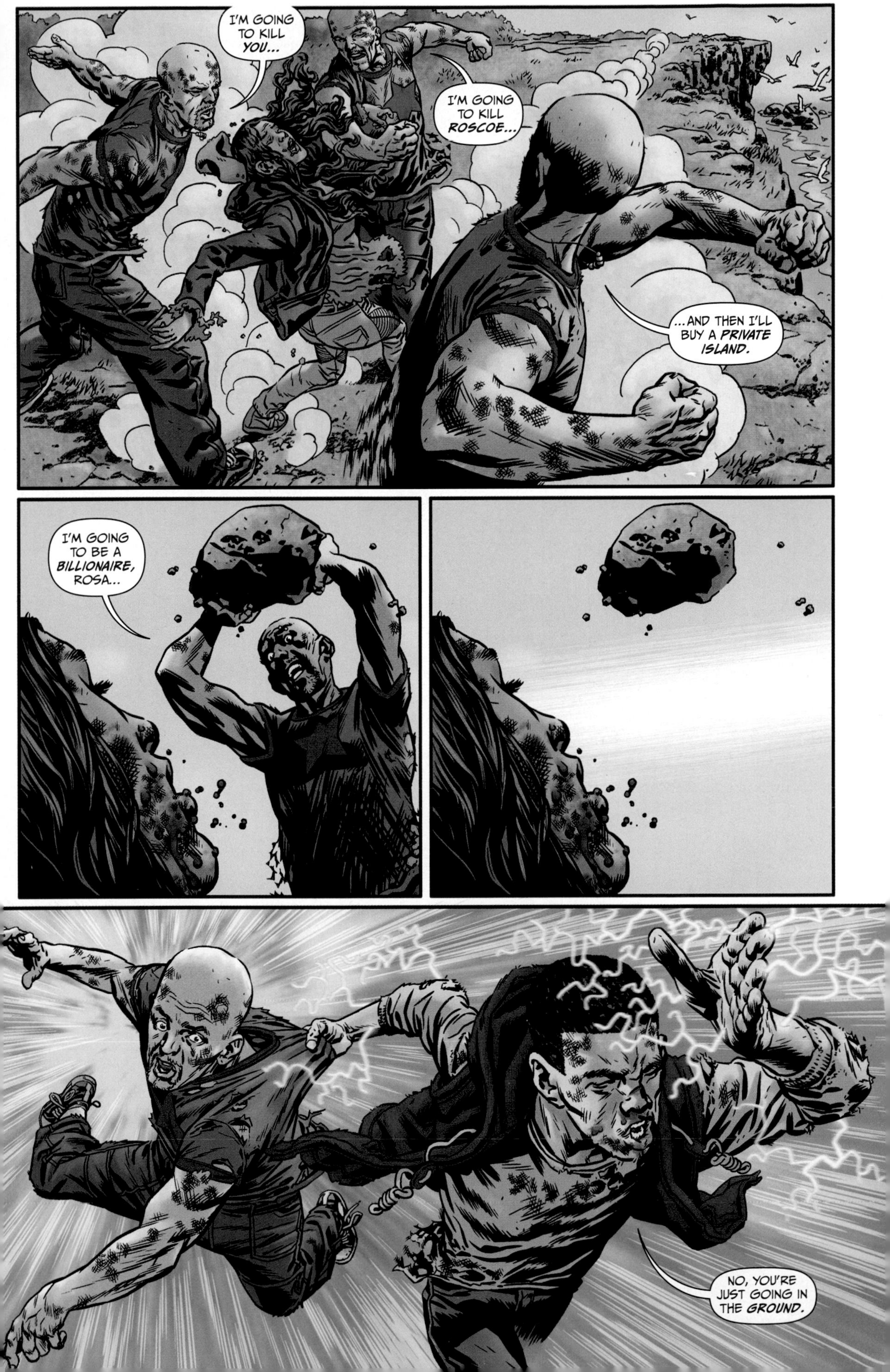
I'M GOING TO KILL YOU...
I'M GOING TO KILL ROSCOE...
...AND THEN I'LL BUY A PRIVATE ISLAND.
I'M GOING TO BE A BILLIONAIRE, ROSA...
NO, YOU'RE JUST GOING IN THE GROUND.

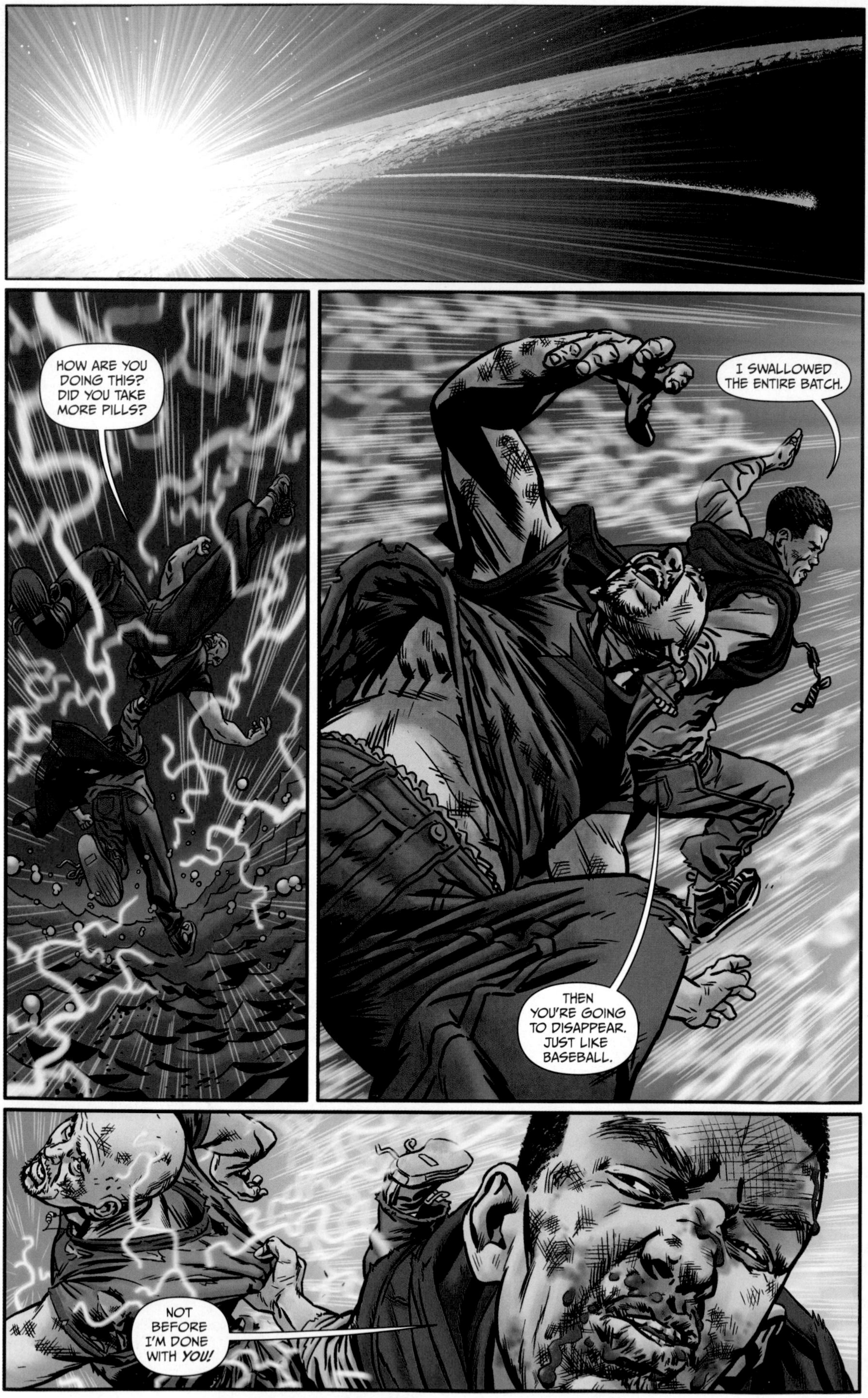
HOW ARE YOU DOING THIS? DID YOU TAKE MORE PILLS?
I SWALLOWED THE ENTIRE BATCH.
THEN YOU'RE GOING TO DISAPPEAR. JUST LIKE BASEBALL.
NOT BEFORE I'M DONE WITH *YOU!*

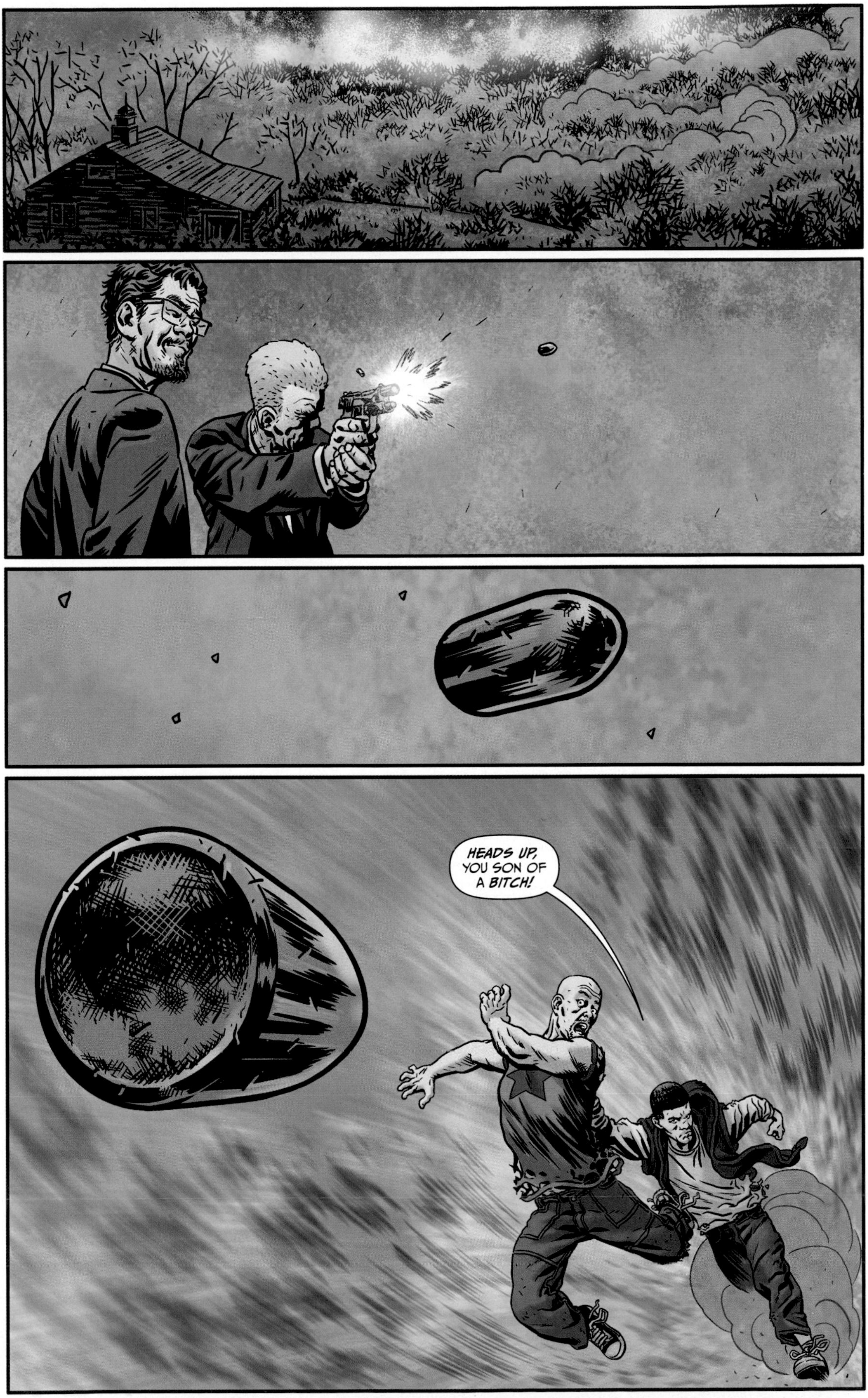
HEADS UP, YOU SON OF A BITCH!

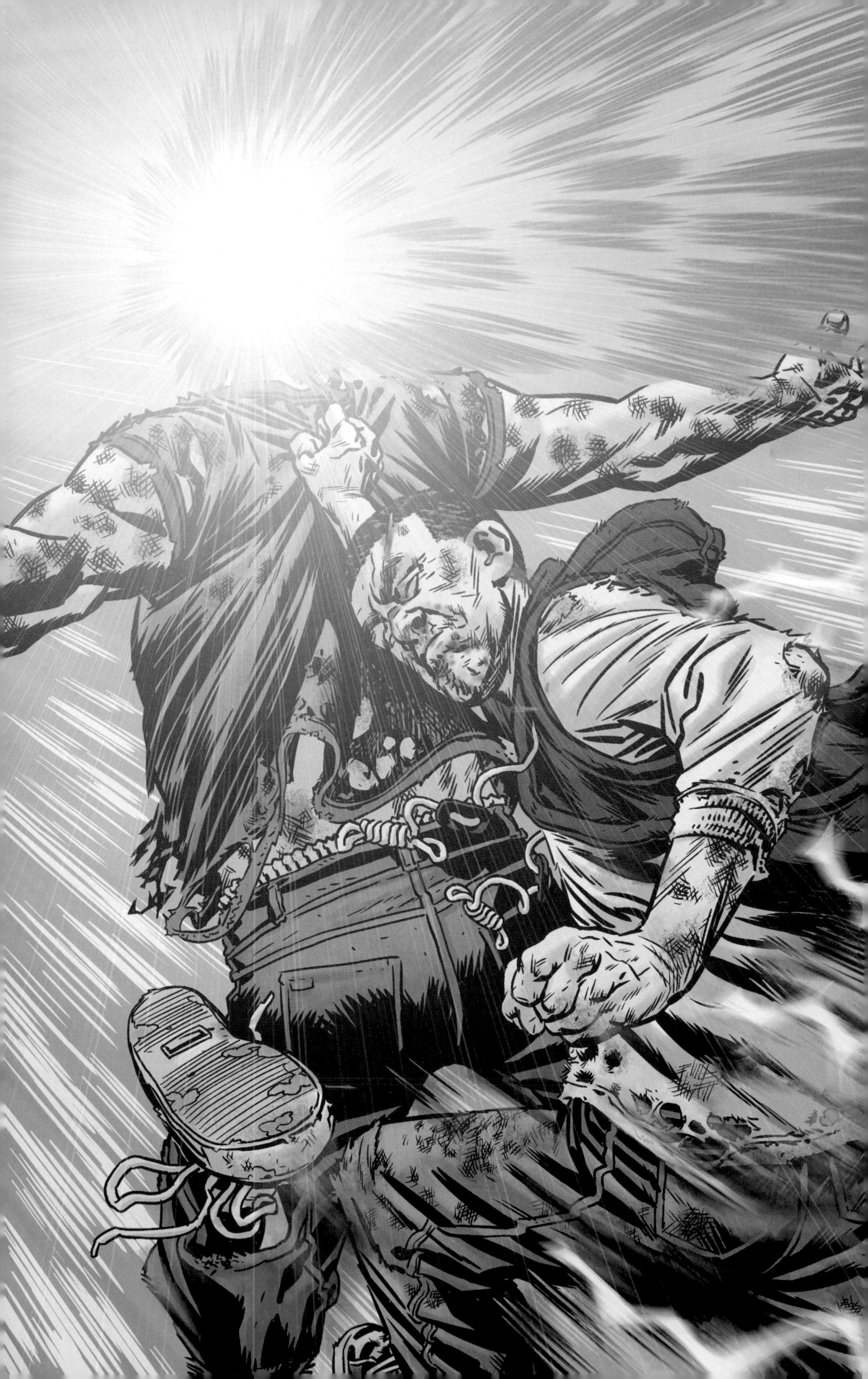

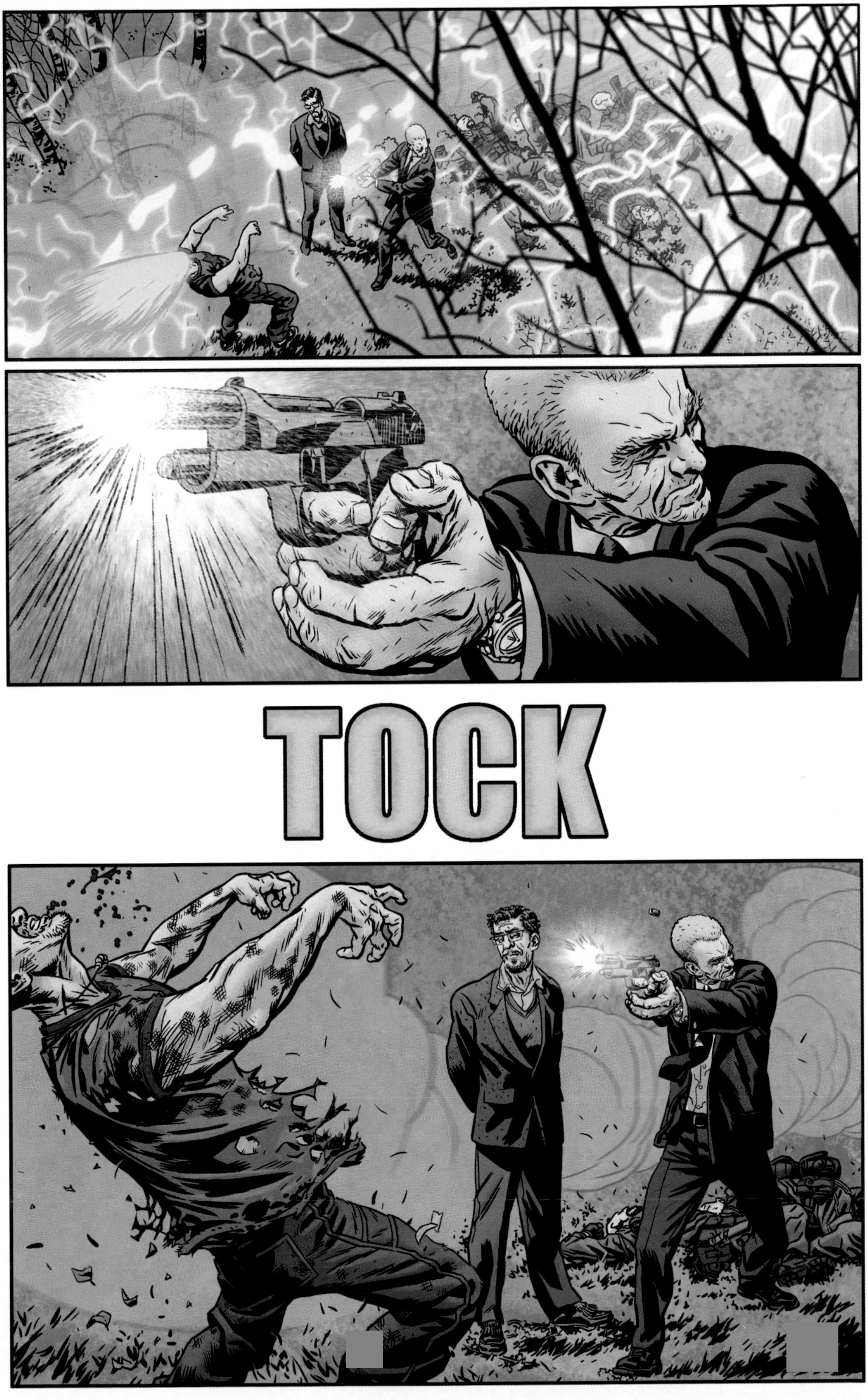
TOCK

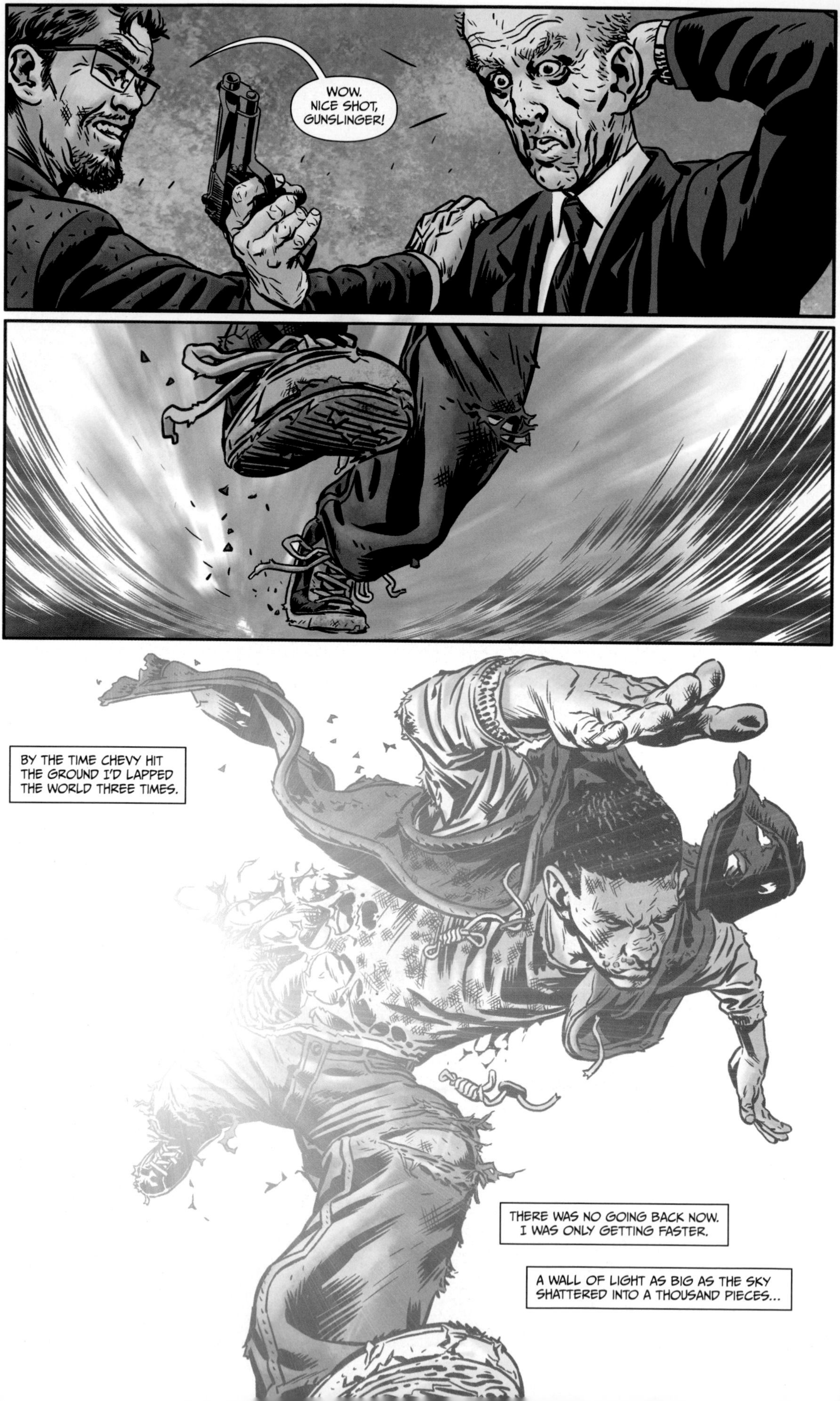
WOW. NICE SHOT, GUNSLINGER!
BY THE TIME CHEVY HIT THE GROUND I'D LAPPED THE WORLD THREE TIMES.
THERE WAS NO GOING BACK NOW. I WAS ONLY GETTING FASTER.
A WALL OF LIGHT AS BIG AS THE SKY SHATTERED INTO A THOUSAND PIECES...

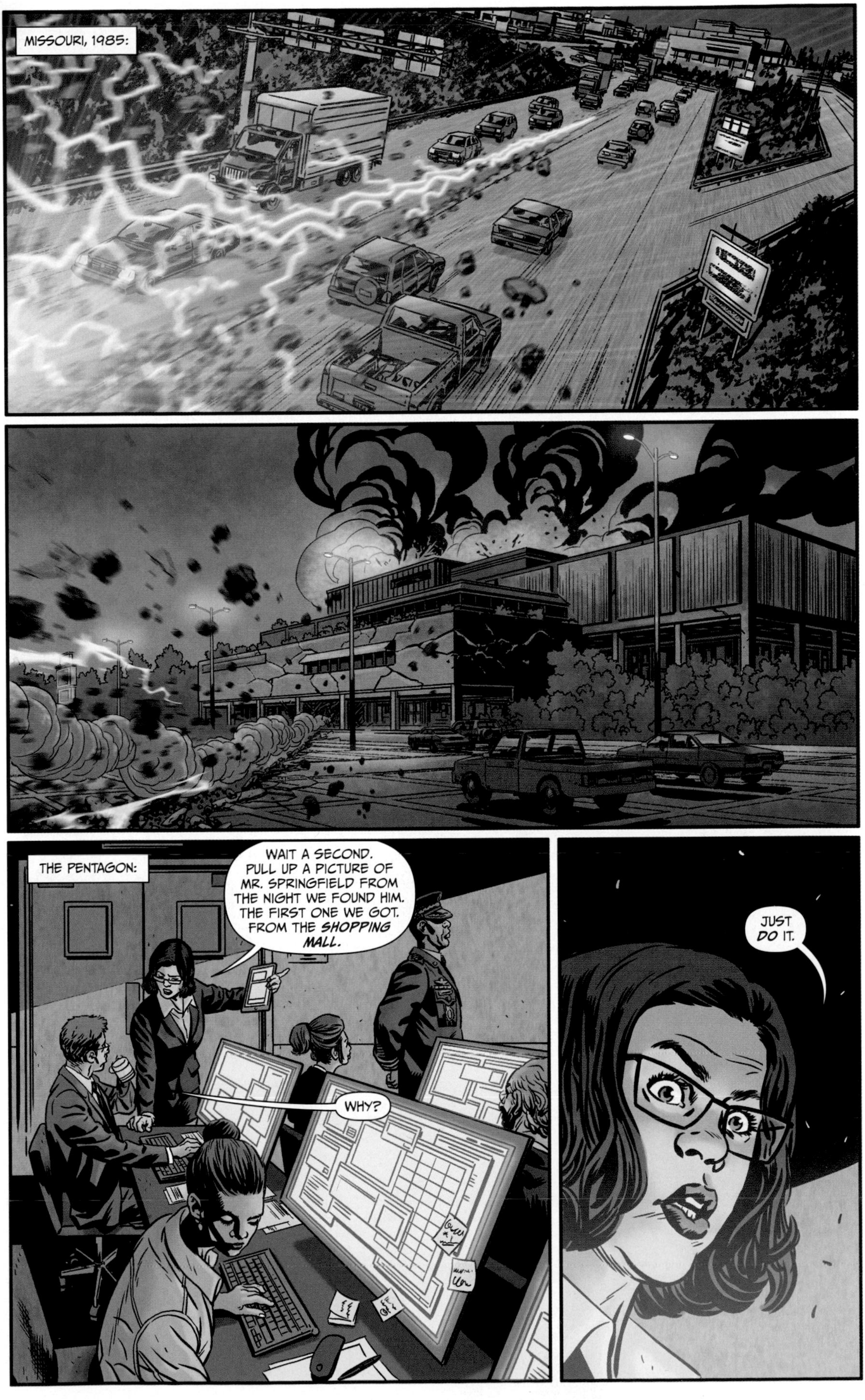
MISSOURI, 1985:
THE PENTAGON:
WAIT A SECOND. PULL UP A PICTURE OF MR. SPRINGFIELD FROM THE NIGHT WE FOUND HIM. THE FIRST ONE WE GOT. FROM THE *SHOPPING MALL.*
WHY?
JUST *DO* IT.

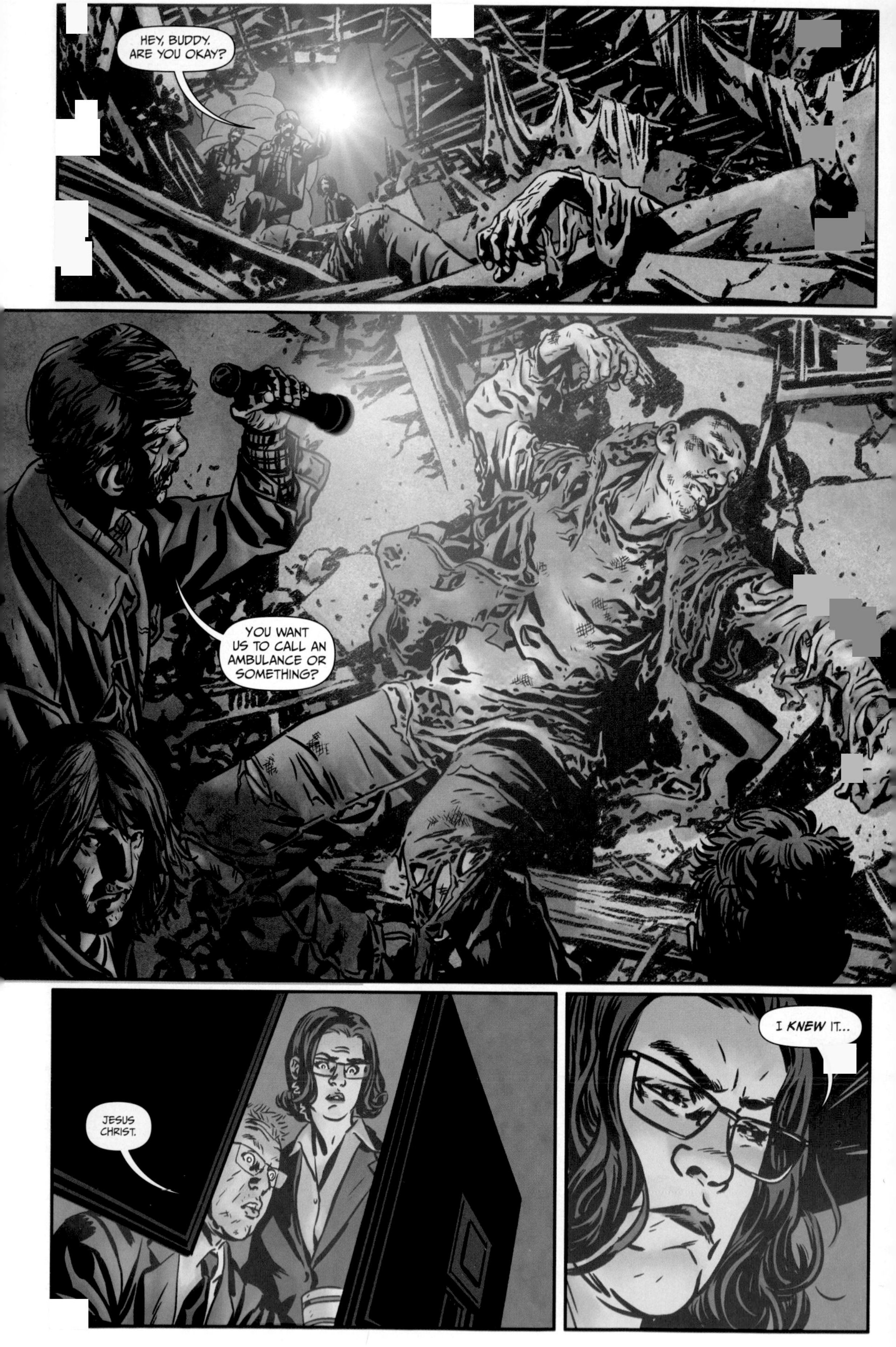
HEY, BUDDY. ARE YOU OKAY?
YOU WANT US TO CALL AN AMBULANCE OR SOMETHING?
JESUS CHRIST.
I KNEW IT...

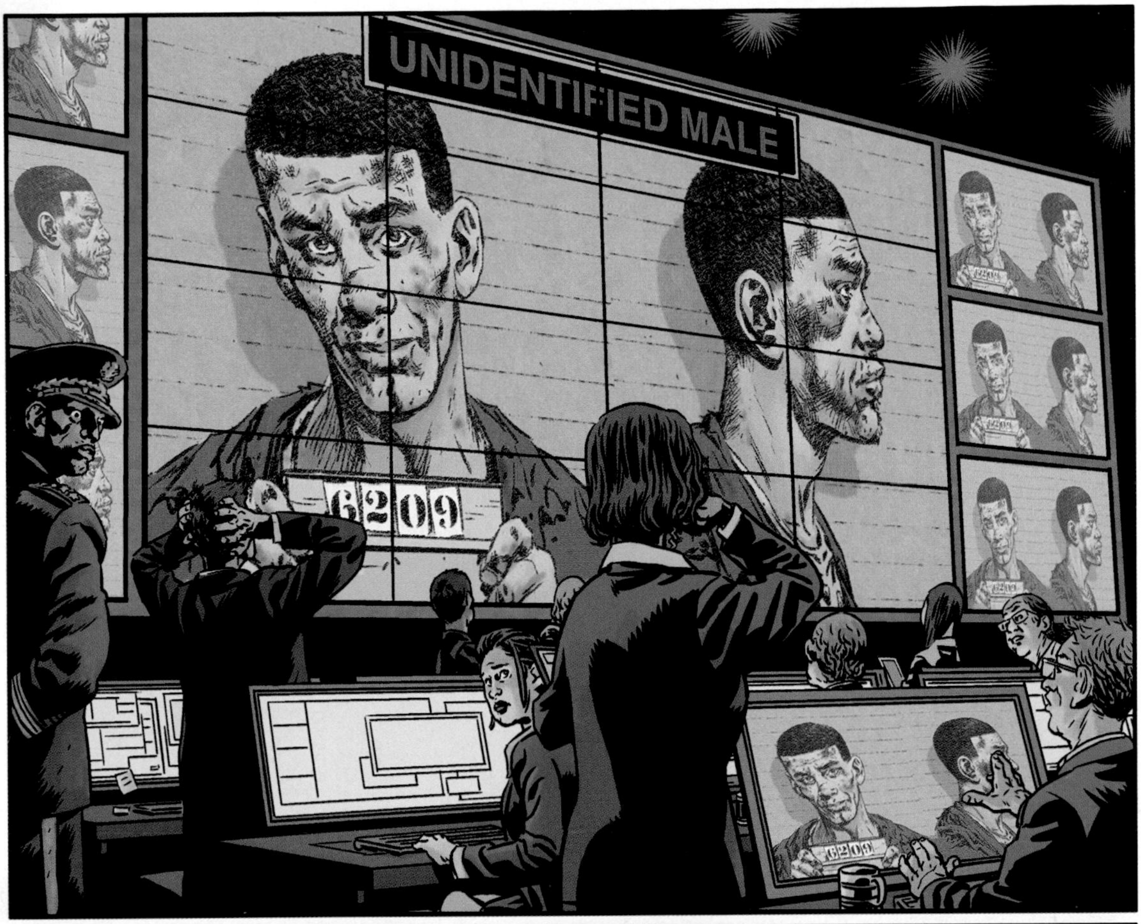
UNIDENTIFIED MALE
6209

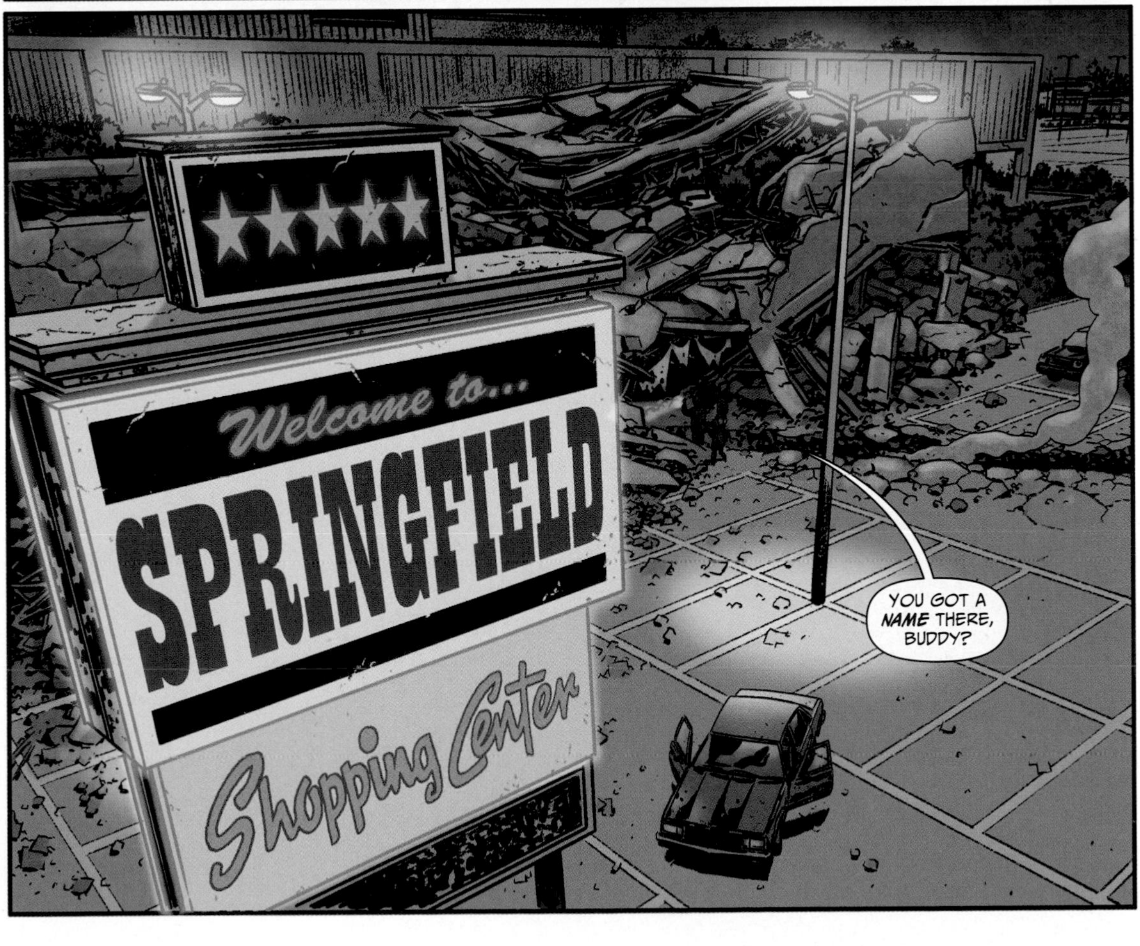
Welcome to...
SPRINGFIELD
Shopping Center
YOU GOT A NAME THERE, BUDDY?

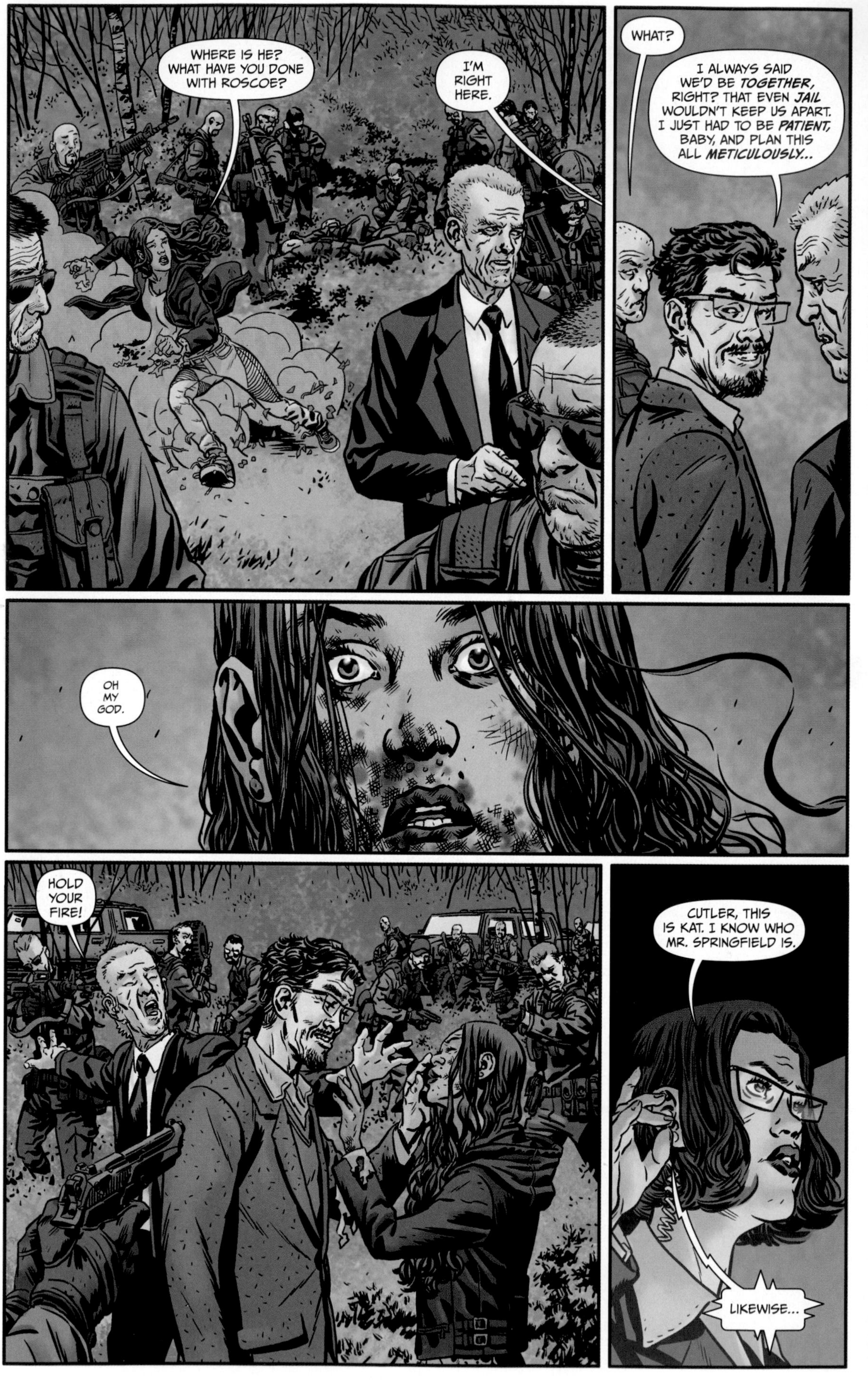
WHERE IS HE? WHAT HAVE YOU DONE WITH ROSCOE?
I'M RIGHT HERE.
WHAT?
I ALWAYS SAID WE'D BE TOGETHER, RIGHT? THAT EVEN JAIL WOULDN'T KEEP US APART. I JUST HAD TO BE PATIENT, BABY, AND PLAN THIS ALL METICULOUSLY...
OH MY GOD.
HOLD YOUR FIRE!
CUTLER, THIS IS KAT. I KNOW WHO MR. SPRINGFIELD IS.
LIKEWISE...

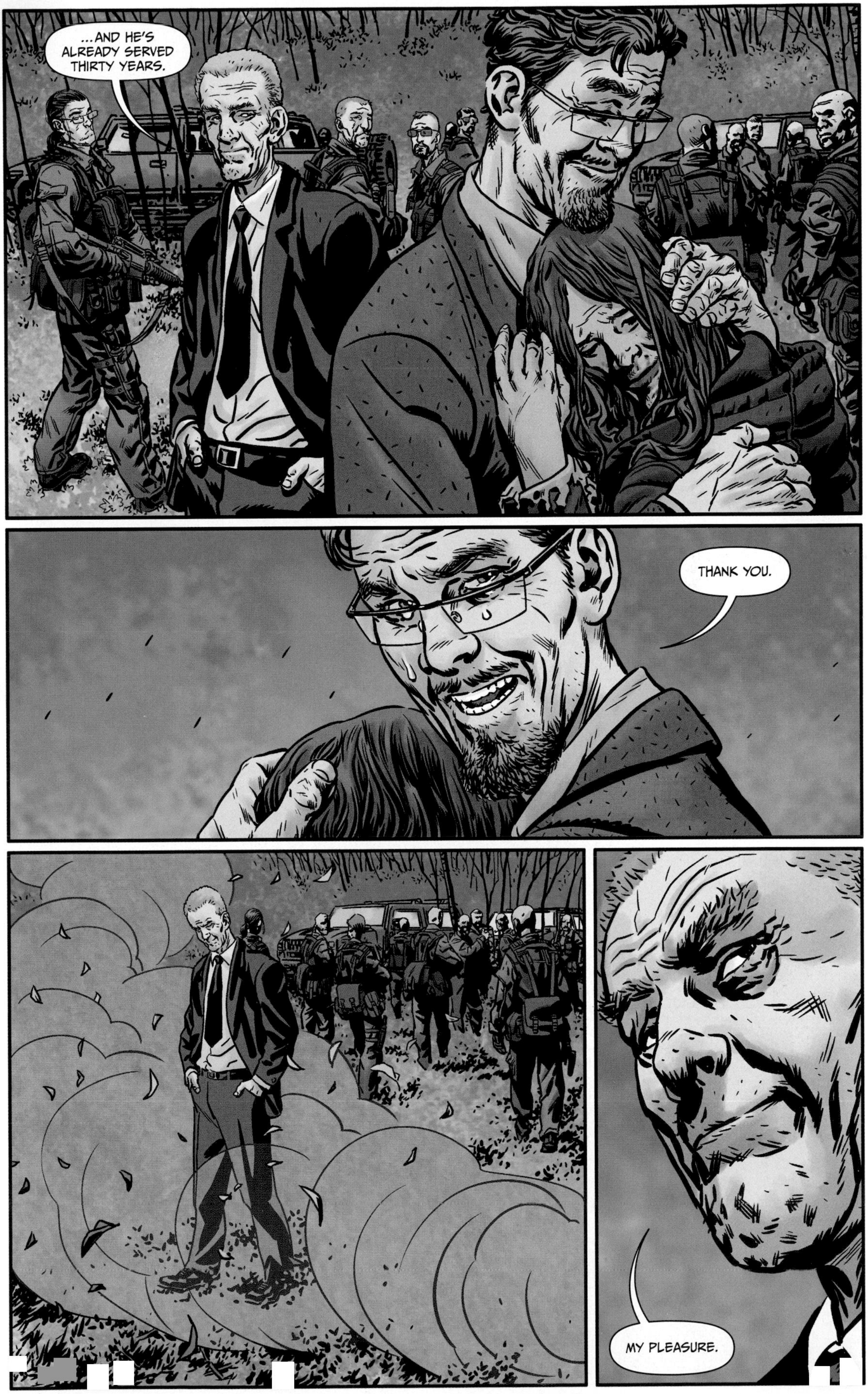
...AND HE'S ALREADY SERVED THIRTY YEARS.
THANK YOU.
MY PLEASURE.

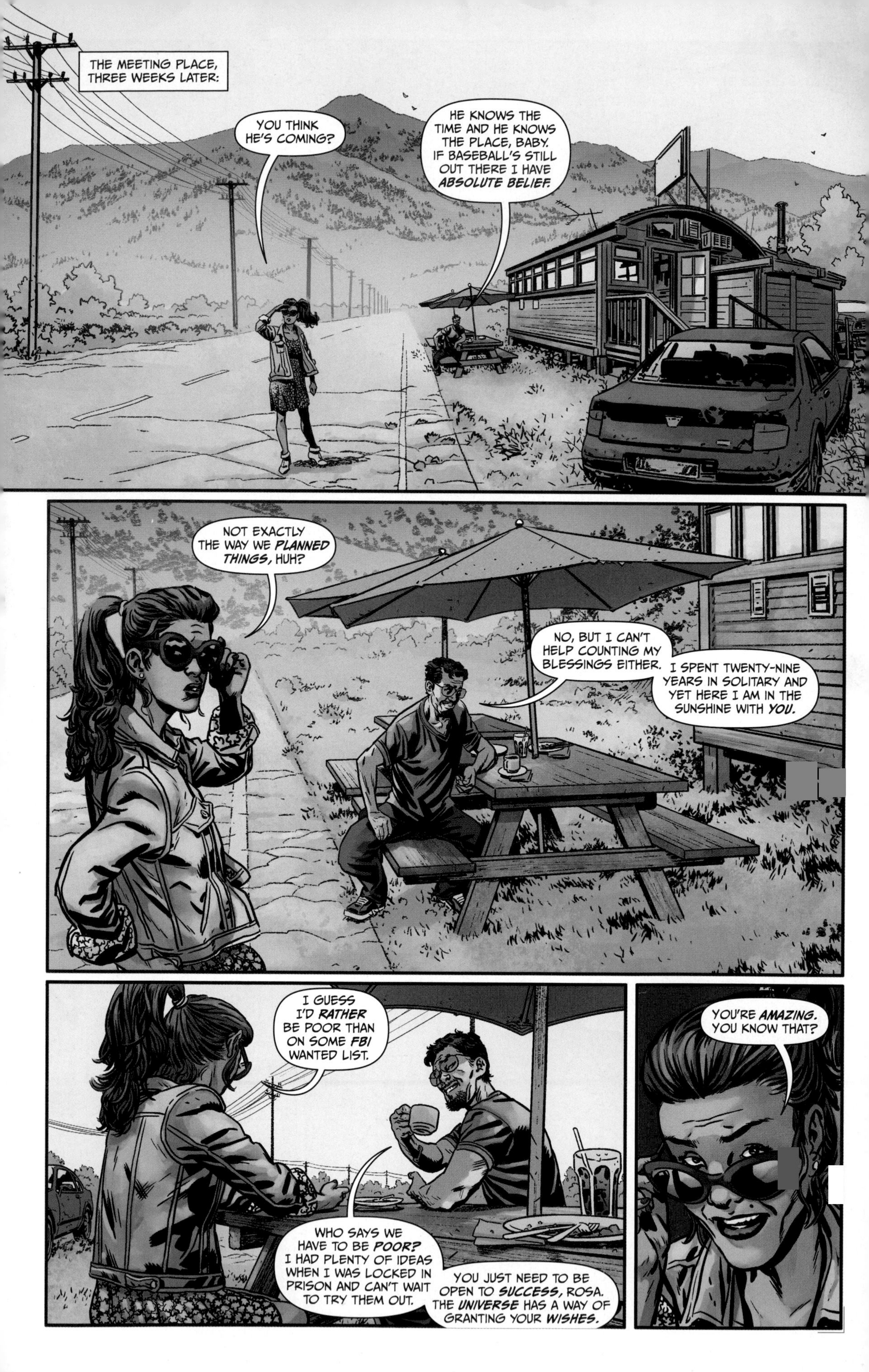
THE MEETING PLACE, THREE WEEKS LATER:
YOU THINK HE'S COMING?
HE KNOWS THE TIME AND HE KNOWS THE PLACE, BABY. IF BASEBALL'S STILL OUT THERE I HAVE ABSOLUTE BELIEF.
NOT EXACTLY THE WAY WE PLANNED THINGS, HUH?
NO, BUT I CAN'T HELP COUNTING MY BLESSINGS EITHER.
I SPENT TWENTY-NINE YEARS IN SOLITARY AND YET HERE I AM IN THE SUNSHINE WITH YOU.
I GUESS I'D RATHER BE POOR THAN ON SOME FBI WANTED LIST.
WHO SAYS WE HAVE TO BE POOR? I HAD PLENTY OF IDEAS WHEN I WAS LOCKED IN PRISON AND CAN'T WAIT TO TRY THEM OUT.
YOU JUST NEED TO BE OPEN TO SUCCESS, ROSA. THE UNIVERSE HAS A WAY OF GRANTING YOUR WISHES.
YOU'RE AMAZING. YOU KNOW THAT?

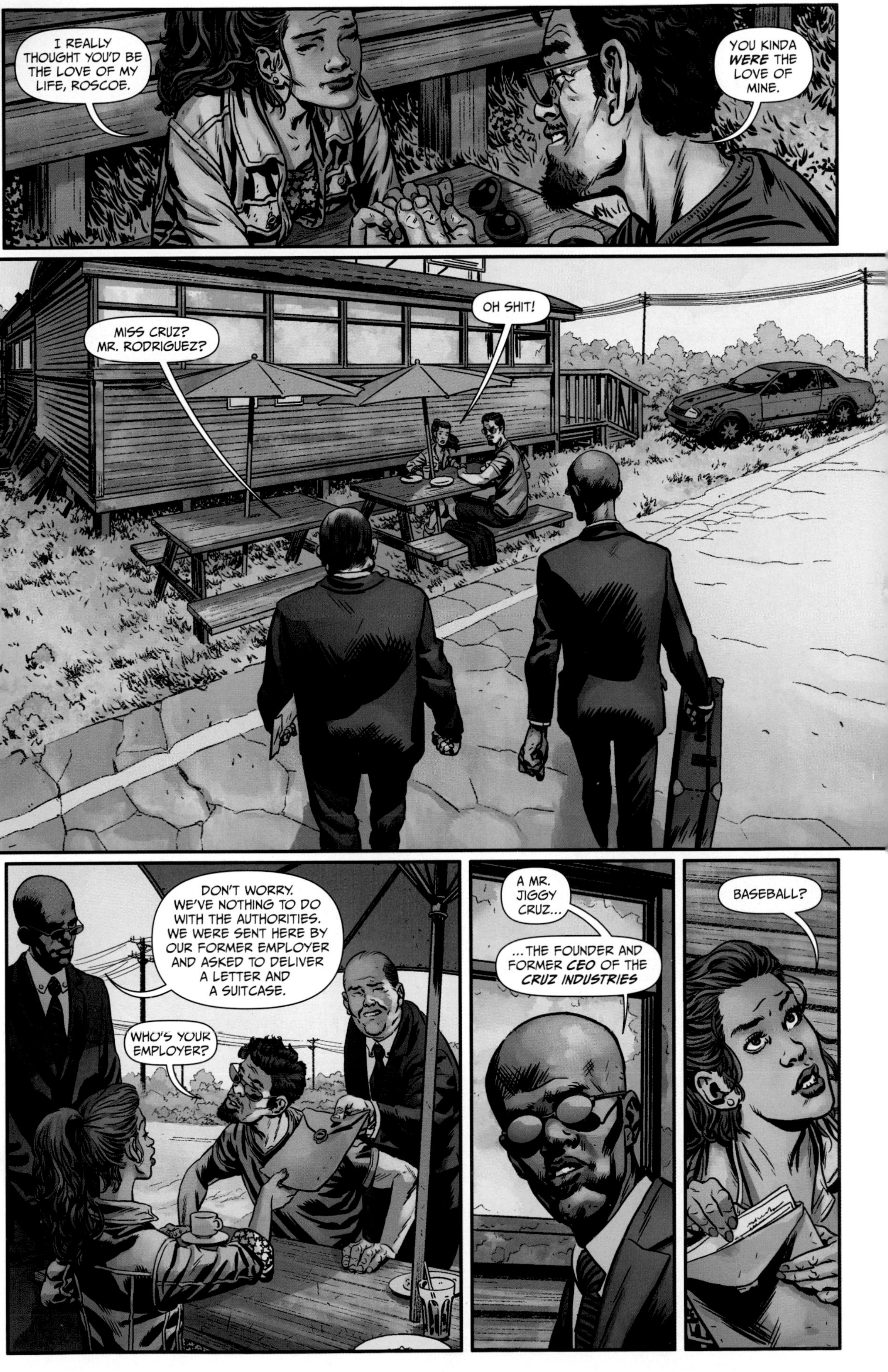
I REALLY THOUGHT YOU'D BE THE LOVE OF MY LIFE, ROSCOE.
YOU KINDA *WERE* THE LOVE OF MINE.
MISS CRUZ? MR. RODRIGUEZ?
OH SHIT!
DON'T WORRY. WE'VE NOTHING TO DO WITH THE AUTHORITIES. WE WERE SENT HERE BY OUR FORMER EMPLOYER AND ASKED TO DELIVER A LETTER AND A SUITCASE.
WHO'S YOUR EMPLOYER?
A MR. JIGGY CRUZ...
...THE FOUNDER AND FORMER *CEO* OF THE *CRUZ INDUSTRIES*
BASEBALL?

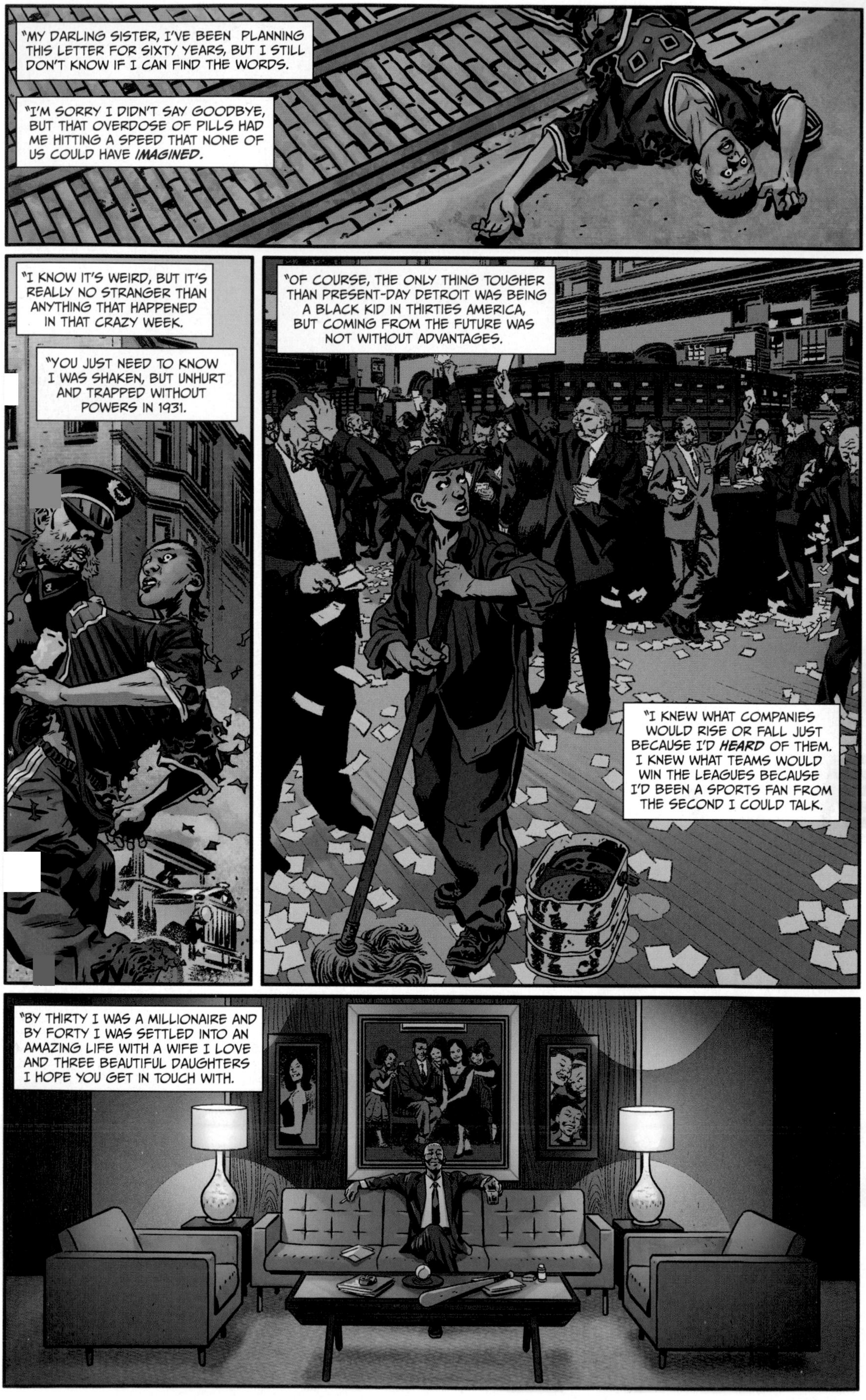
"MY DARLING SISTER, I'VE BEEN PLANNING THIS LETTER FOR SIXTY YEARS, BUT I STILL DON'T KNOW IF I CAN FIND THE WORDS.
"I'M SORRY I DIDN'T SAY GOODBYE, BUT THAT OVERDOSE OF PILLS HAD ME HITTING A SPEED THAT NONE OF US COULD HAVE *IMAGINED.*
"I KNOW IT'S WEIRD, BUT IT'S REALLY NO STRANGER THAN ANYTHING THAT HAPPENED IN THAT CRAZY WEEK.
"YOU JUST NEED TO KNOW I WAS SHAKEN, BUT UNHURT AND TRAPPED WITHOUT POWERS IN 1931.
"OF COURSE, THE ONLY THING TOUGHER THAN PRESENT-DAY DETROIT WAS BEING A BLACK KID IN THIRTIES AMERICA, BUT COMING FROM THE FUTURE WAS NOT WITHOUT ADVANTAGES.
"I KNEW WHAT COMPANIES WOULD RISE OR FALL JUST BECAUSE I'D ***HEARD*** OF THEM. I KNEW WHAT TEAMS WOULD WIN THE LEAGUES BECAUSE I'D BEEN A SPORTS FAN FROM THE SECOND I COULD TALK.
"BY THIRTY I WAS A MILLIONAIRE AND BY FORTY I WAS SETTLED INTO AN AMAZING LIFE WITH A WIFE I LOVE AND THREE BEAUTIFUL DAUGHTERS I HOPE YOU GET IN TOUCH WITH.

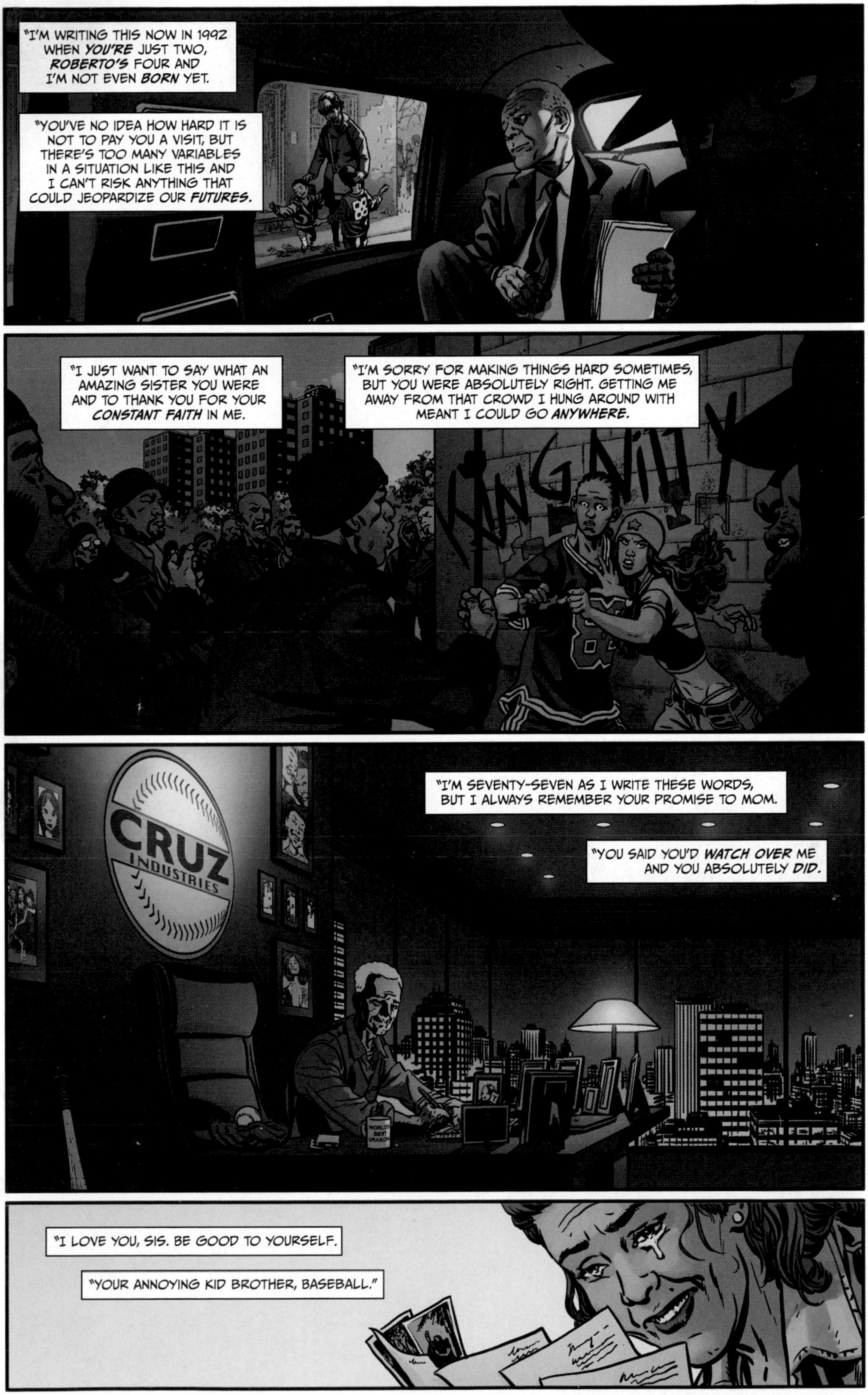
"I'M WRITING THIS NOW IN 1992 WHEN *YOU'RE* JUST TWO, *ROBERTO'S* FOUR AND I'M NOT EVEN *BORN* YET.
"YOU'VE NO IDEA HOW HARD IT IS NOT TO PAY YOU A VISIT, BUT THERE'S TOO MANY VARIABLES IN A SITUATION LIKE THIS AND I CAN'T RISK ANYTHING THAT COULD JEOPARDIZE OUR *FUTURES.*
"I JUST WANT TO SAY WHAT AN AMAZING SISTER YOU WERE AND TO THANK YOU FOR YOUR *CONSTANT FAITH* IN ME.
"I'M SORRY FOR MAKING THINGS HARD SOMETIMES, BUT YOU WERE ABSOLUTELY RIGHT. GETTING ME AWAY FROM THAT CROWD I HUNG AROUND WITH MEANT I COULD GO *ANYWHERE.*
CRUZ INDUSTRIES
"I'M SEVENTY-SEVEN AS I WRITE THESE WORDS, BUT I ALWAYS REMEMBER YOUR PROMISE TO MOM.
"YOU SAID YOU'D *WATCH OVER* ME AND YOU ABSOLUTELY *DID.*
"I LOVE YOU, SIS. BE GOOD TO YOURSELF.
"YOUR ANNOYING KID BROTHER, BASEBALL."

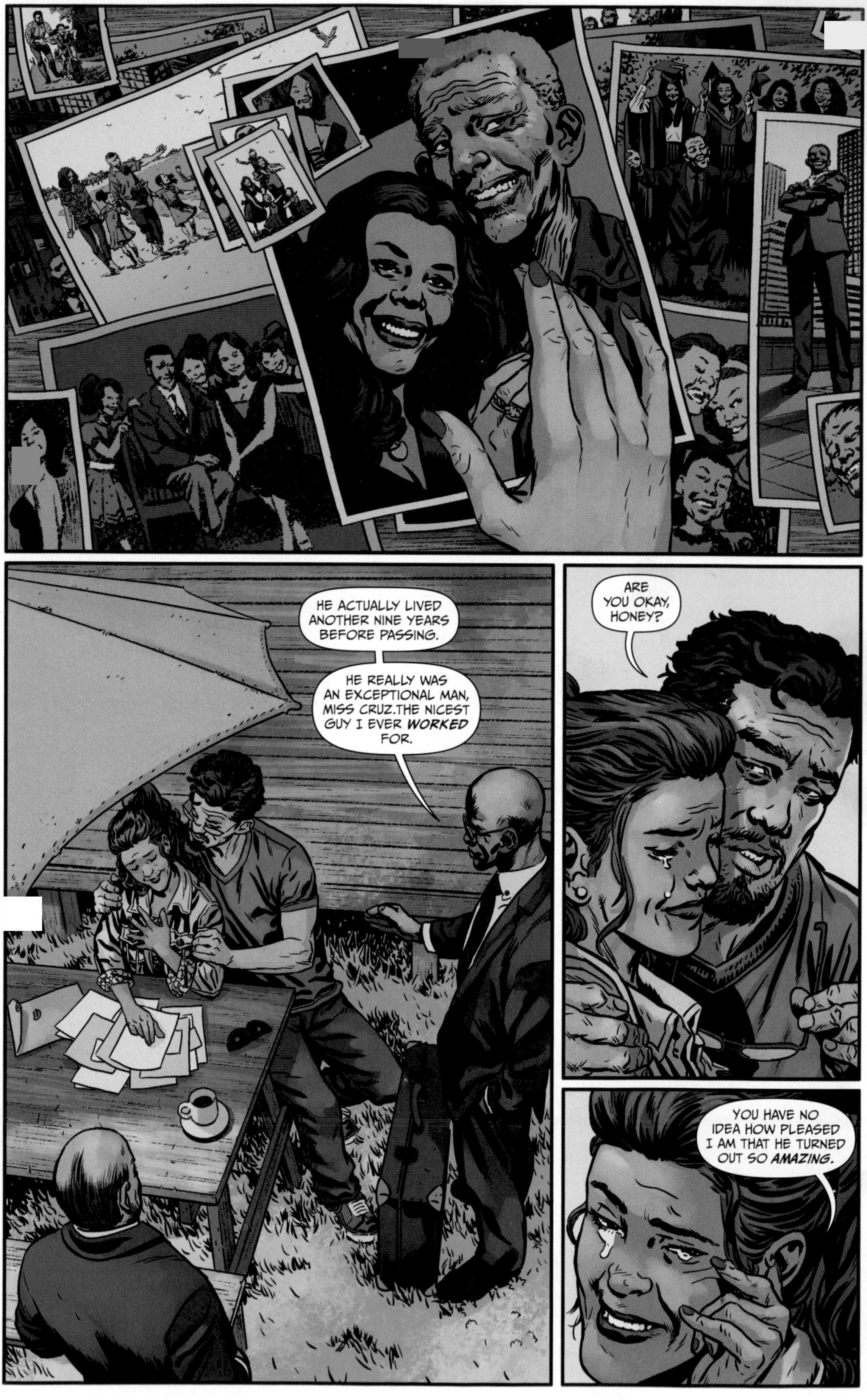
HE ACTUALLY LIVED ANOTHER NINE YEARS BEFORE PASSING.
HE REALLY WAS AN EXCEPTIONAL MAN, MISS CRUZ.THE NICEST GUY I EVER *WORKED* FOR.
ARE YOU OKAY, HONEY?
YOU HAVE NO IDEA HOW PLEASED I AM THAT HE TURNED OUT SO *AMAZING.*

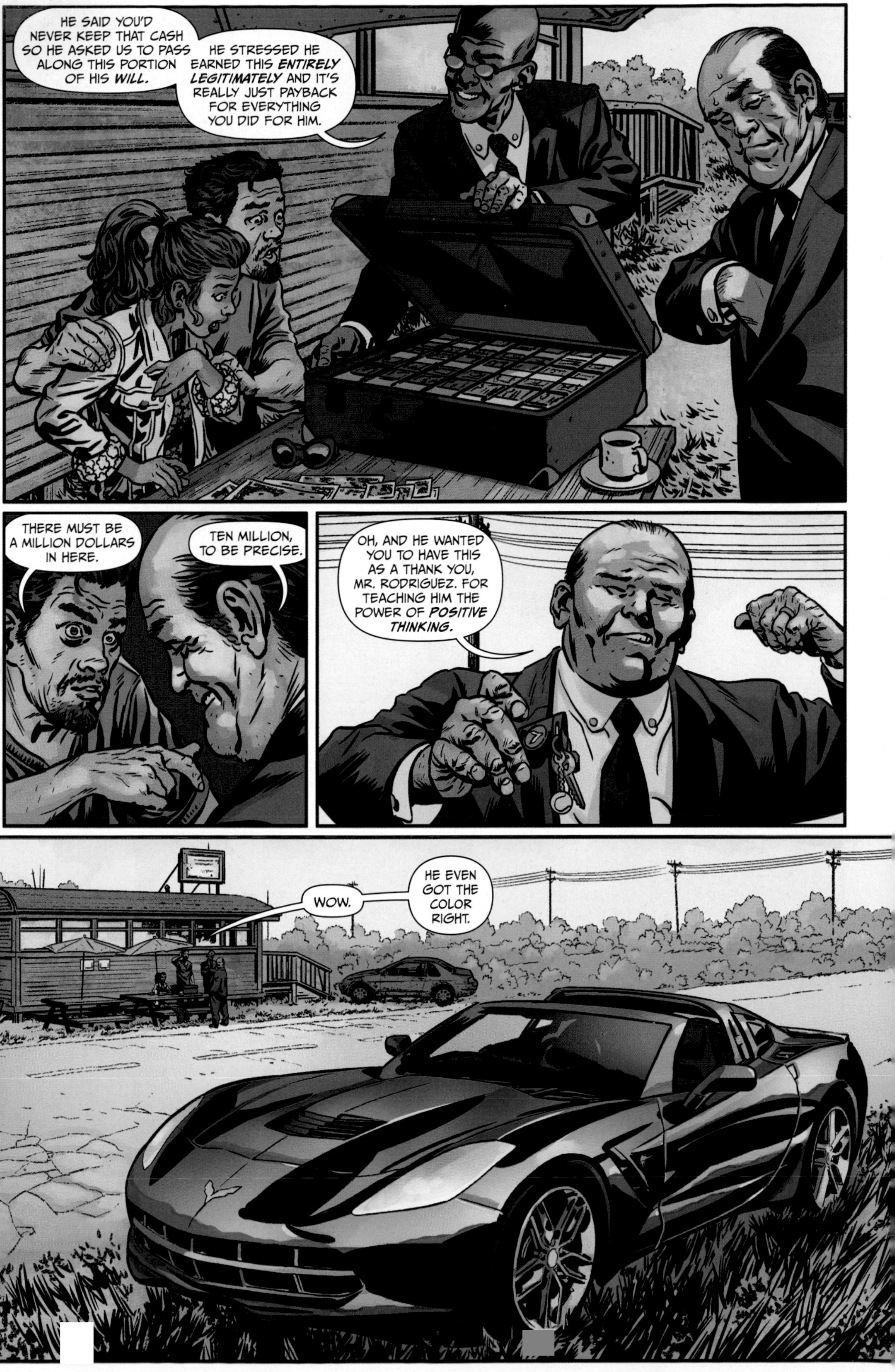
HE SAID YOU'D NEVER KEEP THAT CASH SO HE ASKED US TO PASS ALONG THIS PORTION OF HIS WILL.
HE STRESSED HE EARNED THIS ENTIRELY LEGITIMATELY AND IT'S REALLY JUST PAYBACK FOR EVERYTHING YOU DID FOR HIM.
THERE MUST BE A MILLION DOLLARS IN HERE.
TEN MILLION, TO BE PRECISE.
OH, AND HE WANTED YOU TO HAVE THIS AS A THANK YOU, MR. RODRIGUEZ. FOR TEACHING HIM THE POWER OF POSITIVE THINKING.
WOW.
HE EVEN GOT THE COLOR RIGHT.

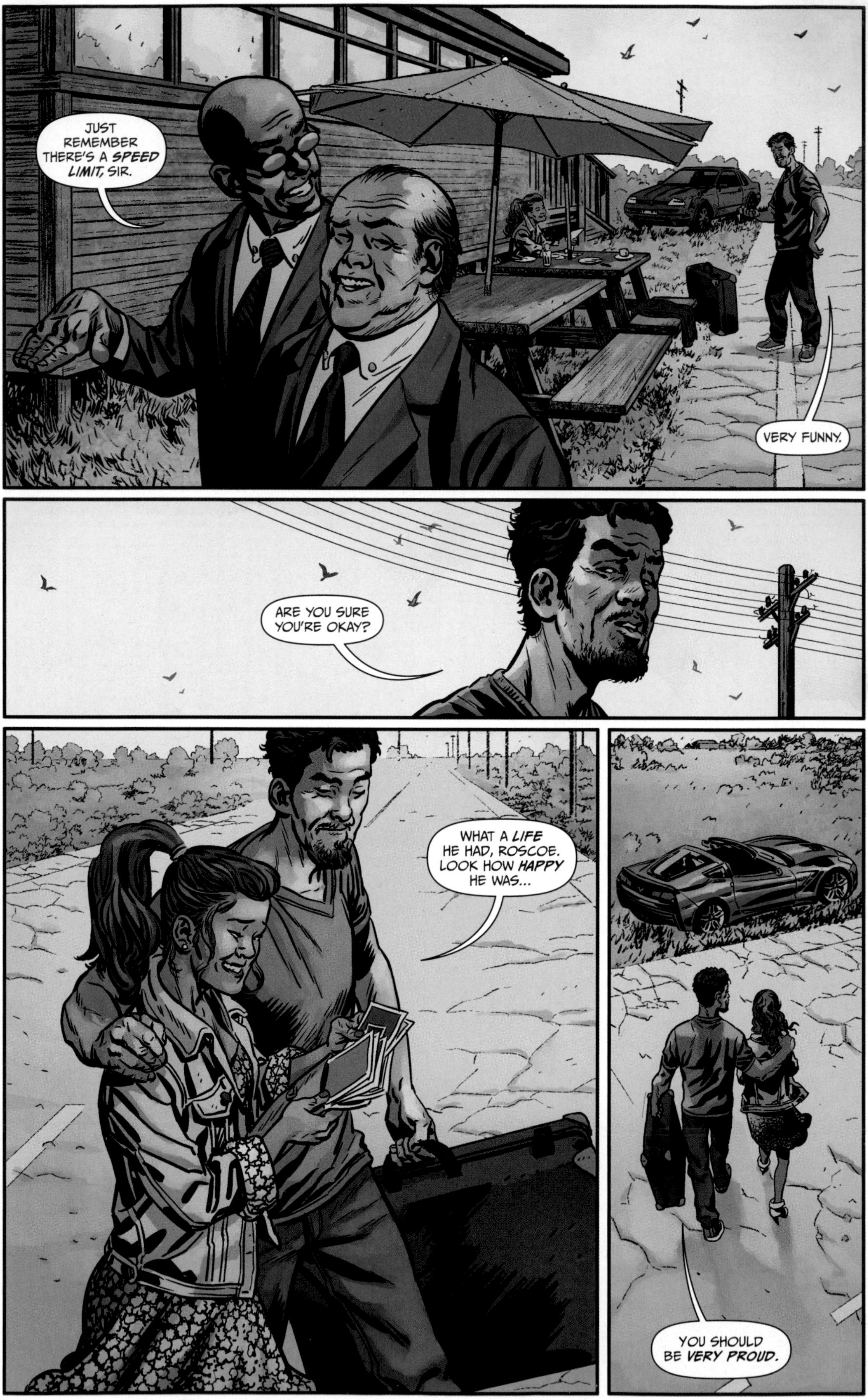

JUST REMEMBER THERE'S A *SPEED LIMIT,* SIR.
VERY FUNNY.
ARE YOU SURE YOU'RE OKAY?
WHAT A *LIFE* HE HAD, ROSCOE. LOOK HOW *HAPPY* HE WAS...
YOU SHOULD BE *VERY PROUD.*

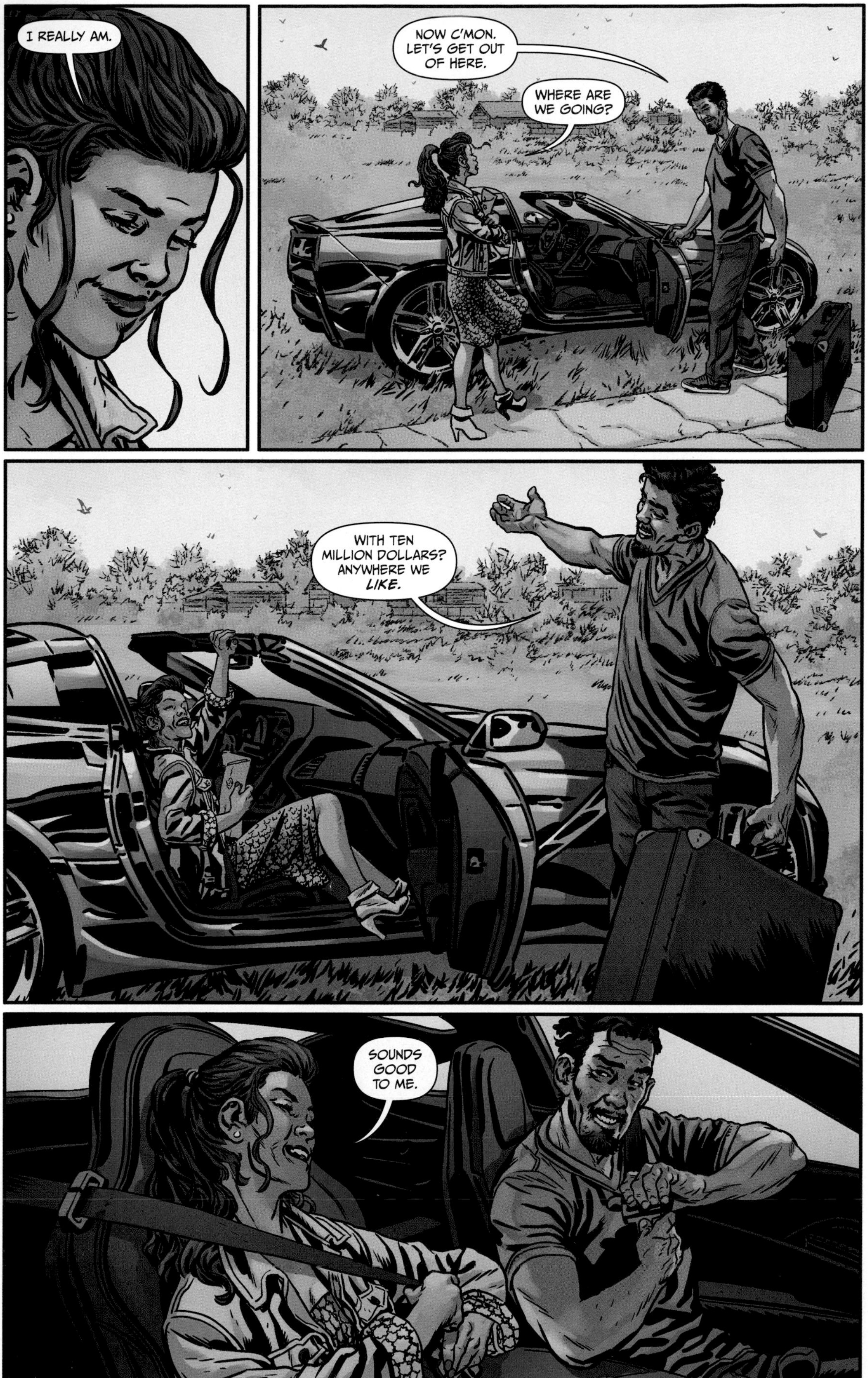
I REALLY AM.
NOW C'MON. LET'S GET OUT OF HERE.
WHERE ARE WE GOING?
WITH TEN MILLION DOLLARS? ANYWHERE WE *LIKE.*
SOUNDS GOOD TO ME.

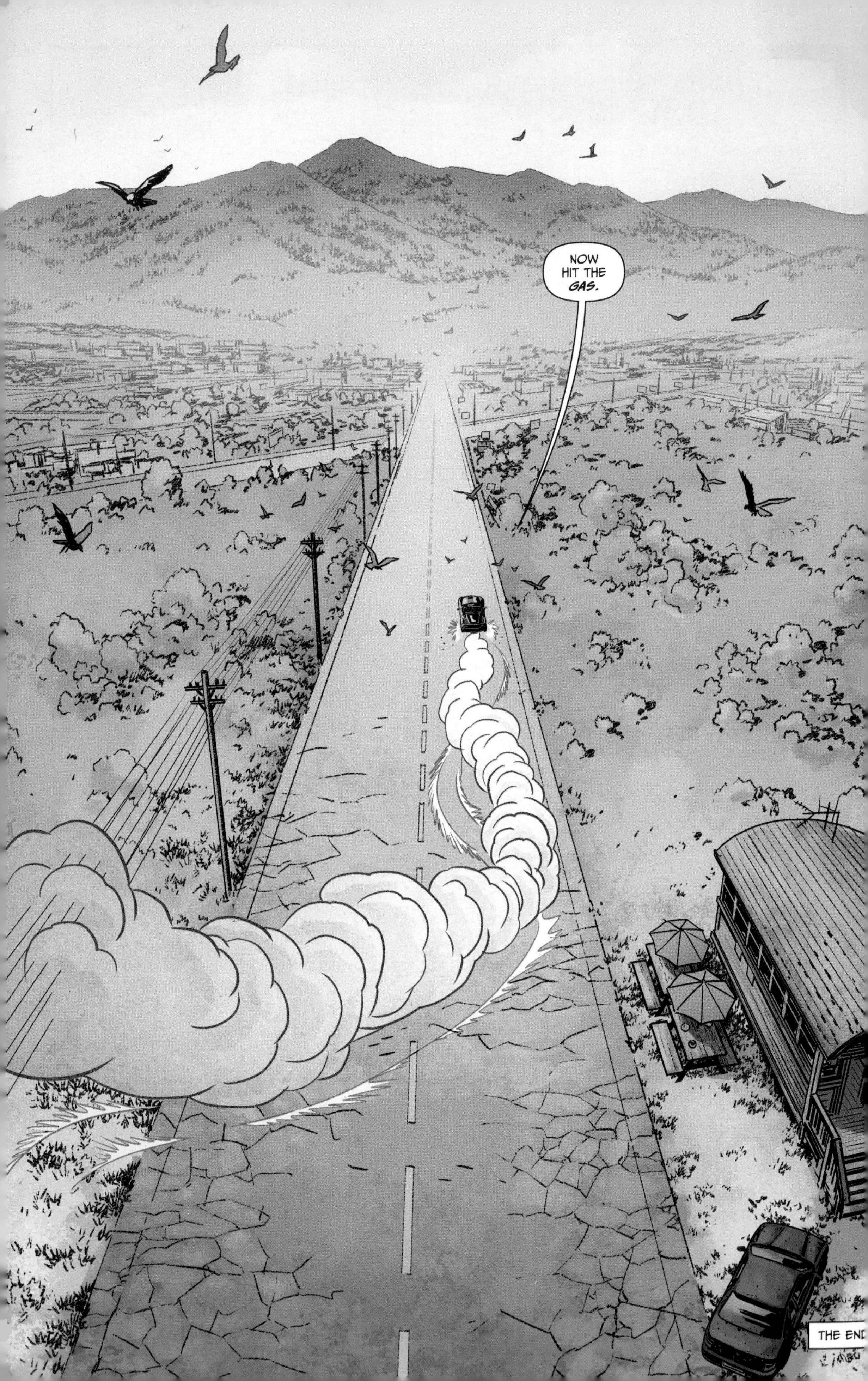

NOW HIT THE GAS.
THE END

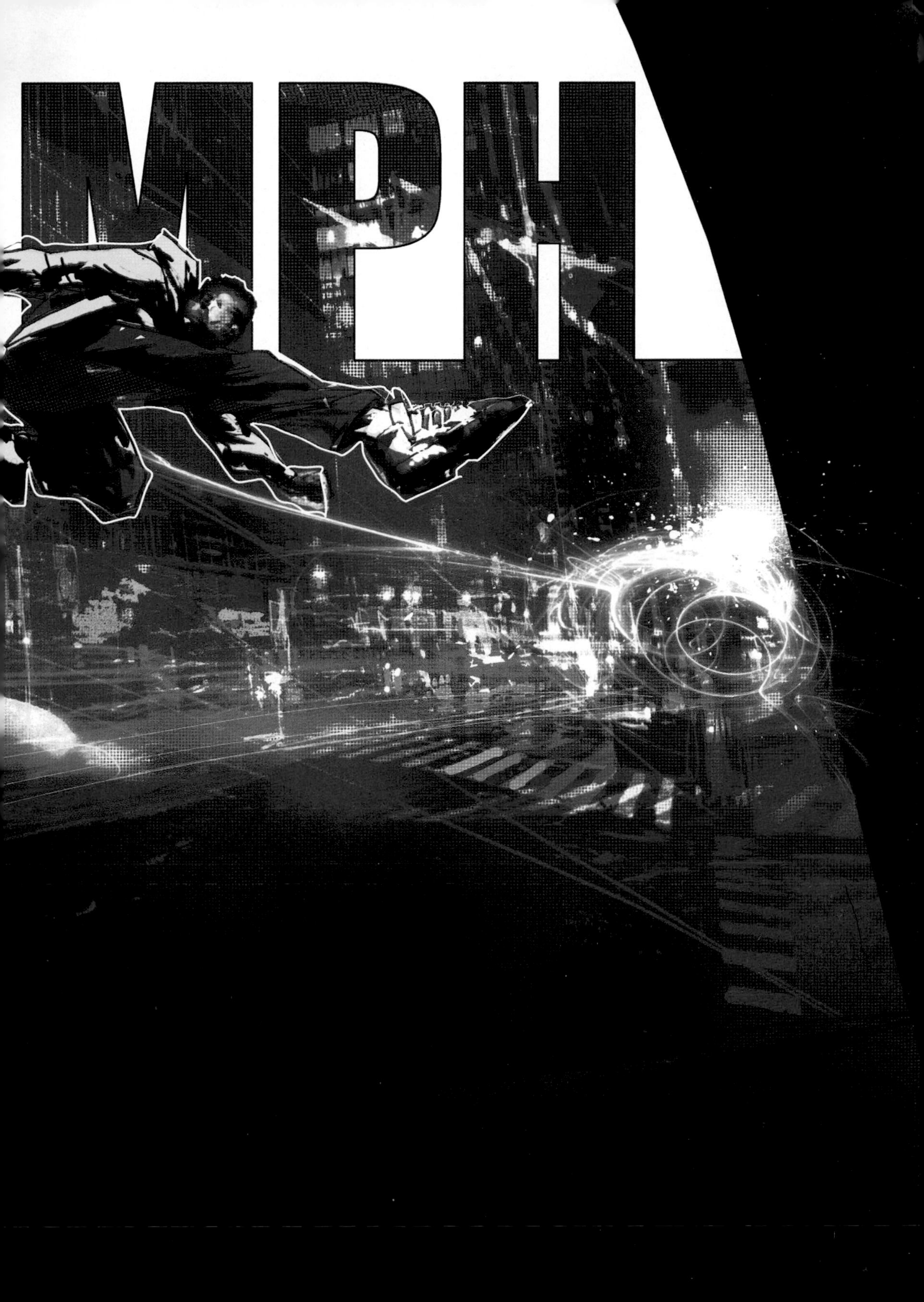
MPH

ISSUE 1 VARIANT

by JOCK

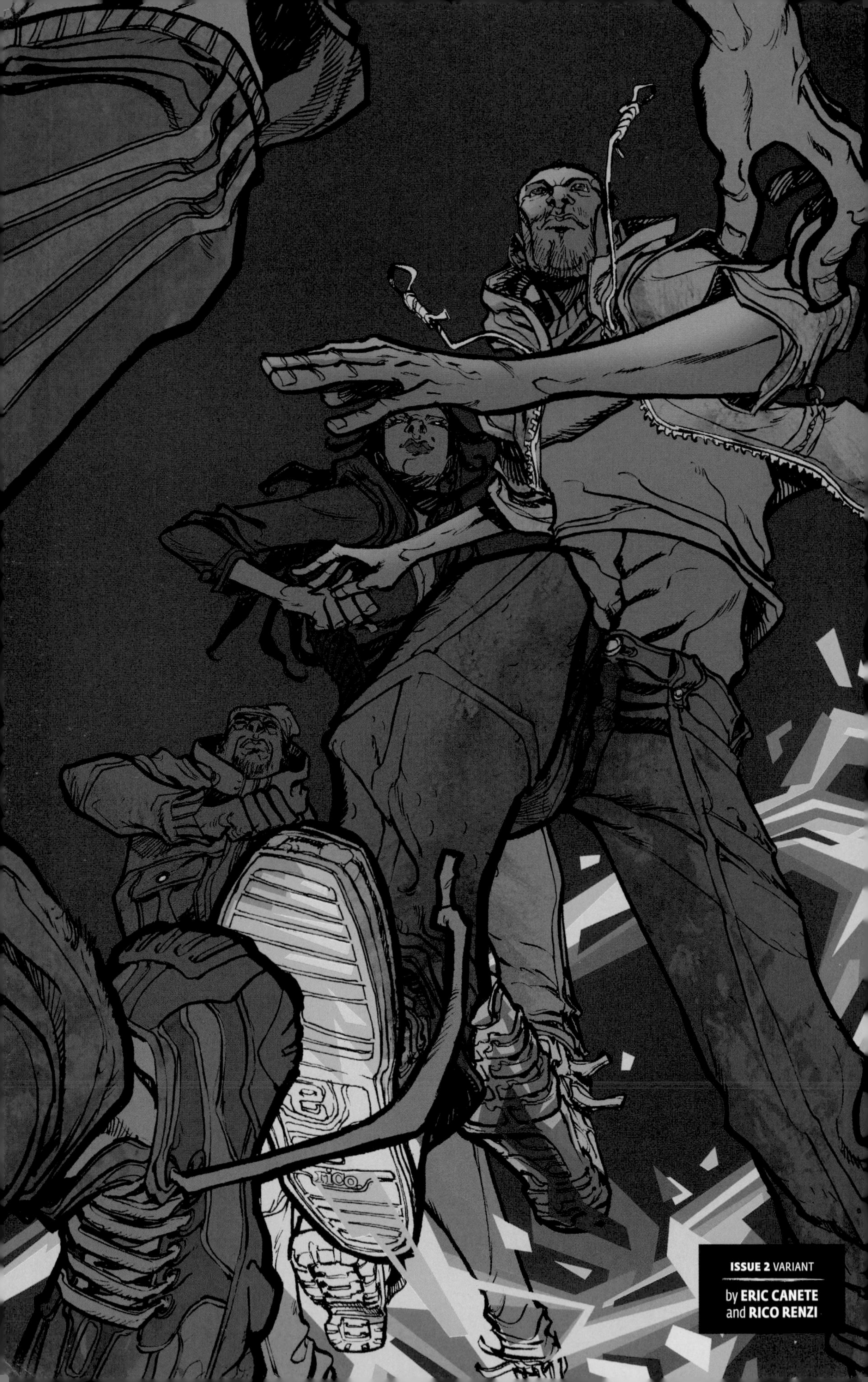

ISSUE 2 VARIANT

by **ERIC CANETE** and **RICO RENZI**

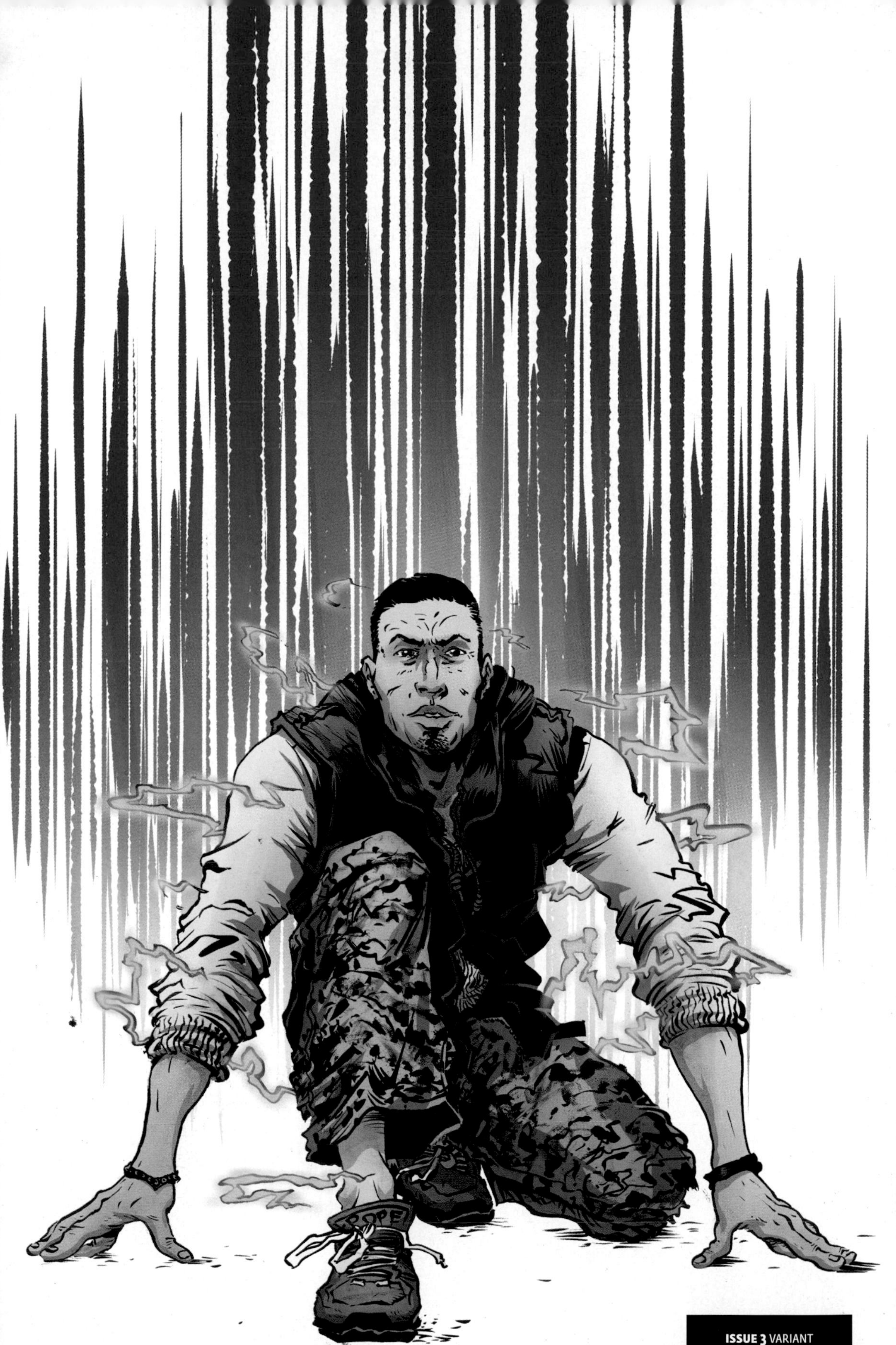
POPE

ISSUE 3 VARIANT

by **PAUL POPE**
and **SHAY PLUMMER**

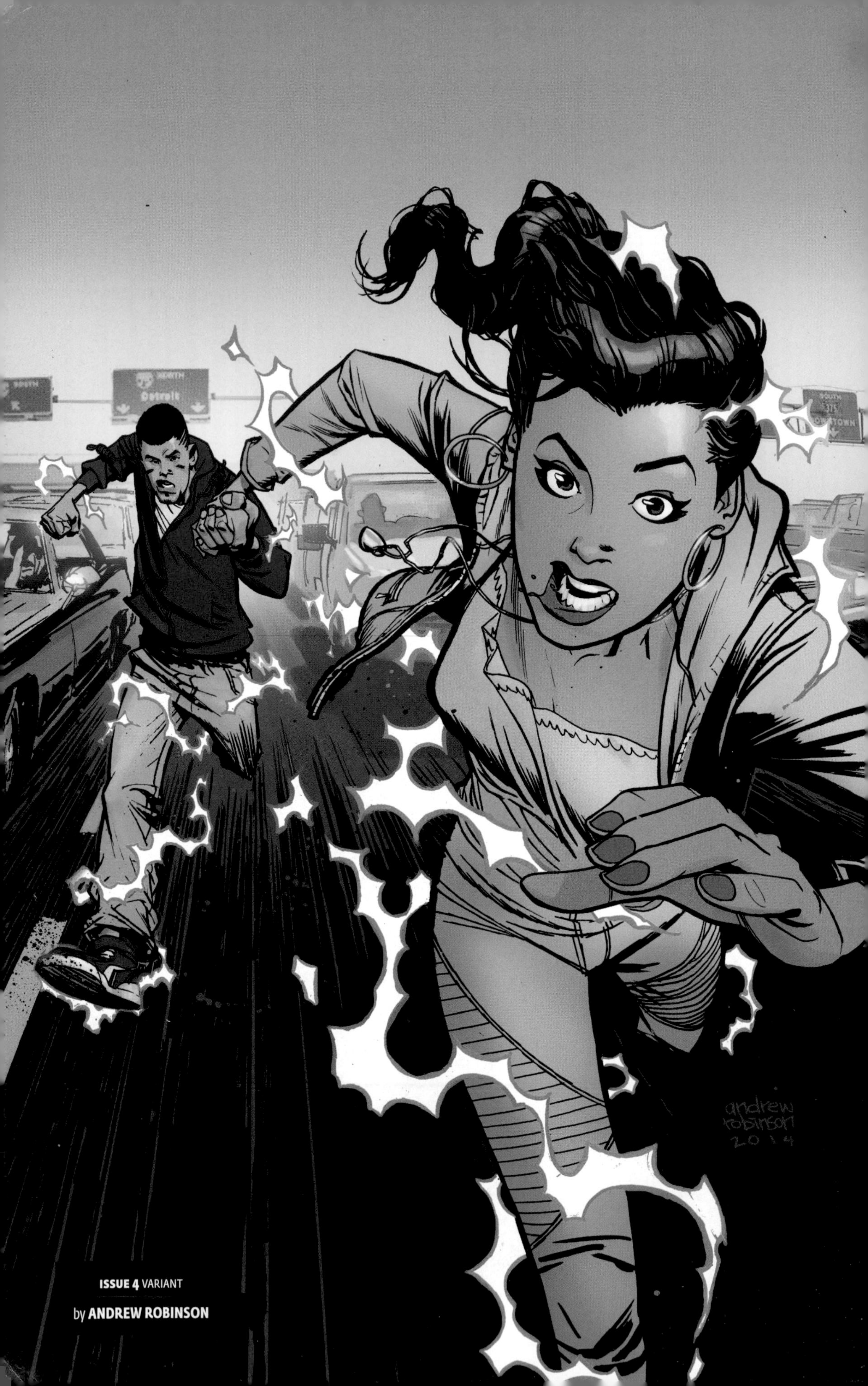
Detroit
andrew robinson 2014

ISSUE 4 VARIANT

by **ANDREW ROBINSON**

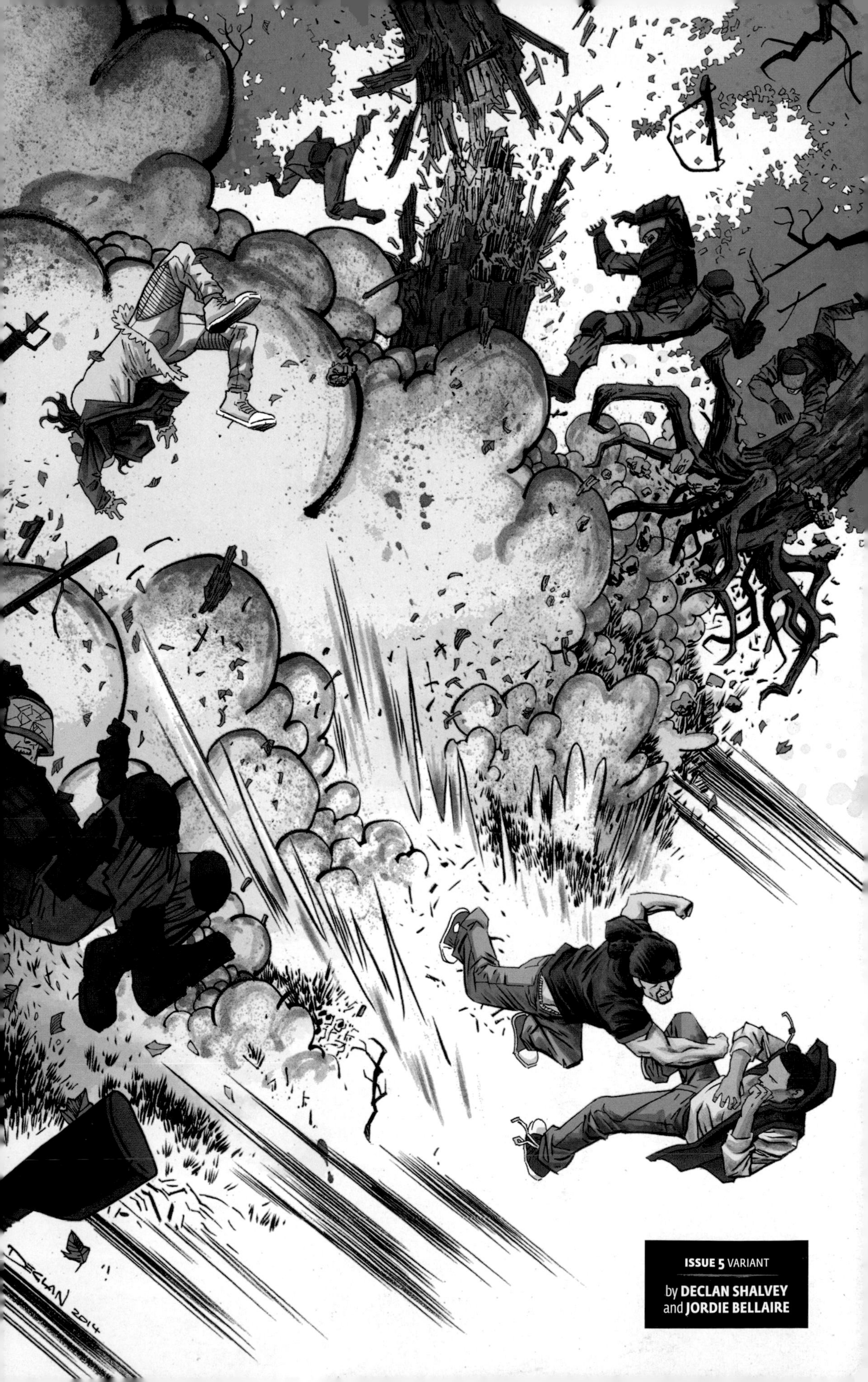
DECLAN 2014

ISSUE 5 VARIANT

by **DECLAN SHALVEY**
and **JORDIE BELLAIRE**

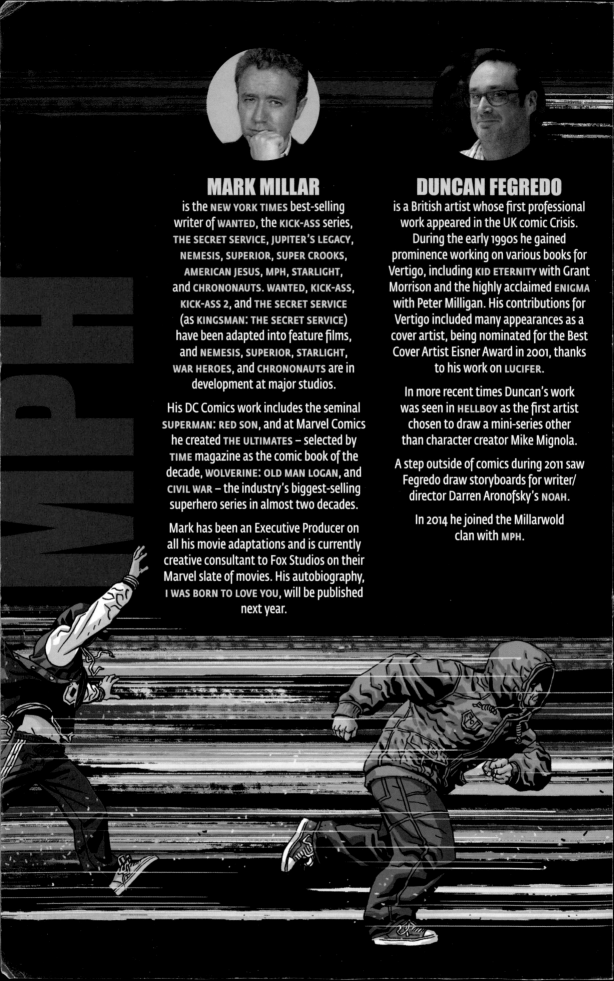

MARK MILLAR

is the NEW YORK TIMES best-selling writer of WANTED, the KICK-ASS series, THE SECRET SERVICE, JUPITER'S LEGACY, NEMESIS, SUPERIOR, SUPER CROOKS, AMERICAN JESUS, MPH, STARLIGHT, and CHRONONAUTS. WANTED, KICK-ASS, KICK-ASS 2, and THE SECRET SERVICE (as KINGSMAN: THE SECRET SERVICE) have been adapted into feature films, and NEMESIS, SUPERIOR, STARLIGHT, WAR HEROES, and CHRONONAUTS are in development at major studios.

His DC Comics work includes the seminal SUPERMAN: RED SON, and at Marvel Comics he created THE ULTIMATES – selected by TIME magazine as the comic book of the decade, WOLVERINE: OLD MAN LOGAN, and CIVIL WAR – the industry's biggest-selling superhero series in almost two decades.

Mark has been an Executive Producer on all his movie adaptations and is currently creative consultant to Fox Studios on their Marvel slate of movies. His autobiography, I WAS BORN TO LOVE YOU, will be published next year.

DUNCAN FEGREDO

is a British artist whose first professional work appeared in the UK comic Crisis. During the early 1990s he gained prominence working on various books for Vertigo, including KID ETERNITY with Grant Morrison and the highly acclaimed ENIGMA with Peter Milligan. His contributions for Vertigo included many appearances as a cover artist, being nominated for the Best Cover Artist Eisner Award in 2001, thanks to his work on LUCIFER.

In more recent times Duncan's work was seen in HELLBOY as the first artist chosen to draw a mini-series other than character creator Mike Mignola.

A step outside of comics during 2011 saw Fegredo draw storyboards for writer/director Darren Aronofsky's NOAH.

In 2014 he joined the Millarworld clan with MPH.

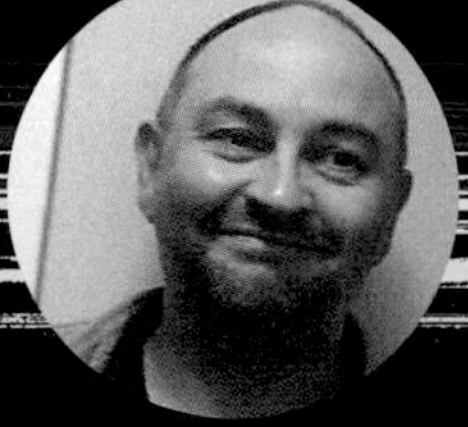

PETER DOHERTY

Peter's first work in comics was in 1990, providing painted artwork for the John Wagner-written "Young Death: The Boyhood of a Super-fiend," published in the first year of the JUDGE DREDD MEGAZINE. For the next few years he painted art for a number of Judge Dredd stories.

During the closing years of the 90s he worked for several comic publishers, most notably DC/Vertigo, and branched out into illustration, TV, and movie work.

After a year as an in-house concept artist at a games company, Peter returned to freelancing. Working digitally for the first time opened the door to coloring work, firstly on the Grant Morrison/Cameron Stewart SEAGUY and with Geof Darrow on his creation THE SHAOLIN COWBOY.

Over the last decade, he's balanced working on projects both as the sole artist and as a coloring collaborator with other artists, most recently with his old friends Frank Quitely and Duncan Fegredo on the Millarworld projects JUPITER'S LEGACY and MPH respectively.

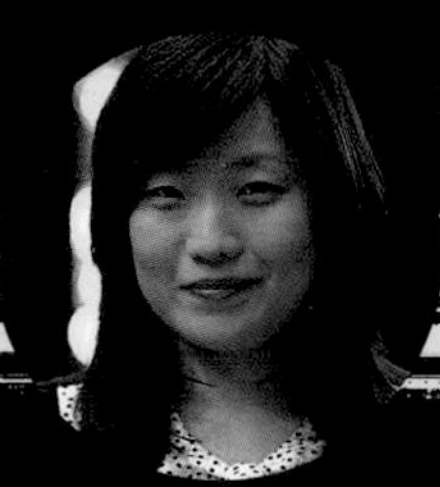

JENNIFER LEE

is a story editor and producer working across film and comics. She's edited for both Marvel and DC Comics, and her credits include WOLVERINE, DAREDEVIL, BLACK WIDOW, 100 BULLETS, TRANSMETROPOLITAN, and the award-winning illustrated prose novel THE SANDMAN: THE DREAM HUNTERS. Other recent comics credits include KICK-ASS 3, HIT-GIRL, and THE ART OF MILLARWORLD.

Film credits include TRUE ADOLESCENTS, UNION SQUARE, and the breakout Sundance hit THE SKELETON TWINS starring Kristen Wiig and Bill Hader.

She lives in New York with her husband, comics illustrator Cliff Chiang.

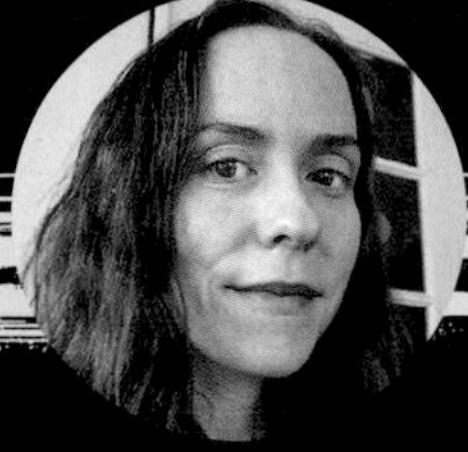

NICOLE BOOSE

began her comics career as an assistant editor for Harris Comics' VAMPIRELLA, before joining the editorial staff at Marvel Comics. There, she edited titles including CABLE & DEADPOOL, INVINCIBLE IRON MAN, and Stephen King's DARK TOWER adaptations, and oversaw Marvel's line of custom comic publications.

Since 2008, Nicole has worked as a freelance editor and consultant in the comics industry, with editorial credits that include the Millarworld titles SUPERIOR, SUPER CROOKS, JUPITER'S LEGACY, MPH, STARLIGHT, and CHRONONAUTS.

Nicole is also Communications Manager for Comics Experience, an online school and community for comic creators.

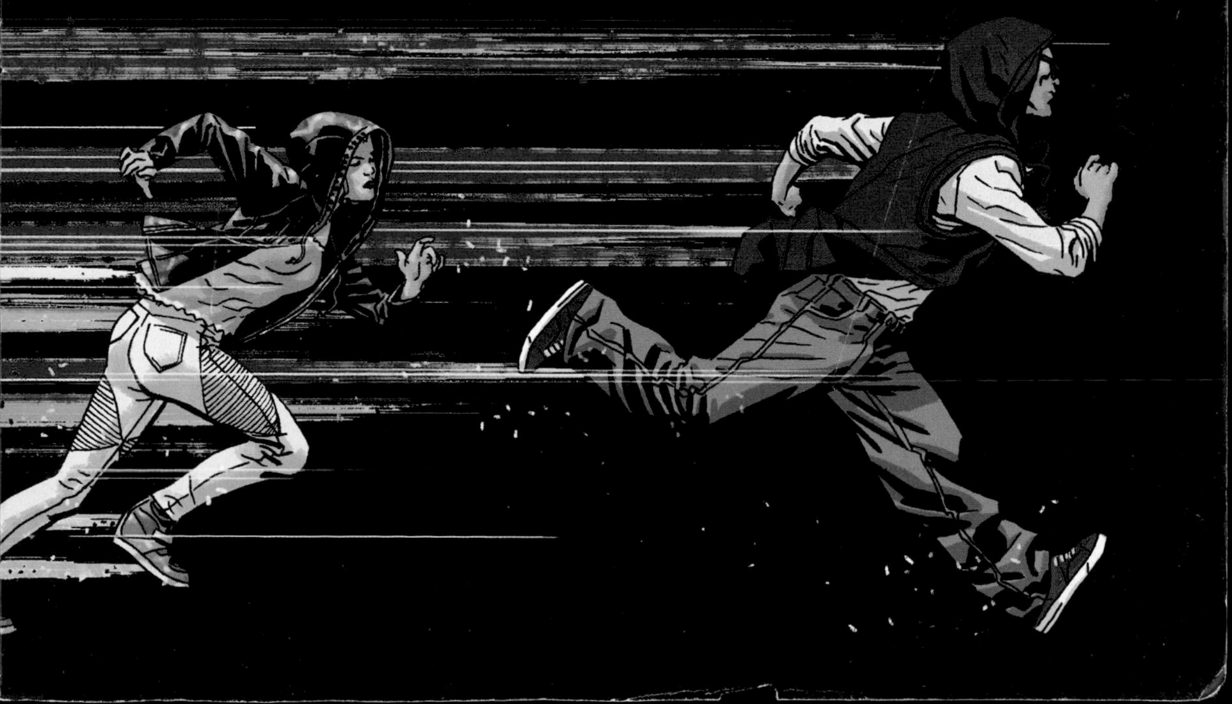

MILLARWORLD®

THE COLLECTION CHECKLIST

KICK-ASS
MARK MILLAR
JOHN ROMITA JR.

KICK-ASS
Art by John Romita Jr.

- [ ] Kick-Ass #1-8

HIT-GIRL
MARK MILLAR
JOHN ROMITA JR.
TOM PALMER and DEAN WHITE

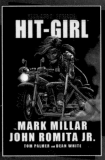

HIT-GIRL
Art by John Romita Jr.

- [ ] Hit-Girl #1-5

KICK-ASS 2
MARK MILLAR
JOHN ROMITA JR.

KICK-ASS 2
Art by John Romita Jr.

- [ ] Kick-Ass 2 #1-7

KICK-ASS 3
MARK MILLAR
JOHN ROMITA JR.

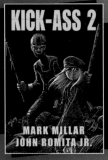

KICK-ASS 3
Art by John Romita Jr.

- [ ] Kick-Ass 3 #1-8

MILLAR MURPHY
CHRONONAUTS
#1
$3.50

CHRONONAUTS
Art by Sean Gordon Murphy

- [ ] Chrononauts #1-4

MARK MILLAR DUNCAN FEGREDO
MPH

MPH
Art by Duncan Fegredo

- [ ] MPH #1-5

MARK MILLAR • GORAN PARLOV
STARLIGHT

STARLIGHT
Art by Goran Parlov

- [ ] Starlight #1-6

KINGSMAN
THE SECRET SERVICE

KINGSMAN: THE SECRET SERVICE
Art by Dave Gibbons

- [ ] The Secret Service #1-6

MARK MILLAR • WILFREDO TORRES
JUPITER'S CIRCLE

JUPITER'S CIRCLE
Art by Wilfredo Torres

- [ ] Jupiter's Circle #1-5

MARK MILLAR • FRANK QUITELY
JUPITER'S LEGACY

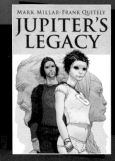

JUPITER'S LEGACY
Art by Frank Quitely

- [ ] Jupiter's Legacy #1-5

MARK MILLAR LEINIL YU
SUPER CROOKS
THE HEIST

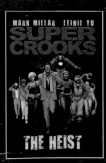

SUPER CROOKS
Art by Leinil Yu

- [ ] Super Crooks #1-4

MARK MILLAR & LEINIL YU
SUPERIOR
FROM THE WRITER OF KICK-ASS

SUPERIOR
Art by Leinil Yu

- [ ] Superior #1-7

MILLAR & McNIVEN'S
NEMESIS

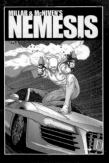

NEMESIS
Art by Steve McNiven

- [ ] Nemesis #1-4

WANTED
MARK MILLAR • JG JONES • PAUL MOUNTS
UNIVERSAL PICTURES

WANTED
Art by JG Jones

- [ ] Wanted #1-6

AMERICAN JESUS
BOOK ONE : CHOSEN
MARK MILLAR • PETER GROSS

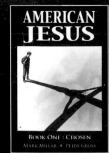

AMERICAN JESUS
Art by Peter Gross

- [ ] American Jesus #1-3